Leaving Children Behind

A Volume in the SUNY series,
The Social Context of Education

Christine E. Sleeter, editor

Leaving Children Behind: How "Texas-style" Accountability Fails Latino Youth

Edited by
Angela Valenzuela

State University of New York Press

Cover Photograph: Getty Images Catalog number AA017132

Published by
State University of New York Press, Albany

© 2005 State University of New York

For information, address State University of New York Press,
90 State Street, Suite 700, Albany, NY 12207

Production by Michael Haggett
Marketing by Anne M. Valentine

Library of Congress Cataloging-in-Publication Data

Leaving children behind : why Texas-style accountability fails Latino youth / Angela
Valenzuela, editor.
     p. cm. — (SUNY series, the social context of education)
  Includes bibliographical references and index.
  ISBN 0-7914-6239-0 (hardcover : alk. paper) — ISBN 0-7914-6240-4 (pbk. : alk. paper)
  1. Hispanic Americans—Education—Texas. 2. Educational accountability—Texas.
  3. Educational tests and measurements—Texas. I. Valenzuela, Angela. II. SUNY
series, social context of education.
  LC2674.T4L43 2004
  371.829'68073—dc22

2004012237

10 9 8 7 6 5 4 3 2 1

Contents

Acknowledgments

I wish to thank all the volume contributors for their contribution to this book and for their support and friendship in our legislative journey in Texas. Special thanks go to Laurie Hammons, Linda McNeil, and Doug Foley for providing me with consistent support and feedback to my own writing and thinking on the Texas case. I am indebted to my friend and colleague, Bill Black, who helped me with the volume throughout its various stages and also for providing helpful, critical suggestions. I also appreciate our editor, Kathy Mooney, who helped us all along with her organizational and substantive suggestions on how to improve the various pieces.

Although too many to name, I also wish to acknowledge other friends and colleagues who have lobbied courageously for the children in our state: Enrique Alemán, Mary Armesto, Sylvia Bruni, Senator Gonzalo Barrientos, State Board of Education member Mary Helen Berlanga, Ernesto Bernal, State Board of Education member Joe Bernal, Oscar Cardenas, David Carrejo, Jere Confrey, Ana Yañez Correa, Albert Cortez, Angelica Cruz, Ray de los Santos, Zoraima Diaz, Deborah Diffily, Jean Ehnebuske, Lewis Ford, Carl Glickman, Michael Guerrero, Rita Haecker, Walt Haney, Will Harrell, Andrea Hinckson, State Representative Scott Hochberg, Carol Holst, Dottie Hooker, Al Kauffman, Deborah Kelt, Leila Levinson, Vincent Lozano, Johnny Mata, Brendan Maxcy, Betty McAdoo, María "Cuca" Robledo Montecel, Monty Neill, State Representative Rick Noriega, State Representative René Oliveira, State Representative Dora Olivo, Gary Orfield, Alba Ortiz, Nina Perales, Alma Perez, Becky Pursley, the late State Representative Irma Rangel, Alejandra Rincon, Ed Rincon, Anna Alicia Romero, Cesar Rossatto, Samantha Smoot, Joe Sanchez, Leticia Saucedo, Becky Stitch, Maricela Urrutia, Senator Leticia Van de Putte, Amanda Walker, Eileen Weinstein, KayDonna Wolfcale, and Senator Judith Zaffarini.

I am blessed to have my mother and father, Helen and Carlos Valenzuela, both of whom remain a constant source of encouragement and inspiration to me. Finally, thanks go to my husband, Emilio Zamora, and two daughters, Clara and Luz, who continue to put up with me and all my projects with such generosity of spirit and grace.

1

Introduction
The Accountability Debate in Texas:
Continuing the Conversation

ANGELA VALENZUELA

The alleged "Texas Miracle" in education (Haney, 2000, 2001), combined with the 2002 reauthorization of the federal Elementary and Secondary Education Act (popularly known as the "No Child Left Behind Act" [NCLB]), has shifted what was once an intrastate debate over educational accountability to a national-level issue. Supporters of accountability claim that it promotes equity by making schools teach poor and minority children who have been historically neglected by our public school system (see Scheurich & Skrla, 2001; Scheurich, Skrla, & Johnson, 2000; Skrla, Scheurich, & Johnson, 2000a, 2000b). Opponents, including the contributors to this volume, argue that the Texas system of educational accountability has failed—and will continue to fail—Latina/o and other minority youth and their communities.[1] We interpret Texas-style accountability as exacerbating historic inequities, mainly through the collateral effects of state policy, but also through a systemwide failure to accommodate the needs and abilities of English-language learners (see the chapters by Alamillo, Palmer, Viramontes, & García; and by Ruiz de Velasco). Moreover, as McNeil points out (see chapter 3), the dramatic educational improvement attributed to Texas' system of accountability is itself questionable. The state's methods of collecting and reporting educational data, including the critically important high-stakes test scores, hide as much as they reveal. When the focus is shifted to Texas' students' performance on nationwide tests such as the American College Test (ACT) and Scholastic Assessment Test (SAT) 1, or when skyrocketing dropout and projected retention rates are factored in (see McNeil and Valencia & Villarreal), the state's "miracle" looks more like a mirage.

That schools should be held accountable is indisputable. This volume does not suggest otherwise. Rather, what we question is the Texas model of accountability. Specifically, the authors reject high-stakes testing, the system's centerpiece. We further contend that the Texas approach is deeply flawed, for three interrelated reasons: for attaching high-stakes consequences—in the areas of retention, promotion, and graduation—to a single measure of students' academic abilities; for attaching high-stakes consequences to schools and districts and thereby encouraging a reductionist, test-driven curriculum; and for promoting a uniform and objectivist way of knowing, to the detriment of other cultures, languages, and approaches to knowledge.

Our collective admonition to the nation is that policies supporting high-stakes testing are harmful to all children, especially for children from poor, minority, or non-English-speaking families.[2] Indeed, these policies curtail or compromise the very achievement the public seeks. Moreover, state policies that attach high-stakes consequences to children's test scores are inherently invalid, undemocratic, and unjust (Heubert & Hauser, 1999). They distort the process of schooling, as well, through the creation of perverse incentives to "lose" children or limit curriculum, or both (see the chapters by Alamillo, Palmer, Viramontes, & García; Hampton; McNeil; Sloan; and Valencia & Villarreal). Finally, when the test is the sole or primary arbiter in decisions with such long-lasting consequences for children, we insist that students have a right to be assessed in a complete and fair manner, using as many criteria as may reasonably indicate children's cognitive abilities and potential.[3]

We would like to see the terms of the current debate over educational accountability overhauled. At issue is not whether schools and districts should be accountable, but what means should be used to accomplish the widely shared goal of ensuring that all children receive a high-quality education. When we allow the state to equate academic excellence with a single test score, when we agree to tie our children's performance on one test to their classroom teachers' jobs and school administrators' bonuses, we implicitly validate the host of values, presuppositions, and attitudes that underlie a flawed version of accountability. Recasting the debate, we hope, will draw necessary attention to the questionable nature of such typically unexamined assumptions.

In calling for a new approach to the ongoing conversation about accountability, we seek to create a larger public space for a Latina/o, research-based perspective and epistemology (see Padilla) in the development of a more just assessment system. In this space, we also see assessment as a tool that can remove schools from public scrutiny with the use of alienating, technical language. In terms of how an "appropriate" or "necessary" educational experience gets defined within a system in which testing drives curriculum, prescribed notions of assessment may also contribute to subtractive cultural assimilation and thereby harm, control, and exclude children and their communities (see Alamillo et al., Hampton, Padilla, and Sloan). At its best, however, assessment affirms a core democratic principle that education is about shared governance and growing healthy children, communities, and citizens for a democracy.

Accordingly, what follows is a description of the current public policy landscape in Texas, providing the backdrop against which my own and others' efforts to pass multiple assessment criteria legislation have taken place. The purpose of this narrative is to situate our modest but significant policy efforts to reclaim education as a publicly shared institution essential to active, democratic participation. This volume does not address such issues as test theory, measurement, or frameworks for assessment in any depth. Abundant scholarship already exists in these areas (e.g., Darling-Hammond, Ancess, & Falk, 1995; Newmann, 1996; Meier, 1995, 2002; Valencia & Suzuki, 2001). Except for the contribution by Alamillo et al., this book engages Texas' unfolding policy debate on accountability and its implementation. This introductory chapter provides an overview of the contributions to the volume. Much as my assessment of the struggle in Texas for multiple-criteria legislation is shaped by my position as a parent of two elementary-school-age children, Latina academic researcher, and community activist, so too do the other authors contribute with their unique experiences and perspectives.

THE UNFOLDING DEBATE ON ACCOUNTABILITY

For reasons that go beyond the scope of this chapter, discussions about educational policy issues, whether they take place among researchers or between researchers and the lay public, often are marred by misunderstandings. Each side unwittingly generates opposition to its views by failing to meaningfully engage challengers' assumptions and perspectives. Specialized language and the tendency to assign multiple meanings to the same term (such as "standards-based reform") only increase the levels of complexity and confusion. As researchers, we are typically somewhat removed from public life; we tend not to participate in the kind of debates and discussions that not only would teach us to think through our evidence and assumptions, but also force us to improve how we articulate our views and positions. My experience as one of a community of scholars engaged in multi-voiced conversations about accountability has prompted me to try to articulate a new, more constructive frame for thinking about and taking action regarding the conceptual and rhetorical quagmire commonly referred to as "accountability."

Background

My expertise on the state's educational system is derived from research I have undertaken in Houston's inner-city public schools over the past 12 years, first as a research associate at the Rice University Center for Education in Houston and now as a faculty member in the Department of Curriculum and Instruction and in the Center for Mexican American Studies at the University of Texas at Austin. While at Rice, I conducted, from 1992 to 1995, an in-depth case study of a large, overcrowded, predominantly Mexican, segregated high school. Most of the findings from this study are presented in my book, *Subtractive Schooling: U.S.-Mexican Youth and the Politics of Caring* (1999).

Subtractive Schooling critiques schools and state education policy as culturally and linguistically subtractive. Rather than building on the assets that children bring with them to schools, public education in Texas subtracts students' linguistic, cultural, and community-based identities, to their academic and personal detriment. My more recent work links Texas' system of testing to this practice of subtractive cultural assimilation (McNeil & Valenzuela, 2001; Valencia, Valenzuela, Sloan, & Foley, 2001; Valenzuela, 2000, 2002). A core idea here is that the state's testing system is embedded within the larger edifice of "accountability," and that it is this overarching framework that perpetuates a subtractive approach to the education of racial, cultural, and linguistic minorities. Children, along with their parents and communities, are treated as objects. The very notion of a mainstream, standardized educational experience implies a systemic disregard of children's personal, cultural, and community-based identities. Rather than providing children with an empowering sense of how their lives can connect productively to the world that they inhabit, a test-centric curriculum compelled by the long arm of the state through standardized, high-stakes testing reduces children's worth to their test scores.

Taking Action

In 2000, I joined two other contributors to this volume (Linda McNeil and Richard Valencia) to testify on behalf of plaintiffs (represented by the

Mexican American Legal Defense and Education Fund [MALDEF] in a federal court trial, *GI Forum et al. v. Texas Education Agency et al.* (2000). The focus of the suit was the adverse impact of the testing system in Texas: 87 percent of all students who fail the state's high school exit exam are either African American or Latina/o.[4] All nine Latino and African American plaintiffs in the case were high school students who had been denied diplomas because they had failed to pass at least some portion of the reading, writing, or mathematics segments of the Texas Assessment of Academic Skills (TAAS) tenth-grade exit exam.[5] Based on both their grades and completion of required course credits for graduation, all of the plaintiffs would have graduated, were it not for their performance on the TAAS test (Kauffman, 2000; Saucedo, 2000). In an ironic turn, MALDEF won the adverse impact argument but lost the case. Judge Edward Prado ruled that the harm against the students did not reach a "constitutional level" because the state had followed due process in the design and implementation of the test.[6]

The trial, and MALDEF lead attorney Al Kauffman's efforts, in particular, helped raise the issue of high-stakes testing to a higher level of public awareness in Texas. Following the trial, a small, multiethnic group of university faculty, graduate students, and grassroots advocates for children (Parents United to Reform TAAS Testing) united into a coalition working toward twin goals: to increase awareness of the harmful effects of high-stakes testing and to promote the use of multiple compensatory criteria for academic assessment (see the chapter by Valencia & Villarreal; and Valenzuela 2002). Through our published work, as well as through opinion-editorial pieces, scholarly conferences, community presentations, and the dissemination of pertinent information through listservs and websites (especially www.texas-testing.org), we have been able to reach a variety of audiences. One especially successful effort to educate communities of color and other stakeholders throughout the state and nation took place during the opening days of the Texas legislative session on January 26, 2001. The event brought nearly all the contributors to this volume together with legislators, legislative staff, and an 800-strong, statewide representation of Latino students, parents, educators, and community activists. During the open-mike session, researchers, community members, and Latino educational leaders repeatedly voiced concern over test abuse. This public exchange, along with the federal trial and a rally organized by League of United Latin American Citizens (LULAC) activists in Houston on January 27, 2001 to challenge the accountability system, were among the first broad-based expressions of disenchantment in the Latino community regarding high-stakes testing.

From the start, our coalition also undertook action at the legislative level, joining forces with MALDEF, LULAC, and the Intercultural Development Research Association, a nonprofit, education advocacy organization for Texas' Mexican American community. When State Representative Dora Olivo (D-Rosenberg) indicated her willingness to sponsor our legislation during the 77th biennial meeting (2001) of the Texas legislature, we began working for the passage of HB 2118 and HB 2570. These bills called for the use of multiple compensatory criteria at the tenth-grade exit level, as well as at the third-, fifth-, and eighth-grade levels affected by SB 4, the state's new policy on social promotion (see the chapter by Valencia & Villarreal for details on SB 4's provisions and effects). SB 4, passed in 1999 when George W. Bush was governor, phases in new promotion gates, beginning in 2002–2003, with the state's third-grade cohort. Under this law, promotion to the fourth grade hinges heavily on the student passing the reading section of the state-mandated third-grade test, regardless of their overall academic accomplishments. The law also stipulates that promotion gates at the fifth- and eighth-grade levels be in place by 2007–2008.[7]

HB 2118 and HB 2570 explicitly addressed the need for *multiple alternative* assessment tools by proposing provisions to allow teacher recommendation, average grades in core subjects, and other test score information to compensate for poor performance on the Texas Assessment of Knowledge and Skills (TAKS) test, a newly devised and approved replacement for the TAAS. The state claims that a multiple-criteria system is already in place: Students must pass the TAAS/TAKS; they must maintain a 70 grade-point average; they must accumulate a specific number of credits for graduation; and they must attend school a certain number of days annually. However, since the decisive hurdle for graduation or promotion to the next grade level remains the student's TAAS/TAKS test score, what the state actually has in place is a multiple conjunctive criteria system, not a compensatory system. A student who met all criteria for graduation but failed the TAAS/TAKS would not graduate, because none of the other required criteria are allowed to compensate for poor test performance (Heubert & Hauser, 1999; Valencia & Bernal, 2000; Valenzuela 2002). As the plaintiffs in *GI Forum et al. v. Texas Education Agency et al.* (2000) remind us, far from being an extreme hypothetical scenario, this situation is painfully real for many Texas high school seniors.

The analogue we frequently offer is the college admissions process. Test scores typically are not the sole arbiter of college admittance. Most colleges assess applicants using multiple sources of information, often with the explicit intent of avoiding the possibility of losing otherwise excellent candidates because of their low scores on a single measure such as the SAT. Moreover, decades of research on college testing shows that multiple criteria and a sliding scale of test scores and grades results in more valid decisions (Linn, 1982; Willingham, Lewis, Morgan, & Ramist, 1990). Decisions based on multiple criteria rather than on test scores in isolation also have been shown to have a smaller adverse impact on minorities and women (Haney, Madaus, & Lyons, 1993).

HB 2570 cleared its first major hurdle when it passed in the House with a majority vote; it did not receive a hearing in the Senate, however. HB 2118, on the other hand, never saw the light of day in either chamber. On the day that Representative Olivo was scheduled to testify on HB 2570, that fellow legislators told her as she was making her way toward the House floor that they had received word from the office of President George W. Bush not to support the legislation. As a result, many were reluctant to vote in favor of the bill. With hindsight, it is easy to see why the president's office would have taken such an active interest in HB 2570 and HB 2118. The federal NCLB legislation was in the process of being developed in Congress. A perceived substantive shift in "accountability" in Texas would have potentially made the president look weak at the national level.

We never viewed the legislation Representative Olivo sponsored as either partisan or as weakening President Bush's national goals for improving education. To the contrary, we believed—and still believe—that a fair assessment system could form the backbone of a more just and valid accountability system (Valenzuela, 2002). What this first foray into legislative action taught us (apart from the lesson regarding the power of political ties) was that we had failed to appreciate how many legislators fully equated "testing" with "accountability." To them, our anti-high-stakes-testing stance constituted an attack on the accountability system itself (see McNeil, 2000, for an excellent historical discussion of the evolution of accountability in Texas). For instance, when we testified on HB 2570 before the House Committee on Public Education on March 27, 2001, a lobbyist from the Texas Federation of Teachers expressed opposition to the legislation (www.house.state.tx.us/committees/audio77/400.htm). Claiming his organization's support for the development of the accountability system, he argued that the legislation weakened it. He felt that the legislation would nullify the driving force for change that a single-indicator system represents. These lessons have left us wiser and undeterred in our overall effort. HB 2570 and HB 2118 were refiled for the 78th legislative session in 2003, bearing new numbers (HB 336 and HB 337, respectively).

Implementation of the state's new TAKS test, administered on March 4, 2003, gave our efforts a special urgency. The TAKS is an espe-

cially troubling instrument, not only because it is a longer and more difficult exam than the TAAS, but also because its implementation collided in
time with the enforcement of the state's new anti–social promotion policy
(the centerpiece of SB 4; see Valencia & Villarreal, this volume). Using
data provided by the State Board of Education (Texas State Board of Education, 2002), the state had estimated that 42,000 third-grade first-time
test takers would fail the TAKS. It was our hope that the prospect of such
high failure rates (and the possible retention in grade of so many children)
would combine with our collective efforts to educate the public sufficiently to create an opening for the passage of Representative Olivo's bills.
Before addressing the fate of the bills in the 2003 session, I first need to
mention the results of the first TAKS administration.

The passage rate on the third-grade English and Spanish versions
of the reading exam in the first administration were 89 percent and 82
percent, respectively (Texas Education Agency, 2003a). Numerically,
this meant that "only" 32,659 students failed the exam. In state newspapers, the passing rate was hailed in positive, if not glowing, terms
(e.g., Blackwell, 2003). A month later, on April 18, 2003, the editors of
the *Houston Chronicle* argued explicitly against the Olivo legislation,
citing the need for an accountability system that relies on "objective"
test score data for determining "academic mastery." They further suggested that despite the "dire predictions" for third graders, the test results were "fairly good." To my knowledge, they were never charged
with displaying a "soft bigotry of low expectations," one of President
Bush's favorite campaign slogans against the critics of the Texas
accountability system.

Privately, I wondered how a thirty-two-thousand-plus failure rate
could be spun into a victory for the state. Were their expectations even
more dire than the actual outcome? Should not the fact of tens of thousands of young children adversely affected be sufficient for us to take
pause, particularly in a state that takes pride in the great strides it has allegedly made? As Valencia and Villarreal's (this volume) analyses demonstrate, failure rates are not only high—especially when considering their
impact on retention and an enhanced probability of dropping out—they
also obscure important subgroup variation that reveals a disproportionate impact of the system on Latina/o and African American youth. I also
wonder why the burden was on us to demonstrate that *more* information
should be used when judging children on decisions of such long-lasting
consequence to them. The burden should be on the state to demonstrate
that *less* information is better and that current failure rates are adequate,
reasonable, and acceptable.

Representative Olivo was able to get nearly enough Republican and Democrat sponsors in the House to pass HB 336 and HB 337. However, the legislation never came out of committee (see the final chapter in this volume for a comprehensive analysis of the conservative legislative climate in the 2003 session). Olivo quickly adopted a new strategy to salvage the content of HB 336 and 337. She successfully amended a dropout prevention bill that the Chairman on the Committee on Public Education, Kent Grusendorf, had coauthored in the House. The legislation passed without a single nay vote in the chamber. However, when an appointed subcommittee "ironed out" the differences between the Senate and House versions of the bill, the Olivo amendment was removed. Although the Olivo legislation did not address many problems that Texas school children face, we believe that its passage could have constituted a first step in promoting a more just, valid, and pedagogically robust assessment system.

Reframing the Debate

An excellent point of departure for crafting a new discourse on accountability is the most high-profile, scholarly debate in Texas, appearing in the December 2000 and December 2001 issues of the *Phi Delta Kappan*. In this section, I summarize the positions and concerns expressed by Scheurich, Skrla, and Johnson (2000), the response by Valencia, Valenzuela, Sloan, and Foley (2001), and Scheurich and Skrla's (2001) rebuttal. Revisiting this debate provides an opportunity to examine the assumptions that underlie Texas-style accountability and to contrast those with the assumptions that underlie the alternative approach of assessment based on both authentic assessment and multiple compensatory criteria. Identifying and evaluating these assumptions is more than an academic endeavor. What is meant and not meant, and what is articulated and what is left unspoken when we declare ourselves for or against "accountability" have direct bearing on real-world public debate and policy making.

In "Thinking Carefully About Equity and Accountability," Scheurich and colleagues (2000) present a general argument justifying the Texas accountability system by pointing to the state's "miserable record" in educating children of color, including a historic problem with deficit thinking and subtractive schooling. Moreover, they posit that with an emphasis on results, as measured by test scores, it will be possible to establish a new "national equity norm" for measuring poor and minority childrens' achievement across the fifty states. By this they mean that equity in achievement would be a taken-for-granted assumption in the context of a national consensus to eliminate the achievement gap between Anglo children and children of color.

Scheurich and colleagues (2000) then propose that we are at a critical crossroad; that for the first time, there is an alignment of factors that make the historically elusive goal of educational equity an attainable possibility. First, the high level of public attention currently being paid to poor and minority children is unprecedented. Second, both major U.S. political parties now support a major public commitment to ensuring high academic performance from poor and minority youth. Last, in some states, including Texas, where accountability systems are in place, there are signs of rising academic achievement among some poor and minority children in particular schools and districts. As evidence of this last point, they refer primarily to their own research among Texas schools and districts populated by low-income children of color, where they have witnessed improved test performance, as well as rising test scores on the National Assessment of Educational Progress (NAEP), often referred to as the "nation's report card." Scheurich and colleagues' research findings, based on interviews with school and district administrators, reveal that it was not until the establishment of the accountability system that administrators came to believe that they could hold all children to high standards and achieve positive results.

In the remainder of the article, Scheurich, Skrla, and Johnson (2000) turn their attention to elaborating a taxonomy of multiple, interacting components of accountability, through which "equity effects" should be both studied and judged. Their taxonomy consists of (1) system elements, covering comprehensive factors that would allow equity to be judged on the basis of similar criteria across all fifty states; (2) curriculum issues, particularly the relationship of state tests to state academic standards; (3) teaching issues, including how accountability system components affect instructional quality; (4) assessment issues, especially the validity of tests that purport to measure learning; and (5) other issues, such as whether some system components are increasing dropout and pushout rates within the poor and minority segments of the student population. With regard to this last point, they cite Haney (2000), who makes the case that increasing dropout rates in Texas reflect collateral effects of high-stakes accountability systems.

This taxonomy leads Scheurich and colleagues (2000) to suggest that polarizing "either/or" stances on accountability, which they believe our position represents (particularly McNeil & Valenzuela, 2001), are ill conceived. Empirical observations of failure in one system component (e.g., teaching to the test and narrowing curricula), they argue, should not be read as a failure of accountability as a whole, but rather as the failure of a single component.

Valencia, Valenzuela, Sloan, and Foley (2001) respond to Scheurich and colleagues (2000) by first pointing to common ground. We begin by concurring with their assertion of the state's "miserable record" on educating children of color and the deficit thinking and subtractive schooling practices that have been associated with this history. Although we support the notion of a national agenda to promote equal educational opportunity, we express concern over the use of standards-based reform (to which high-stakes tests are frequently attached) to achieve the new national equity norm envisioned by Scheurich, Skrla, and Johnson (2000).[8]

We then list what we see as the flaws in their "historical possibilities thesis." We discount both the notion of an unprecedented level of public attention and the assertion of a major public political commitment to poor and minority children. Public attention to these children has persisted over decades; and campaign rhetoric does not necessarily translate into equitable reform. We assert that test-centric systems of accountability treat only the symptoms, not the root causes of low student achievement. We also note both political parties' evident lack of will to use already proven means to enhance student performance (e.g., smaller class and school sizes, and improved teacher quality).[9]

We respond to Scheurich and colleagues' (2000) final claim of improved academic performance and substantially improved equity (i.e., reductions in the achievement gap) by noting that their own published research regarding the benefits of accountability (Skrla, Scheurich, & Johnson, 2000b) suggests that empirical examples of high-minority, high-performing schools are hard to come by, at least in Texas. After ten years of accountability and claims of success, we would expect to find a large number of districts with such schools. A search by Scheurich, Skrla, and Johnson (2000) yielded a total of 30 or (2.9 %) of Texas' 1,041 districts. Generalizing, as they do, from outlier districts like these to the state as a whole is problematic. Moreover, external data on those districts point to questionable progress. For example, they note positive outcomes in the Aldine Independent district where only 53.1% of the students have graduated. In a national study of 100 large urban districts cited by McNeil (this volume), Aldine's high school completion rate ranks 80th. Indeed, among the nation's 14 districts with the lowest graduation rates, six of these were in Texas. As of this writing, Texas' lofty claims about the

Houston Independent School District as a reformed district are being significantly challenged (Schemo, 2003a, 2003b; Winerip 2003).

With respect to the NAEP, we acknowledge improvements in scores among Texas students, but we also point out that Barton's (2001) research suggests that in 47 states, including Texas, an achievement gap persists on the NAEP between students in the top and lowest quartiles of White and minority students at the fourth-grade (mathematics and reading) and eighth-grade levels (mathematics) (also see McNeil, this volume). We respond to the allegation of polarization by reiterating that we are for accountability, while implicitly suggesting (through our alternative vision) our opposition to high-stakes testing.

We support an alternative model of accountability that is based on a framework developed by the Coalition for Authentic Reform in Education (C.A.R.E.). The model is centered around the notion of *local control over assessment* (for details, see www.fairtest.org/arn/masspage.html). Standardized examinations would be administered primarily to test for literacy and numeracy, and would be used in combination with multiple sources of information about a student's academic performance when making retention, promotion, and graduation decisions. These non-test sources would include student exhibitions, portfolios, products, and performance tasks. Under this model, state curricular standards reflect an essential but limited body of knowledge and skills that call for broadly defined competencies. Relying on a less regimented, more localized curricular focus that is authentically situated within the values and opportunity structures of communities would promote local innovation and a democratic spirit of parental and community participation, resulting in a more robust and authentic form of assessment.

This alternative proposal also calls for the establishment of quality review boards (QRB) at state and regional levels. At the state level, the QRB would bear the primary responsibility for annually evaluating the quality and availability of resources in schools and districts across the state. At the regional level, QRBs would consist of such stakeholders as teachers, parents, administrators, business representatives, and state education staff. These groups would bear the responsibility of reporting annually to their communities regarding student progress. Schools, in turn, would assume decision-making responsibility for curriculum and assessment, but these decisions would be subject to the review and approval of their districts and regional QRBs. Accountability is thus not to the state, but rather to a citizen public and the communities that schools serve.

Because of space limitations in the *Phi Delta Kappan*, current nationwide efforts toward authentic assessment were not discussed. Rhode

Island and Maine have been developing and experimenting with alternative assessment models. In Rhode Island, students entering the ninth grade in September 2004 will be subjected to alternative graduation criteria rather than to exclusive, test-based requirements (Rhode Island Board of Regents for Elementary and Secondary Education, 2003). That is, they must exhibit proficiency in a common core curriculum that includes the arts and technology. Schools have the option of using results of the state assessment as part of the graduation criteria, but they may not count for more than 10 percent of all the weighted factors contributing to the graduation determination.

Maine's assessment model is founded on overarching systemic change. By law, each district is to develop and implement a Comprehensive Local Assessment System (CLAS). The responsibility of the CLAS is to assess students' performance in relation to the content standards in eight content areas. Each CLAS was required by law to be in place by the end of 2002–2003 and it had to be certified by its superintendent as valid and reliable. Accordingly, each CLAS must guide teaching and learning, certify students' achievement in relation to the standards for high school graduation, and hold its district accountable for students' performance. In addition to administering the Maine Educational Assessment (MEA), students may be assessed with teacher-developed tests, nationally normed achievement tests, exit presentations, portfolios, district-wide administered and scored writing prompts, and other locally developed performance assessments (www.elm.maine.edu/assessments/class/). Another feature of the CLAS is that test scores are used constructively to trigger resources to schools in need.

For both Rhode Island and Maine, scoring children according to multiple assessment criteria is challenging but not impossible with computer technology. In Maine, some districts are developing their own software whereby student report cards are electronically generated. Each report card evaluates the students' mastery of state objectives according to various forms of assessment. By definition, although the model of assessment and accountability that a particular state takes would differ, the principle of multiple assessment criteria (not multiple tests) on which to evaluate students' work would be a common denominator. Moreover, such assessment alternatives are compatible with the requirements of the NCLB legislation.

In "Continuing the Conversation on Equity and Accountability: Listening Appreciatively, Responding Responsibly," Scheurich and Skrla (2001) take issue with our criticisms in several areas. First, they sense that we misunderstand their commitment to addressing systemic problems.

Accordingly, they cite a litany of historic inequities in need of redress: high teacher turnover; a lack of expertise among many teachers in high-poverty schools; chronic tracking, with children of color excluded from high-level classes; unjustifiably high rates of children of color in special education classes; low per-pupil expenditures; subtractive educational classroom experiences in which teachers fail to use the language and culture of the students; and power evasiveness among White teachers who say that they do not see color. Moreover, in light of their expressed view that results from state accountability systems do not exist in isolation from the effects created by other changes in state policies (such as increased state funding for public schools, mandatory class-size reductions, etc.), they wonder why "everyone seems to hear only that we support accountability" (p. 324).

Schuerich and Skrla also take issue with our characterizing their research results as an outlier effect. They suggest that to characterize schools and districts in this manner is to invoke a bell curve assumption, whereby most schools located in the middle of the curve are presumed to be doing little to nothing to promote student achievement. Finally, in response to the C.A.R.E. proposal, they urge us not to "romanticize" the notion of local control. They refer to the historic necessity for communities of color to seek statutory assistance from the federal government because of racist and exclusionary practices at the local level. They note that historic civil rights legislation was literally forced on local communities steeped in a culture of racism, but, they maintain, over time these changes came to be viewed positively. Top-down accountability, they suggest, should play out similarly.

Continuing the Conversation

Here, I offer some clarification of our position regarding the role of high-stakes testing in educational accountability. First, although we all share a deep concern over historic inequities, Scheurich and Skrla (2001) respond to these paradigmatically. They suggest adding opportunity-to-learn (OTL) measures to accountability scores for all schools and districts. Presumably, this would involve using an accountability reporting matrix that incorporates either additional or weighted results as part of the calibration of test scores according to available resources. This recommendation is consistent with their assumption that measurement can resolve the problem of unequal opportunities to learn the state curriculum.

Our continuing concern is that, at least in Texas, such "mathematical leveling" in performance reporting still would be premised on a misuse of tests through high-stakes testing. Scheurich and Skrla (2001) express some reservations about test validity, but generally they assume that the tests are valid—or valid enough—for accountability purposes. We disagree. A single measure of academic performance is not a valid indicator of achievement and thus cannot be an acceptable basis for holding the test taker or her teacher or his school or their district "accountable." The test makers themselves do not suggest otherwise (Valenzuela, 2002). Moreover, the act of adjusting scores by adding or subtracting OTL units could have the insidious effect of replacing constructive action—such as increasing funding or adding staff to resource-poor schools—with complex accounting techniques. Perhaps because their view of the state's testing system is based on interviews conducted with top-level administrators (school and district officials) rather than with teachers and parents, Scheurich and Skrla do not see Texas-style accountability as problematic. They also place great stock in the power of measurement to increase attention to existing problems and stimulate the downward flow of resources from district superintendents to classroom teachers. They anticipate that where the numbers show a need for improvement, more resources will be allocated for more hours of instruction. The result will be more equitable educational outcomes.

We recommend that instead of bringing in yet another measure of inequities as part of an accountability rubric, the state's obligation would be to redistribute material and human resources across districts and also to assist districts in redistributing resources equitably. Overhauling enduring structural problems that are the root cause of equally enduring educational inequities is the change that we seek. Rather than continuing to rate and diagnose the inequities, we call for putting in place a more democratic and balanced model that is as concerned with inputs (resources) and processes (quality of instruction) as our colleagues are with outputs (test scores). This case is forcefully made by Ruiz de Velasco (this volume), who maintains that the basic elements for the academic success of English-language learners are simply not in place. Our aim is not to banish testing. Rather, as explained earlier, in our vision of equity and accountability, test scores would be only one of many different kinds of assessment criteria.

With regard to Schuerich, Skrla, and Johnson's (2000) concern that readers seem to misunderstand their position, two explanations come to mind. First, in their discussion of OTL, the authors themselves suggest the centrality of accountability. A tortured circular logic guides their thinking: If there are persistent inequities, we need to measure them to make them "visible, obvious, and public" (p. 324). If there is a reduction in inequities, it is because they were made visible, obvious, and public. Perhaps because accountability "worked" in the schools where they conducted their research, Schuerich and colleagues seem unable to set aside their silver-bullet, cause-and-effect approach long enough to consider not only that responses to test-based accountability are varied, but also that in many instances accountability actually widens the achievement gap (see McNeil, this volume).

When the authors elaborated their five system components in their first article, they failed to address whether the high-stakes tests in Texas are appropriate, either as sole or primary indicators of academic competence. Their utter silence on this issue undermines their stated agreement with scholars (e.g., Hood, 1998) who argue that the current state tests favor middle-class Whites and are culturally biased against children of color. Not addressing this aspect of high-stakes testing suggests that Schuerich and colleagues believe that these considerations are secondary to the greater goal of equity that results-based accountability, in their view, promises. Similarly, despite their expressed concern over the absence of culturally and linguistically relevant curricula in schools, the authors do not include them into the curriculum section of their taxonomy. Finally, when Scheurich and colleagues acknowledge the collateral effects of testing reported in our research (McNeil & Valenzuela 2001; McNeil, 2000), they view this more as a lapse or breakdown within a system component than as evidence of a flawed design.

Logic alone dictates that when assessment doubles as the tool for monitoring student, teacher, school, and district quality, assessment is vulnerable to corruption. A strength of the C.A.R.E. model of accountability is that it separates these functions of assessment from monitoring. Scheurich, Skrla, and Johnson's model of accountability posits conceptually distinct components, but then negates this separation by failing to make provisions for the varying influence of the determinative weight of high-stakes tests. For example, curriculum issues (component 2), such as teaching to the test and "dumbing down" course materials, are intimately related to assessment issues (component 4) in a context in which high-stakes consequences for both children and schools are attached to children's scores.

For those of us who share a deep concern over extant inequities, the fact that Scheurich and colleagues' framework stops just short of addressing the adverse impact of high-stakes testing on minorities provokes an especially strong reaction to their thesis of historic possibilities. This aspect of their position also encourages our reading of their model of accountability as uncritically wedded to the notion of high-stakes testing. Such facile coupling of high-stakes testing to accountability presumes, on the one hand, that this kind of testing is a necessary feature of accountability systems and, on the other hand, that such tests actually measure what they purport to measure.

Our proposal of a more democratic form of accountability separates the concept of high-stakes testing from accountability. We posit that it is possible to have an accountability system that does not harm children. Stated more positively, we insist that accountability can and should be consistent with the use of locally derived, authentic assessments, academic rigor, and rich learning experiences. Children need not bear the brunt of unequal OTL through their graduation or nongraduation, or their promotion or nonpromotion. Absent these considerations, Scheurich and colleagues' vision of equity and accountability rings hollow.

The issue of outlier effects needs clarification. We did not intend to suggest the existence of a bell curve along which schools and districts could be ranked. Rather, our concern was and is with the generalizability of the claim that accountability works to change mindsets that previously were deficit oriented and subtractive. Does this mean that in all other schools where performance ratings have shown improvement, changed perspectives coupled with a marshaling of resources have been the decisive factor? Does a marshaling of resources signify a fundamental transformation of a poorly performing school into one that is staffed with certified and trained teachers, more advanced curricular offerings, well-stocked libraries, and fully functioning science laboratories? Or does it mean the channeling of dollars into the purchasing of test prep materials and activities of limited instructional value (see the chapters by McNeil; Hampton; Alamillo, Palmer, Viramontes, & García; and Sloan)? Does a marshaling of resources for targeted improvement qualify such schools and districts as nonracist? As culturally and linguistically relevant? What are we to make of the fact that the state-mandated, culturally chauvinistic curriculum remains intact?

Another concern we registered was that ten years of accountability in Texas have done little to alter the state's educational landscape. When Scheurich, Skrla, and Johnson's (2000) search for high-performing schools and districts attended by children of color, many of them poor, yields a subset of fewer than 3 percent of all Texas schools, this renders untenable their claim that accountability results in increased equity. In a state as large as Texas, we are not surprised that there would be entire districts where accountability data have been used responsibly. However, that some schools and districts are acting responsibly does not allay our concerns over test abuse, collateral effects, or adverse impact on poor and minority youth.

Finally, in cautioning us not to romanticize the notion of local control, Scheurich and colleagues cite top-down reforms accomplished by the civil rights movement. They note that people in power complained about integration and Title IX but grew accustomed to these changes over time. This analogy implies that the "movement" toward standards-based reform emanates from the mobilization efforts of poor, disenfranchised communities. This characterization could not be further from the truth.

The standardized accountability system has been unilaterally and undemocratically foisted on poor and minority communities. Poor, minority and immigrant communities may have been led by the rhetoric of "standards-based reforms" to believe that the state's accountability system would deliver to their communities the educational resources to help their schools—and their children—receive a highly academic education, one that attained high academic standards more typical of the education of children in more privileged districts. Little prepared, many of these parents felt encouraged to support the standardization of their children's schools and the reduction of their children's educational achievement to a single score on a single measure. A single-measure accountability system based on a standardized test, however, occupies no organic space in the wishes, desires, or mobilization efforts of poor, minority communities in Texas or elsewhere (see especially McNeil, 2000; Trujillo, 1998).

The case of desegregation is instructive, though, to the extent that it reminds us that when the statutory engines of change commanded restraint, they targeted not the victims of Jim Crow, but rather the perpetrators of discriminatory practices. Just as it would have been unreasonable—indeed, nonsensical—for either the lowest-level workers or business clientele to have assumed the primary burden of change to integrate lunch counters, hotels, and other public establishments, so too is it unreasonable for both children and their teachers to bear the burden of change under the banner of accountability. Using a market metaphor, it is similarly illogical to make either students or teachers responsible for the quality of their product when they do not control the resources or flow of finances to which the outcomes are tied (Dye, 2002).

It is important to note, however, that from a rational-choice, decision-making perspective (which is the underlying framework of the voucher/school choice movement), holding children—and by extension, their families—responsible for test score "products" does make sense.

That is, families *as consumers* can make use of the test scores and school ratings that accountability systems provide as a basis for their decisions regarding which schools their children should attend. From this perspective, school quality is less an issue of structural inequities, and more a matter of individual choice based on the "objective" information that accountability provides. Hence, an unintended consequence of the accountability model advanced by Scheurich, Skrla, and Johnson (2000) is a latent effect of advancing a conservative, consumer-oriented agenda that seeks nothing less than the privatization of public education (Labaree, 1997; Meier, 1995; Valenzuela, this volume). In light of their expressed concern for minorities, it is ironic, then, that Scheurich and colleagues' model should open the door to consumer-minded, often deficit-oriented individuals who have abandoned even the pretense of striving for equity.

One final point: Rather than being "romantic," the C.A.R.E. proposal implicitly reflects a studied consideration of the appropriate role of the state. Its aim—to limit the power of the state to make assessment and curricular decisions—is hardly an endorsement of a conservative, states' rights or return-to-local-control perspective. The equitable distribution of resources is an appropriate role of the state. The premise underlying our position is that the community is in a better position than the state to define not only what constitutes a quality education but also to assess children's talents, abilities, and potential. In contrast, one-size-fits-all performance standards conceived and administered at the highest bureaucratic levels encourage a regimented, test-driven curriculum and increase the chances that inaccurate decisions will be made on children's behalf.

Guiding Assumptions

The preceding analysis suggests, first, that proponents of Texas-style accountability view high-stakes testing as the driver for equity. Second, it suggests that they conceptually equate high-stakes testing with educational accountability, so much so that our anti-high-stakes-testing position gets construed as anti-accountability. This lack of precision helps explain why we are often accused of polarizing the debate on accountability. The truth of the matter is that although each side in this debate uses the same or similar terminology, we often mean different things. Third, for all their misgivings concerning the testing system's imperfections, they view "the test" as both an essential feature of accountability and a valid measure of educational knowledge and skills. Fourth, alternative epistemologies, values, and ways of knowing are secondary to the greater goal of equity that results-based accountability promises. And last, control over assessment properly resides in the hands of the state.

Opponents of Texas-style accountability bring a different set of assumptions to the table. First, we view high-stakes testing as unethical and inappropriate for measuring students' talents, abilities, and potential. Moreover, through collateral effects (such as narrowing curricula and marginalizing students), Texas-style accountability systems rob children of a quality education, fostering their psychic, emotional, and, sometimes, literal physical withdrawal from the schooling process.

Second, we distinguish accountability from high-stakes testing. Our insistence that accountability can be pursued without making children bear the brunt of it through their retention/non-retention or graduation/nongraduation on the basis of a single exam may be our most important contribution to the debate. Getting this message across to policy makers and the lay public is crucial because, at least in Texas, these stakeholders often equate accountability with high-stakes testing.

Third, using a single test to judge whether a student has mastered the state curriculum is inherently invalid. More valid decisions are made when educators use multiple and authentic sources of assessment of student learning. Additionally, coupling the assessment instrument with the monitoring function of accountability not only corrupts the assessment, but also makes children assume primary responsibility for both educational quality and inequality.

Fourth, Texas-style accountability is subtractive to the degree that the curriculum and the testing instrument reinscribe relations of domination and subordination between Anglos and Latina/os through a culturally and linguistically chauvinistic curriculum that privileges the English language while devaluing fully-vested bilingualism and biculturalism. In the current incarnation of accountability, alternative epistemologies or ways of knowing are not encouraged because the system is said to be culture-blind. Last, control over assessment properly resides not at the end of the long arm of the state, but rather in the caring hands of those who are in the best position to know our children, namely, their teachers, parents, and community. With our proposal for a more reciprocal and responsible form of accountability, the state's proper role is recast in terms of its central obligation, which is to provide the material and human resources that schools need to promote their equity goals.

The structuring out of culturally relevant schooling through the standardized educational experience that is reflected in Texas' current model of accountability results in enormous sacrifices that we as a society cannot afford (see McNeil, this volume). These include closing off teaching that draws from the richness of children's experiences, depriving them of our deepest and broadest understandings of our particular and shared cultural heritages in an increasingly interconnected global economy and planet. Standardized curricula, as argued in the chapters that follow, also lessen children's access to our greatest scientific achievements and our myriad ways of knowing (see Padilla, this volume).

Although the C.A.R.E. proposal insufficiently addresses the importance of culture in education, it creates space for this by calling for other ways of knowing, and teaching, to children's abilities and potential. Particularly in a context of rapidly changing demographics where the increasing presence of Latinos is reshaping entire communities, our sense of what children can learn should be based less on the limited goal of whether they can pass centrally designed, computer-scored tests, and more on a rigorous and challenging vision of schooling. Neither children nor their communities, languages, or identities represent liabilities, or "problems" to be overcome. From an asset-based perspective, they offer needed qualities in an increasingly globalized world.

Within an additive schooling model, caring for children in an authentic manner means honoring their community-based identities in a respectful, relational manner—*con propio respeto* (with due respect). Through a culture of engagement as Padilla (this volume) suggests, we can rekindle our democratic impulse to both search out our commonalities while respecting difference and affirming as Americans our commitment to shared principles like hard work, fair play, tolerance, due process, and social and economic justice. Resistance to high-stakes testing is thus not a ploy to water down quality or requirements, but rather a call to citizens and parents to exert democratic and community-based authority to rectify a system out of balance.

CHAPTER SUMMARIES

In chapter 2, "Performance-Based School Reforms and the Federal Role in Helping Schools That Serve Language-Minority Students," Jorge Ruiz de Velasco assesses the federal role by focusing attention on perhaps one of the most vulnerable student populations in our schools, namely, immigrant, English-language learners (ELLs). Ruiz de Velasco makes the case that typical assumptions that hold for English-speaking children's classrooms do not generally hold true for those filled with ELL youth. He investigates assumptions undergirding standards-based reforms and suggests reasons why those reforms that rely on high-stakes testing are not likely to be sufficient in meeting the needs of ELL youth. For starters, ELLs vary widely with respect to the number of languages that they speak, their prior levels of former schooling, their parents' levels of education, and the kinds of literacy practices that take place in their homes. Indeed, many enter our schools significantly under-schooled. Such students not only find it difficult to work at age-appropriate levels in required subjects, they also have difficulties doing so in their native languages. Nor are schools sufficiently equipped with trained staff and appropriate technologies for teaching to this wide diversity. Ruiz de Velasco also elaborates on what he thinks the appropriate role of the federal government should be at this historic juncture.

Chapter 3, "Faking Equity: High-Stakes Testing and the Education of Latino Youth," by Linda McSpadden McNeil, carries forward the critique of an allegedly objective accountability system by providing a thorough analysis of numbers-based accountability in Texas. She finds that accountability not only fails to tell the whole story, but depends on a partial accounting for the story to be true. Specifically, McNeil challenges the claim widely made in Texas that achievement is improving. She finds that on every indicator of academic achievement other than the TAAS, school children in the state not only register poor performance levels, they also are growing increasingly weaker academically.

McNeil portrays accountability as a system of controls governing nearly every aspect of public schooling in Texas. Moreover, these controls hinge on a standardized test that all children must take, which then becomes a basis for rating schools. This results in pressures to raise scores by narrowing curricula and marginalizing students who threaten school ratings. She maintains that the state is faking its claims of improving test scores. McNeil counters with evidence from other indicators, including SAT, ACT, and NAEP scores, and high school graduation rates. She concludes by suggesting that the evaluation of adults' (district administrators, school principals, and classroom teachers) performance must be decoupled from children's test scores. She also calls for an *educación* model of schooling that respects the cultures and values of children's families. In short, McNeil makes a persuasive case for why Texas-style accountability is not a model that other states should follow.

In chapter 4, "Texas' Second Wave of High-Stakes Testing: Anti–Social Promotion Legislation, Grade Retention, and Adverse Impact on Minorities," Richard R. Valencia and Bruno J. Villarreal review more than five decades of research on grade retention. They find clear evidence of its harmful impact on students, particularly with respect to academic outcomes. They point out that results in social science are rarely unequivocal. Yet study after study shows that although a few students perform better after being retained, most demonstrate either no progress or lower academic achievement when followed over time. Indeed, grade retention significantly increases the likelihood that students will drop out.

Valencia and Villarreal's analysis of projected third-grade retentions in Texas as a result of the state's new anti–social promotion policy provides sobering evidence of the disparate impact of SB 4 on Latinos, particularly Mexican Americans, and African Americans, relative to Anglos. They critique policy makers' penchant for attributing minorities' chronically low achievement to individual-level factors such as cognitive ability, motivation, and family background characteristics. Inasmuch as minority youth attend poor, segregated schools staffed by teachers who frequently are not certified to teach the courses they are assigned, high failure rates on standardized tests are scarcely reducible to individual aptitude, motivation, and decision making. Instead, poor test performance, alongside retention and dropping out, are better construed as symptomatic of many children's inferior schooling experiences (see also Valencia & Bernal, 2000).

In chapter 5, "Playing to the Logic of the Texas Accountability System: How Focusing on 'Ratings'—Not Children—Undermines Quality and Equity," Kris Sloan reports on his investigation of a Houston-area elementary school and school district. In considering accountability proponents' claim that it can be used to leverage educational reform, Sloan cites examples of places where such leveraging has occurred, drawn from research by Scheurich, Skrla, and Johnson (2000). He contrasts these findings with those of McNeil and Valenzuela (2001), whose investigation of accountability shows the system contributing to a reduction in the quality and quantity of curricula delivered to poor, minority children. Sloan reconciles these two strands of research by noting important differences in the focus of the studies. Scheurich and colleagues' research is top-down, gathered mostly from district-level personnel, while McNeil and Valenzuela provide a bottom-up view from the classroom. Sloan maintains that these divergent approaches help explain divergent conclusions. He situates his own two-year study within the latter approach.

As a matter of interest, if Sloan had conducted only a one-year ethnographic study, he would have concurred with Scheurich and colleagues' position. During the first year of his two-year study, teachers at Glendale Elementary school used the accountability system to successfully leverage reform through authentic approaches to curricula, activity-based learning, and an ethic of care. During the second year of the study, however, their reformist agenda was subverted into a ratings-focused response, largely through district-level mandates. Higher test scores and an accompanying positive school rating were achieved, but the cost was high—Glendale was transformed into a "factory model" school that aligned "people, customers, strategy, and processes" (Sloan, 2002, p. 171). The earlier, child-centered reform efforts were abandoned. The "TAAS discourse" that ensued, Sloan maintains, was able to dominate issues of educational quality precisely because of the composition of the school's student population—mainly poor children of color.

In chapter 6, "Standardized or Sterilized? Differing Perspectives on the Effects of High-Stakes Testing in West Texas," Elaine Hampton presents interview, survey, and focus group data from nine elementary and three middle schools in the Ysleta Independent School District in El Paso. Hampton's survey respondents and focus group members reported their perceptions of the effects of mandated testing on curriculum, students, and school climate. The data provide support for Sloan's view that perceptions of accountability are affected by individuals' position in the system. Across the schools that Hampton studied, administrators were much more positive about the effects of mandated testing than were the teachers in their schools.

Hampton also builds on Sloan's and McNeil's contributions with her findings that in response to administrators' demands, a test-centric curriculum unfolded at the classroom level. In one middle school, for example, teachers from every class in all subject areas taught math during their own class time. Students also took one to three math classes, per week (during their two-day block schedule), that focused exclusively on TAAS objectives. Professional development for teachers in the middle school was reduced to establishing teaching teams whose members then trained colleagues to design TAAS-like tests for use in their own classrooms. The elementary schools in Hampton's sample followed a similar path, supporting her contention that the accountability system is creating a standardized, sterilized curriculum and classrooms where rote, fragmented learning and monotony prevailed.

Laura Alamillo, Deborah Palmer, Celia Viramontes, and Eugene E. García highlight in chapter 7, "California's English-Only Policies: An Analysis of Initial Effects," policy and practice changes that have occurred in bilingual education programs under the rule of California's Proposition 227. Passed by voters in 1998, Proposition 227 restricts the use of the student's primary language in classroom instruction. Alamillo et al. collected interview data from teachers and principals statewide who work with language minority, elementary school students. Some of the educators in the sample continue to teach in their students' primary language because they work at sites where exemptions have preserved the bilingual programs, despite the recent policy mandates. Others work in schools that have dismantled their bilingual education programs. Across these two settings, increased frequency of assessments in English have resulted in a push for more English curricula and instruction, as well as in greater pressures on teachers to transition students into mainstream English to raise test scores.

Alamillo and colleagues find, as do McNeil, Sloan, and Hampton, that these pressures have reduced both the quality of learning and teacher autonomy, while increasing control over teacher practices. Teachers in schools with waivers that allow them to continue teaching bilingually even in the wake of Proposition 227 felt that the state's English-only testing system "was even more damaging to their primary language programs than Proposition 227 had been" (p. 217). Several participants in the study also cited racism against Latinos as an explanation for increased mass testing in English only.

In chapter 8, "The Centurion: Standards and High-Stakes Testing as Gatekeepers for Bilingual Teacher Candidates in the New Century," Belinda Bustos Flores and Ellen Riojas Clark examine the records of 20 students from a state university teacher education program who had been teaching in public schools located in a large, urban district. The analysis reveals how accountability logic attaches to teacher certification requirements to the detriment of prospective Latino, bilingual college students in pursuit of bilingual certification. Bustos Flores and Riojas Clark show how these students got caught in a web of university policies that were not designed for teachers who were seeking bilingual certification.

Specifically, by imposing a qualifying test, the university screened out potential failures on the "real" (state-mandated) exit test upon which both program accreditation and federal aid are based. This (along with other test-centric bureaucratic hurdles) negatively impacted Latina/o teachers seeking bilingual certification because it required them to take an exam outside of their specialty area; the exam presumed training commonly given to mainstream prospective teachers but not typically included in bilingual teacher programs. The test did not reflect, for example, differences in Spanish language arts training compared to English language arts training.

As a consequence of this and other gatekeeping mechanisms, many of these demonstrably qualified preservice teachers were unable to find stable employment. No matter how effective they were in the classroom, they had to take and pass the state-mandated exit exam to remain in their teaching positions. Bustos Flores and Riojas Clark note that at a time when there is a critical shortage of Latina/o teachers, these roadblocks preserve teacher training programs in the state universities but disproportionately sacrifice Latina/o students in the process.

The following chapter, "'High-Stakes Testing' and 'Educational Accountability' as Social Constructions Across Cultures," by Raymond V. Padilla, frames the contributions to this volume with a Latina/o epistemological perspective. He develops three major topics: (1) testing in relation to our present culture of measurement; (2) the underlying reductionism of accountability; and (3) alternative social constructions of educational reform that provide a richer sociocultural learning context for culturally diverse students. Padilla draws on the Spanish language terms *saber* and *conocer* to differentiate between objectivist and relational ways of knowing, respectively. He then shows how these epistemological differences are associated with distinctive cultural frameworks, which he terms the *culture of measurement* and the *culture of engagement*, respectively. He writes critically of the culture of measurement, which includes the currently popular model of de-contextualized accountability with high-stakes testing. The culture of measurement arises from a context-free perspective that privileges a numbers-based, objectivist way of knowing, and holds students solely responsible for school performance. It departs dramatically from the context-based culture of engagement that ascribes value and meaning to relationships and community, alongside a responsibility to care for children.

For Latina/os and other culturally diverse students, the culture of measurement can have harsh implications. An objectivist, decontextualized curriculum promotes a systemic disregard for the languages, cultures, and assets that children bring with them to the classroom, with the result that these students often are marginalized and alienated, to their academic and personal detriment. Padilla also notes the shared meaning of accountability within English and Spanish (*contabilidad*), where "to count" (*contar*) and "to recount," either with numbers or through narrative, are alternating options. Due to the culture of measurement, however, the semantic space accorded to "accountability" in the English language has narrowed. Instead of telling a story or providing a full accounting, the meaning of accountability is now reduced to numbers-based measurement.

In the final chapter, "Accountability and the Privatization Agenda," I make the case that the current accountability system serves as handmaiden to the privatization agenda in Texas. The political agenda behind the current accountability system became transparent while witnessing the strong push to privatize public education in Texas through various proposals during the 2003 legislative session. I document the presence of a powerful, neoliberal political and economic elite that helped develop and now works within the current framework on educational accountability, while simultaneously supporting privatization efforts, including school vouchers.

I expound on the debate over vouchers both because of my personal involvement in this issue and because of the influential, if unfortunate, role that some Latinos from the League of United Latin Americans Citizens (LULAC), in particular, have played in this evolving debate. The narrative shows that the Latino community is positioned on the sidelines of a much larger drama characterized by a right-wing, conservative agenda that both exploits the long-standing grievances that poor and minority communities hold toward schools and districts and deploys raw, political power to accomplish its goals. This account illustrates how localized issues, people, and cultures intersect when the forces for privatization emerge in a state or community. Building on the preceding chapters, this final piece demonstrates how accountability is more about the politics of control over public education than it is about children's learning and well-being.

In conclusion, as states elaborate their testing systems mandated by the No Child Left Behind Act, we hope educators and policy makers will heed the lessons provided by Texas-style accountability. The particular legislative issues in Texas reveal the complexity of the struggle and the difficulty in changing these top-down, state-mandated systems once they are in place. Increasing numbers of parents, educators, and government officials across the United States realize that accountability systems based on standardized tests carry high costs to districts, and harmful effects on children. Also, efforts involving revision or resistance are taking many forms. In Texas, it is important to note that the locus for change has been in the legislature, where important bills originate.

The evidence and arguments in this volume make clear that to the degree that states attach high-stakes consequences to tests for children, schools, and districts, they are likely to reproduce the uneven, unjust, and unnecessary educational outcomes we have documented in Texas. For the sake of all of our children, we hope that those who design the new systems will seize the opportunity to reconceptualize accountability by first divesting it of its high-stakes testing component and developing in its place multiple and authentic sources of assessment that will provide a more valid, just, and humane picture of student achievement. The purpose of accountability is to make sure that the educational system serves the children. Our earlier statement bears repeating: Accountability is thus not to the state, but rather to a citizen public and the communities that schools serve.

NOTES

1. I use the terms Latina and Latino (or Latina/o) to be inclusive of all Latina/o subgroups in Texas. According to the 2000 U.S. census, U.S.-born Mexican Americans and immigrant Mexicans combined are the largest Latina/o subgroup, numbering 5,071,963 out of the total state population of 20,851,820 (24.3%). (Source: U.S. Census Bureau, Census 2000. Table DP 1. Profile of General Demographic Characteristics: 2000, Geographic Area: Texas.)

2. We presented this position at a Capitol Hill briefing to address the effects of high-stakes testing and social promotion on Latino youth on Friday, March 15, 2002. The event was conducted in conjunction with the Congressional Hispanic Caucus, the Hispanic Education Coalition, and the Center for Mexican American Studies (CMAS) at the University of Texas at Austin.

3. Our position on high-stakes testing is shared with all of the leading national educational and measurement organizations, including the American Educational Research Association, National Academy of Sciences, Association for Supervision and Curriculum Development, American Psychological Association, National Council of Teachers of English, National Council of Teachers of Mathematics, and the National Council on Measurement in Education.

4. I quote here from Kauffman (1999), "In 1997 at the end of the twelfth grade, approximately ten thousand seniors were still taking the TAAS Exit Test (Fassold report, PX 26). Of these, 87% were either Hispanic or African American. On this 'final' administration of the TAAS Exit Test, 41% of Whites, 32% of African Americans and 27% of Hispanics passed the test (Fassold test; Fassold report, PX 26 at pp. 8–9)."

5. Historically, the exit-level TAAS test has been taken beginning during the students' sophomore year, giving them up to eight additional opportunities to take the exam. Beginning this year, the exit exam is to be given in the eleventh grade, giving students fewer opportunities to take the state exam (see McNeil).

6. For an excellent review of this case from a research-based perspective, see the special issue of the *Hispanic Journal of Behavioral Sciences* edited by Valencia and Bernal, 2000.

7. The Urban School Alliance, a coalition of urban district administrators representing a quarter of all children enrolled in the state, made use of a clause in SB 4 that instructs the commissioner to certify whether sufficient funds have been appropriated statewide for the legislation (TEC §28.0211 [m]). The Alliance attempted to make the case that funding was insufficient. However, their concern was subsequently nullified by the commissioner who indicated that sufficient funds were available.

8. According to Ingersoll (2003), as of 2002, nineteen states have high-stakes graduation tests in place. Five states, including Texas, make grade promotion contingent on passing a test. At the school level, all schools that are now receiving Title I monies are subject to high-stakes consequences if adequate yearly progress is not achieved (see the NCLB website at http://www.ed.gov/legislation/FedRegister/finrule/2002-3/070502a.html for Title I regulations).

9. See Ingersoll (2003) for a national-level analysis of the determining influence of teacher quality on improved student performance.

REFERENCES

Barton, P. (2001). *Raising achievement and reducing gaps: Reporting progress toward goals for academic achievement. A report to the National Education Goals Panel*. Washington, D.C.: National Education Goals Panel.

Blackwell, K. (2003, March 19) Students rise to challenge of tougher test in reading. *Austin American-Statesman*, pp. B1, B6.

Darling-Hammond, L., Ancess, J., & Falk, B. (1995). *Authentic assessment in action: Studies of schools and students at work*. New York: Teachers College Press.

Dye, J. (2002). *A natural yet overlooked feature of accountability in public education: Accountability is supposed to go both ways*. Unpublished manuscript.

Fassold, M. (1999). Expert report supplemental. Submitted to plaintiffs' counsel, Albert H. Kauffman. GI Forum et al. v. Texas Educational Agency et al. 87 F. Supp.2d 667 (W.D. Tex. 2000).

Fassold, M. (2000). Disparate impact analyses of TAAS scores and school quality. *Hispanic Journal of the Behavioral Sciences, 22*(4), 460–480.

GI Forum et al. v. Texas Educational Agency et al., 87 F. Supp.2d 667 (W.D. Tex. 2000).

Haney, W. (2000). The myth of the Texas miracle in education. *Education Policy Analysis Archives, 8*(41), 1. Retrieved August 24, 2000. Available at: http://epaa.asu.edu/v8n41/

Haney, W. (2001). *Revisiting the myth of the Texas miracle in education: Lessons about dropout research and dropout prevention*. Paper presented at the Dropout Research: Accurate Counts and Positive Interventions Conference, Harvard Civil Rights Project, Cambridge, MA, January 13, 2001.

Haney, W., Madaus, G., & Lyons, R. (1993). *The fractured marketplace for standardized testing*. Boston: Kluwer Academic Publishers.

Heubert, J. P., & Hauser, R. M. (Eds.). (1999). *High stakes: Testing for tracking, promotion, and graduation*. Committee on Appropriate Test Use, Board on Testing and Assessment, Commission on Behavioral and Social Sciences and Education, National Research Council. Washington, D.C.: National Academy Press.

Hood, S. (1998). Culturally responsive performance-based assessment: Conceptual and psychometric considerations. *Journal of Negro Education, 67*, 187–96.

Ingersoll, R. M. (2003, January 9). Special report: Quality counts 2003: "If I can't learn from you." *Education Week.*

Kauffman, A. (1999). Post-trial brief. In the United States District Court for the Western District of Texas, San Antonio Division.

Labaree, D. F. (1997). *How to succeed in school without really learning: The credentials race in American education.* New Haven: Yale University Press.

Linn, R. L. (1982). Ability testing: Individual differences, prediction and differential prediction. In A. K. Wigdor & W. R. Garner (Eds.), *Ability testing: Uses consequences and controversies, Part II* (pp. 335–388). Washington, D.C.: National Academy Press.

McNeil, L. (2000). *Contradictions of reform: Educational costs of standardized testing.* New York: Routledge.

McNeil, L., & Valenzuela, A. (2001). The harmful impact of the TAAS system of testing in Texas: Beneath the accountability rhetoric. In M. Kornhaber & G. Orfield (Eds.), *Raising standards or raising barriers? Inequality and high stakes testing in public education* (pp. 127–150). New York: Century Foundation.

Meier, D. (1995). *The power of their ideas.* Boston: Beacon Press.

Meier, D. (2000). *Will standards save public education?* Boston: Beacon Press.

Meier, D. (2002). *In schools we trust: Creating communities of learning in an era of testing and standardization.* Boston: Beacon Press.

Murdock, S., Hoque, M. N., Michael, M., White, S., & Pecotte, B. (1997). *The Texas challenge: Population change and the future of Texas.* College Station: Texas A&M University Press.

Newmann, F. M. (1996). *Authentic achievement: Restructuring schools for intellectual quality.* San Francisco: Jossey-Bass.

Rating TAKS: State must not waver in reaching accountability goals. (2003, April 18). *Houston Chronicle,* p. 36A.

Rhode Island Board of Regents for Elementary and Secondary Education. (2003). *Regulations of the Board of Regents for elementary and secondary education regarding public high schools and ensuring literacy for students entering high school.* Cranston: Rhode Island School-to-Career. Retrieved March 31, 2004, from http://www.riste.org/hsrules.htm

Saucedo, L. M. (2000). The legal issues surrounding the TAAS case. *Hispanic Journal of Behavioral Sciences, 22*(4), 411–422.

Schemo, D. J. (2003a). Questions on data cloud luster of Houston schools. New York Times. Retrieved July 11, 2003, from http://www.nytimes.com

Schemo, D. J. (2003b). For Houston schools, college claims exceed reality. *New York Times.* Retrieved August 28, 2003, from http://www.nytimes.com

Scheurich, J., & Skrla, L. (2001). Continuing the conversation on equity and accountability: Listening appreciatively, responding responsibly. *Phi Delta Kappan, 83*, 322–326.

Scheurich, J., Skrla, L., & Johnson, J. (2000). Thinking carefully about equity and accountability. *Phi Delta Kappan, 82*(4), 293–299.

Shepard, L. A., & Smith, M. L. (1989). *Flunking grades: Research and policies on retention.* London: Falmer Press.

Skrla, L., Scheurich, J., & Johnson, J. (2000a). *Accountability for equity: Can state policy leverage social justice?* Paper presented at the annual meeting of the American Educational Research Association, New Orleans, LA, April 24–28, 2000.

Skrla, L., Scheurich, J., & Johnson, J. (2000b). *Equity-driven achievement-focused school districts: A report on systemic school success in four Texas school districts serving diverse student populations.* Austin, TX: Charles A. Dana Center.

Sloan, K. (2002). *A ratings-focused response to the Texas accountability system and the professional lives of teachers: An ethnography.* Doctoral Dissertation: University of Texas at Austin, Texas.

Texas Education Agency. (1996). *The development of accountability systems nationwide and in Texas (Statewide Texas Educational Progress Study (STEPS) 1).* Austin, TX: Texas Education Agency.

Texas Education Agency. (2003a, March 18). *Texas third-grade students exceed predictions; 89 percent pass reading exam.* Press Release. Retrieved July 14, 2003, from http://www.tea.state.tx.us/press/89percent.html

Texas Education Agency. (2003b, July 23). Passing rate hits 96 percent on crucial third-grade TAKS reading test; retention may be only slightly higher than past years. Press Release. Retrieved August 20, 2003, from http://www.tea.state.tx.us/press/taks31.html

Texas State Board of Education. (2002). *Texas Assessment of Knowledge and Skills [TAKS] standard setting: Summary of projected impact.* Unpublished document.

Trujillo, A. (1998). *Chicano empowerment and bilingual education: Movimiento politics in Crystal City, Texas.* New York: Garland Publishing.

Valencia, R. R., & Bernal, E. M. (Eds.). (2000). Special Issue. The Texas Assessment of Academic Skills (TAAS) Case: Perspectives of plaintiffs' experts. *Hispanic Journal of the Behavioral Sciences, 22*(4), 403–561, 423–444.

Valencia, R. R., & Suzuki, L. A. (2001). *Intelligence testing and minority students: Foundations, performance factors, and assessment issues.* Thousand Oaks, CA: Sage.

Valencia, R. R., Valenzuela, A., Sloan, K., & Foley, D. (2001). Let's treat the cause, not the symptoms: Equity and accountability in Texas revisited. *Phi Delta Kappan, 83*(4), 318–326.

Valenzuela, A. (1999). *Subtractive schooling: U.S.-Mexican youth and the politics of caring.* Albany: State University of New York Press.

Valenzuela, A. (2000). The significance of the TAAS test for Mexican immigrant and Mexican American adolescents: A case study. *Hispanic Journal of the Behavioral Sciences, 22*(4), 524–539.

Valenzuela, A. (2002). High-stakes testing and U.S.-Mexican youth in Texas: The case for multiple compensatory criteria in assessment. *Harvard Journal of Hispanic Policy, 14,* 97–116.

Valenzuela, A., and Maxcy, B. (in press). Limited English proficient youth and accountability: All children (who are tested) count. In J. Ruiz deVelasco & M. Fix (Eds.), *School reform, immigrants, and native minorities.* Washington, D.C.: Urban Institute.

Willingham, W., Lewis, C., Morgan, R., & Ramist, L. (1990). *Predicting college grades: An analysis of institutional trends over two decades.* Princeton, NJ: Educational Testing Service.

Winerip, M. (2003). The "zero dropout" miracle: Alas! Alack! A Texas tall tale. *New York Times.* Retrieved August 13, 2003, from http://www.nytimes. com

2

Performance-Based School Reforms and the Federal Role in Helping Schools That Serve Language-Minority Students

JORGE RUIZ DE VELASCO

The 1980s and 1990s were a period of enormous ferment in American public education. Still, few reforms of the period have had as much impact on classroom practice as the federal push to encourage states to establish curriculum standards in core subjects and to hold teachers and local school administrators accountable for student performance on state-administered tests. Educators have focused much attention on this movement's implications for classroom teaching and learning.[1] Considerably less attention has been paid to implications for Latinos, English-language learners (ELLs),[2] and other student subpopulations. Yet, the measurement of performance through school-level results on standardized achievement tests is so pervasive that, to be meaningful, any discussion of Latino education today must take place within that framework.

This chapter, by analyzing the fundamental assumptions embedded in the performance-based accountability movement, extends criticisms of the movement originally formulated by such groups as the Citizens' Commission on Civil Rights, the Mexican American Legal Defense and Education Fund (MALDEF), and the Harvard Civil Rights Project. However appropriate accountability assumptions may be for the typical classroom, they generally do not hold true for ELL classrooms. What would work best for ELL students remains uncertain. The gap between the educational needs of English-language learners (especially those in secondary

Work on this chapter was supported, in part, by the Spencer Foundation and the U.S. Department of Education, Office of Educational Research and Improvement. Opinions expressed herein are those of the author.

schools) and professional knowledge about how to meet these students' needs is wide. This chapter argues that despite efforts such as additional resources, professional development, and school capacity building, this gap is unlikely to be bridged in the short run. Federal programs that focus greater attention on basic research in language and literacy development for second-language learners could be of help; additionally, federal programs should support professional development for those who teach ELL students and should promote innovative demonstration programs. This chapter's analysis also makes clear that public school systems must work toward a greater reciprocal accountability that includes measurable standards for holding state and district leaders accountable for providing teachers and students with adequate resources and opportunities to meet new standards. In the absence of such reciprocity, accountability systems are likely to continue to net poor results.

HISTORICAL OVERVIEW: FROM EQUAL ACCESS TO PERFORMANCE OUTCOMES

Between 1960 and the mid-1980s, the center of gravity in federal efforts to improve ELL education lay in ensuring equal access and in building the capacity of state and local agencies to mount effective programs for a steadily growing ELL student population. A long civil rights crusade led by minority advocates resulted in these imperatives being codified in key legislation, including the Civil Rights Act and the Elementary and Secondary Education Act of 1964, the Bilingual Education Act of 1968, the Equal Educational Opportunity Act of 1974, and the Emergency Immigrant Education Act of 1984. This legislation also reflects federal policy makers' awareness that local educators often lacked the capacity and expertise to meet the needs of a changing school population without federal help.

By the mid-1980s, the strongest voices for school reform were animated by a different set of imperatives: school productivity and accountability for student performance. Following the 1983 release of *A Nation at Risk* by the National Commission on Excellence in Education, school reform advocates in many states began calling for higher curriculum standards, more ambitious instructional frameworks, and new student assessments tied to the new, more rigorous standards (Lowry & Buck, 2001). Moreover, most reformers thought that schools should be held accountable for student results on the new assessments (Cohen, 1996). Early promoters of performance-based reform—

business élites, public officials, and education experts[3]—were joined by a wider coalition of educators and reform advocates who saw an opportunity to harness the standards movement to equity concerns[4] (Smith & O'Day, 1991).

In 1994, the Clinton administration convinced Congress to require all states to implement comprehensive accountability systems for schools receiving federal funds under Title 1 of the Elementary and Secondary Education Act. This new federal requirement addressed civil rights advocates' concerns that schools serving large numbers of poor, minority, and limited-English-proficient students set lower standards for their education and thus ratified lower expectations for their performance (Citizens' Commission on Civil Rights, 1999). The Title 1 program changes broke with past practice by requiring states to replace minimum standards for poor and academically disadvantaged children with challenging standards for *all* students. These new accountability systems were to be based on state-established content standards for reading and math and on assessments aligned with those standards. The new law required states to hold all students to the same performance standards and to hold schools and districts accountable for student performance. Most states subsequently developed performance-based accountability systems for a wider number of core subjects and for all public schools. Some states went a step further and attached high stakes to performance-based assessments (e.g., relying on test scores to assess teacher or principal performance or to determine student promotion and graduation). In 2001, Congress reauthorized Title I legislation when it passed the No Child Left Behind Act. Congress now mandates annual testing of every child in grades three to eight and strengthens requirements that states hold schools and districts accountable for student performance, including, specifically, minority and economically disadvantaged students, as well as those with limited proficiency in English.

CHALLENGING PERFORMANCE-BASED SCHOOL ACCOUNTABILITY REFORMS

As more and more states adopted performance-based accountability reforms, civil rights and minority group advocates began to challenge several aspects of the reforms. These challenges have taken three broad approaches. Civil rights advocates who were early supporters of the accountability movement, including the Citizens' Commission on Civil Rights, continue to embrace the argument that accountability reforms can benefit disadvantaged students (Citizens' Commission on Civil Rights, 1999). They argue, however, that the movement's promise has not been realized because, too often, ELL and other disadvantaged students are effectively excluded from accountability systems. The Citizens' Commission thus directs attention to the need to enforce existing Title 1 requirements that states provide adequate resources and training to staff in poor and low-performing schools. The Commission also has insisted that states avoid creating dual performance standards for advantaged and disadvantaged students and instead include all students within the same accountability system and hold all schools and students to the same standards.

Other groups, including the Mexican American Legal Defense and Education Fund (MALDEF), initially sought to forestall implementation of some accountability reforms by challenging them directly in court. In Texas, for example, MALDEF filed suit on behalf of nine Black and Latino students denied high school diplomas after they did not pass the required state assessments prior to their scheduled graduation dates. MALDEF asserted that the Texas assessment system placed the onus of accountability on students themselves and discriminated against Black, Latino, and ELL students who were disproportionately and adversely affected by the state test requirements (Horn, 2001).[5]

Still others, including participants in the Harvard Civil Rights Project, have focused on extralegal aspects of state accountability systems as they affect schools where poor and minority students predominate. Angela Valenzuela and Linda McNeil, for example, have argued that the Texas accountability system has often had the effect of crowding out instruction in non-tested subjects (e.g., science and social studies) and has reduced the depth and quality of instruction in subjects that are tested (e.g., writing). Moreover, they point to field research suggesting that accountability systems discriminate against minority students insofar as they reward cultural literacies and understandings that African American and Latino students do not possess and/or effectively separate these students from (and thus fail to capitalize on) the experience, language, and cultural knowledge that they do bring to the classroom (McNeil & Valenzuela, 2000).

A key reason performance-based school reforms have so frequently worked against student subpopulations such as language, racial, and ethnic minorities lies in the movement's basic assumptions about classroom practices, student demographic and skill profiles, and teacher preparation and expertise. The next section examines these assumptions.

FUNDAMENTAL ASSUMPTIONS OF THE PERFORMANCE-BASED ACCOUNTABILITY MOVEMENT

Early proponents of performance-based reforms envisioned that, prior to implementation of high-stakes assessments, states would ensure that schools had the support needed to respond to new curriculum and student performance standards. At a minimum this meant an adequate supply of high-quality textbooks, technological software, and other instructional materials aligned to the new standards. In some states, standards-based reforms also implied a concerted effort to reform and align preservice and in-service professional development systems with the imperatives of the curriculum standards. As Smith and O'Day (1991) explained, states must first ensure that teachers "know well *and* know how to teach the content set out in the [curriculum] frameworks" (p. 249).

Unfortunately for students and teachers, many states have put standards in place ahead of the instructional support and teacher preparation that are prerequisites to success. Indeed, most standards-based reforms implemented today make two important—and fundamentally flawed—assumptions about the classroom:

1. The basic elements for academic success already exist in the classroom[6] (i.e., classrooms are staffed by trained and skilled educators with appropriate resources and know-how).
2. Students are ready to perform at or near the desired performance level.[7]

As Stanford education historian Larry Cuban reminds us, these assumptions are consistent with the "business model" of reform that dominates today: "Restructure operations so that managers and employees who actually make the product decide how it is to be done efficiently and effectively. Then hold those managers and employees responsible for the quality of the product by rewarding those who meet or exceed their goals and punishing those who fail" (Cuban, 2001, p. 178). In this approach, the production level of an organization is treated as a black box. Success at the production level is measured as the difference between the cost of needed inputs (resources and materials) and the market value of outputs (final products).

In school settings, the classroom becomes the black box; however, only test scores (outputs) are measured and they become the sole basis for rewards and consequences. Little attention is given within the accountability system to inputs (resources and conditions necessary for students and teachers to succeed). The tacit assumption is that teachers and students already possess whatever is required to work and compete successfully. All that is needed is for administrators, teachers, and students to be given clear signals about what is expected (performance standards) and the right incentives (accountability systems and high-stakes assessments) to get them to focus on production (meeting the standards). Yet, there is ample evidence that these assumptions are most often not true for immigrant and other language-minority students and the teachers who work directly with them. The sections that follow offer a glimpse into the black box of the classroom and explain why the inclusion of ELL students in one-sided performance-based accountability systems is problematic today and why it will likely remain problematic in the coming decade.[8]

Increasing Demographic Diversity Among ELL Students

The wide diversity of ELL students and their needs is one of the biggest challenges schools have in fitting ELL students into performance accountability regimes. English-language learners vary considerably with respect to the number of languages they speak, the level of prior schooling in their native languages, the level of their parents' education, and the nature of home literacy practices (e.g., whether students are read to at home). These students also differ in the degree to which they are linguistically isolated from English learning outside the classroom setting. These factors all bear on classroom learning and may require different kinds of interventions, teaching strategies, and curricula. Some educators have speculated that the level of diversity found among ELL immigrants might require abandoning the practice of offering one basic language development program and embracing an approach similar to that taken with special education, in which schools develop an individualized education plan for each student. Some states, including Texas, have taken some steps in this direction.[9] Indeed, some educators suggest that the growing diversity of students' needs and skill levels demands a new, student-centered pedagogy (Reyes, Scribner, & Paredes Scribner, 1999).

Recent studies of immigrant secondary education programs have identified two ELL subpopulations as being of special concern. One is the set of immigrant children who arrive after the fourth grade, often as teenagers. Because these late-arriving students have limited time to master a new language and pass subjects required for promotion and high school graduation, language and content instruction must be offered simultaneously rather than sequentially. Yet, we know very little about how best to help these students meet these twin objectives while also meeting new state standards (August & Hakuta, 1997; Ruiz de Velasco & Fix, 2000; Wiley, 1996).

The other subgroup of special concern is the growing number of under-schooled newcomers who must overcome critical literacy gaps and the effects of interrupted schooling in their home countries. Schools rarely collect data on the prior schooling of immigrant students, so their precise number in U.S. schools is not known. One estimate indicates that 20 percent of all ELL students at the high school level and 12 percent of ELL students in middle schools have missed two or more years of schooling since age six (Fleishman & Hopstock, 1993). Under-schooled ELL students most often arrive with a weak literacy foundation for learning a second language and have difficulty working at age-appropriate levels in required subjects, even when taught in their native or primary languages (García, 1999). Moreover, most English as a Second Language (ESL) and bilingual education programs for secondary school youth assume some native language literacy. Thus, such programs are not designed to develop the basic literacy that children would normally have acquired in elementary schools (García, 1999; Mace-Matluck, Alexander-Kasparik, & Queen, 1998; Ruiz de Velasco & Fix, 2001).

Lack of critical resources. Another challenge to ELL student education in the performance-based accountability environment is that even the best of schools often lack the capacity to meet student needs. Here the problem is not just a need for *more* resources. There is, in addition, a critical need for *new*, as yet undiscovered, resources.

Lack of Reliable and Scientifically Valid Assessment Instruments

The lack of reliable and valid assessment instruments available for testing ELL students' core subject knowledge in Spanish (or other native languages) is a problem of long standing. Although some states (e.g., Texas) have produced Spanish-language versions of their state performance assessments, others have found this approach problematic. Illinois officials, having determined that there is no appropriate way to translate any part of the state's performance test Illionis Standards Achievement Test (ISAT) into other languages, specifically prohibit local officials from doing so.[10] Illinois is not alone in this regard. The lack of reliable content area assessments or information on appropriate assessment accommodations for ELL students is a challenge in all states developing performance-based accountability systems.

Long-Term Shortage of Trained Teachers

Critical shortages of language-development and other specially trained staff place special burdens on schools as they struggle to meet the needs of a growing number of ELL students. In the Department of Education's last national Schools and Staffing Survey, only 30% of public school teachers instructing limited-English students nationwide reported receiving any special training for working with these students. Moreover, 27% of all schools with bilingual/ESL staff vacancies—and 33% in central city school districts—reported finding these positions "difficult" or "impossible" to fill (U.S. Department of Education, 1995). In Illinois, as elsewhere, the state board of education has identified both certified bilingual and ESL teachers as likely high-demand areas in which teacher shortages are expected over the next 10 years (Illinois State Board of Education, 2000).

The long-term shortage of new teachers specially trained to work with ELL students underscores the importance of training *veteran* teachers to work more effectively with new populations of ELL immigrants. This imperative is especially strong in secondary schools. Training around ELL issues (e.g., language acquisition, ELL assessment, and multicultural awareness) for high school administrators and teachers of mainstream subjects is often absent or sketchy, even though ELL students frequently are in mainstream subject classes for at least part of their school day.[11]

ELL CURRICULUM AND INSTRUCTION: THE DEBATE OVER EFFECTIVE STRATEGIES

A review by the National Academy of Science (NAS) suggests that professional knowledge about how to help ELL students develop academic English reading and composition skills (as opposed to basic oral English speaking and comprehension skills) is thin. This problem is particularly acute in secondary schools where learning in mainstream-content classes requires background knowledge and advanced literacy skills (both linguistic and cultural) that second-language learners may not possess (August & Hakuta, 1997). In the typical social science class, for example, students must be able to construct arguments and discuss alternative solutions to social problems in English. In mathematics, students must work with English texts containing vocabulary specific to math (e.g., integer, algebraic), as well as everyday words that have different meanings in mathematics (e.g., table, irrational). This level of academic English may take four to seven years to acquire under the best of circumstances (August & Hakuta, 1997; Hakuta, Butler, & Witt, 2000; Thomas & Collier, 1997); for many ELL students, the amount of time available to master the subjects required for graduation is much shorter (Anstrom, 1997).

The NAS study also noted the continuing uncertainty regarding how students' age, intelligence, and attitudes mediate their language learning. As well, much remains unknown about the specific relationship between the social and linguistic environments of schools and the linguistic attainments of students (August & Hakuta, 1997). For example, immigrant residential patterns and ESL bilingual programming may result in school settings in which ELL immigrant students are concentrated with other language-minority students. The effects of the resulting linguistic isolation may be more pronounced in secondary schools where, studies have found, students tend to self-segregate in nonclassroom contexts (Olsen, 1997). Although this area remains under-studied, there is evidence that immigrant ELLs may encounter difficulties in language and subject matter learning because of limited exposure to English speakers in their home and peer-group settings. Nonclassroom contact has been found to accelerate language and subject learning by exposing ELL students to novel word meanings and standard and academic discourse styles that are rewarded in classroom work (August & Hakuta, 1997).

ELL STUDENTS AND THE IMPACT OF SECONDARY SCHOOLS' WORK AND TIME ORGANIZATION

The organization of work and time in the typical secondary school is often incompatible with the needs of English-language learners and tends to isolate them and their language development teachers from the mainstream school program.[12] These concerns are all the more important as ELL students are expected to meet the same content performance standards as all other students to graduate.

Staff Organization

Studies of secondary schools serving large numbers of language-minority students indicate that the organization of school staff into subject or functional departments (e.g., English and science departments or special education and ESL departments) often has important and largely negative consequences for ELL students and their language development teachers. This is so principally because, at the organizational level, the task of preparing ELL students to participate effectively in mainstream classrooms is conceived of as a special or add-on activity outside the "normal" functions of the secondary school (Adger & Peyton, 1999).

Rigid departmentalization often excludes ESL/bilingual teachers from such functions as school-wide curriculum planning and standards development. These responsibilities, which fall squarely within ESL/bilingual teachers' professional competence, often are executed from within regular academic departments. This is especially true in high schools where larger student enrollments and wider grade spans compel greater specialization among teachers. In one study, departmentalization was found to encourage mainstream subject teachers to believe that addressing the language development needs of their ELL students was the exclusive responsibility of other school staff or departments. This belief was reinforced by the fact that school administrators did not support or encourage mainstream subject teachers' participation in training that might help them incorporate language development strategies into their classes. Core subject teachers also reported that their lack of knowledge about ELL students' needs often led them to have low expectations of these students' performance (Ruiz de Velasco & Fix, 2001).

Providing all students with effective access to the full range of a school's programs (e.g., libraries, computers, counseling, and health services) requires that key nonclassroom staff be aware of ELL/immigrant student needs and act to eliminate language and cultural barriers to the services they provide. Yet, principals, counselors, librarians, and other support staff typically have no special training to work with ELL immigrant youth and often do not possess the language skills necessary to communicate directly with them. As a result, ESL and bilingual teachers often must take on duties normally handled by administrative and support staff. In high schools, for example, it is not uncommon to find ESL teachers charged with conducting library orientations, computer classes, and counseling sessions, and asked to participate in student discipline conferences in which parents are present. ELL students in such schools have fewer adults who are specifically charged with their education. And the long-term outlook is poor where more veteran teachers and administrators are not encouraged to retool their skills to meet ELL student needs.

Time Organization

Teachers in secondary schools with large numbers of language-minority students often report that the typical school class schedule (50-minute time blocks) and academic calendar (180 school days) are not long enough to promote the kind of sustained, interactive, and comprehensive instruction ELL secondary students need. Teachers cite two critical needs that go unmet when these students and their teachers confront an inflexible schedule. First, teen ELL students need to spend more time on all tasks that require English language proficiency to master the content required for graduation in the short time available. Accomplishing this often requires access to extended day programs, specially designed summer school, and after-school tutoring. But such extended programming requires district or state-level support that frequently is not available.

Likewise, teachers who work closely with ELL students need to devote more time to planning and collaboration when facing greater skill diversity in their classrooms. Yet the typical teaching schedule—five classes per day, 150 students, and a single 50-minute planning period—makes it exceedingly difficult for teachers to prepare for students with special needs, give struggling students individualized attention, and collaborate with other teachers. The complex task of teaching students at differing levels of language and literacy development, coupled with the limited body of professional knowledge about effective teaching strategies, only increase the importance of not working in isolation. Collaboration among ESL/bilingual teachers is necessary because it promotes a greater awareness of the approaches that other teachers are taking with ELL youth. And collaboration between language development and mainstream subject teachers is essential for teachers to develop school-wide strategies for helping ELL students make successful transitions to mainstream instruction. This collaboration requires flexible scheduling that permits common planning periods and opportunities for team teaching—activities not often supported in secondary schools.

PERFORMANCE-BASED REFORM: EARLY WARNING SIGNS OF PROBLEMATIC OUTCOMES

As states implement new performance standards, some are finding troubling signs that reform efforts are not translating into improved outcomes for all students. This is particularly so where states attach consequences, such as promotion or graduation eligibility, to performance on state assessments. The Texas Education Agency, for example, has reported that only 20% of ELL 10th graders met minimum qualifications on all three exit-level tests (reading, writing and math) the state requires for graduation (Texas Education Agency, 2001). The other 80% will face steep challenges because they have only two years in which to master the English language and content skills required for a high school diploma. These numbers are troubling because recent studies confirm that low-performing teens are the most likely to drop out, absent special intervention by their teachers and schools (Jacob, 2001; Roderick & Engel, 2001).

Aggregate data on African American and Latino student persistence in school provide reason for serious concern.[13] In Texas, there is evidence that high school dropout rates have increased for Black and Latino students as a result of the state's implementation of a high-stakes exit test for 10th graders (Haney, 2001; McNeil, chapter 3, this volume). Similarly, a nationwide study finds that stricter high school graduation requirements resulted in a 3–7% jump in the dropout rate during the 1990s. The Cornell and University of Michigan economists who conducted the study say this may translate to between 26,000 and 65,000 more high school dropouts a year nationwide (Lillard & DeCicca, 2001).

The relationship between higher standards and dropout rates is not hard to understand. Researchers have found that early disaffection with school programs that fail to meet their needs and subsequent poor school performance cause students and their families to look on early labor market entry as a rational alternative to continued schooling (Steinberg, Fegley, & Dornbusch, 1993). Although some work during high school may have positive effects on student outcomes (Grasky, 1996), students who work intensely at paid jobs tend to have lower grades and to drop out (Chaplin & Hannaway, 1996). Thus, raising graduation standards (without first ensuring that students have the time and support they need to meet those standards) significantly changes short-term calculations of the relative payoffs between schooling and early entry into the labor market. The push to leave school before graduating is particularly acute among teen ELLs (who, as previously noted, often are further behind academically than their non-ELL peers) and undocumented students, whose path to post-secondary education is effectively blocked by limited access to financial aid and whose eligibility for higher paying jobs in the post-secondary job market is effectively barred by law.

Given these circumstances, the role of federal policy makers is especially important. The next section examines the steps the government should take to promote accountability for student outcomes while creating reasonable and positive incentives for improving those outcomes.

POTENTIAL STRATEGIES AND POLICY CHOICES: THE ROLE OF THE FEDERAL GOVERNMENT

The exclusion of ELL immigrant youth from standards-based accountability systems threatens to widen performance differences between ELL students and others. At the same time, applying a one-sided accountability system to a special needs population in schools with low capacity to meet their needs threatens equally undesirable consequences. These include increased grade retention and dropout rates among language-minority students and low morale among their teachers and administrators. Clearly, the challenge is to extend accountability systems to ELL students in ways that realistically reflect and respond to the state of knowledge and capacity among school-level educators. Moreover, if ELL students are to meet the same performance standards applied to all other students, state and local policy makers must pay greater attention to strategies that promise to advance what educators in the field know and can do. Some suggestions for roles the federal government might play in meeting these and other, related challenges follow.

Over the past three decades, the lion's share of the federal Department of Education's ELL-targeted grants have focused on helping individual schools or districts mount comprehensive language-development programs.[14] Prior to 2001, these grants were made to schools on a competitive basis and thus, in any given year, reached only a fraction of eligible schools. Beginning in 2002, ELL-targeted dollars are to be distributed to all ELL-serving districts on a formula basis. This shift, if adequately funded, will mirror and support the broader capacity-building efforts long funded through the larger Title I program. Arguably, these changes put the Office of English Language Acquisition (OELA)[15] in a better position to make a significant contribution in three areas in which national leadership is needed: (1) meeting key research needs; (2) supporting demonstration programs that use promising new curricula, assessments, and innovative approaches; and (3) supporting professional development programs that prepare new and veteran teachers to work with language-minority youth. These priorities are discussed in the following section.

Research Agenda

There are four key areas in which leadership and financial support from the OELA would make a significant contribution:

- ELL student data collection and analysis
- Basic research in second-language learning
- Studies of ELL student subpopulations
- Development of valid assessment instruments

Data-driven reform can be the linchpin of a sound accountability system. Some of the most salient predictors of educational outcomes for ELL students, regardless of national origin, are native language literacy and prior schooling. Teachers report that it is helpful to know how recently their students have immigrated, and the level of the students' previous education in the home country. Yet schools rarely collect and examine these data. Such information might also help school-level staff identify subpopulations of students (e.g., under-schooled newcomers) whose literacy needs are not fully met by standard ESL/bilingual programming.

Similarly, there are few efforts to collect school-level data on the number of ELL students who drop out or who are retained in grade (a factor that has been found to correlate with dropping out). Nor do districts routinely collect and report school-level data on how many ELL students are served in support programs other than ESL/bilingual classes (e.g., number also served in Title I or special education programs). This type of data would help state and district-level educators measure local program effectiveness and identify unmet needs.

Basic research needs that bear on English language learning were identified by the National Academy of Science after an exhaustive investigation the agency conducted in 1997. The results of that study now need to be put into concrete action. The OELA could assert leadership by setting research priorities and providing funding.

Research on ELL student subpopulations is inadequate. There is a growing need for data collection on the size, distribution, and needs of this subcategory of students. Such information could help school-level staff identify specific groups (e.g., under-schooled newcomers) whose literacy needs are not fully met by standard ESL/bilingual programming.

The tests most states use to assess students' competence in core subjects are not valid forms of assessment for English-language learners. Policy makers continue to struggle with how best to include ELL students in accountability systems in the absence of reliable, field-tested assessment instruments for measuring their mastery of math, science, and social studies content. This problem is particularly acute in the secondary school grades. The OELA should assist in the development of modified assessment instruments in various primary languages. The agency also could lead the way in developing standards for appropriate accommodation of English-language learners taking core subject tests written in English.

Demonstration Programs

The challenges presented by the organizational features of the typical secondary school suggest that a narrow focus on improving language development programs will yield only limited success with ELL students. Several studies of ELL and immigrant-serving schools indicate that exemplary schools focus on linking ELL students to whole-school reforms. Exemplary schools tend to share the following four overarching elements: (1) all teachers, administrators, and counselors are involved in the reforms; (2) there is a focus on bringing language development and mainstream subject teachers together; (3) ELL immigrants spend an expanded amount of time receiving direct instruction in English and core subject areas; and (4) there is an emphasis on sustained, long-term professional development for all school professionals (Ruiz de Velasco & Fix, 2001, pp. 70–80).

Exemplary strategies the OELA should ensure receive opportunities for further demonstration and attention include:

- Devising ways to implement whole-school reforms that take the special needs of ELL students into account (e.g., school-wide professional development efforts; organizational changes, including block scheduling; and extended day/year initiatives).
- Developing alternative courses of instruction for special needs populations (including under-schooled youth and newcomer immigrants).
- Finding creative ways to identify gifted or talented ELL immigrants and guiding their preparation for post-secondary education.
- Promoting innovative programs to encourage parent-school involvement among language-minority parents.

Professional Development Programs

During the past decade, the federal Department of Education has emphasized teacher recruitment and professional development initiatives, but these programs thus far have received only a fraction of the funding they deserve. Some key professional development initiatives are:

- Grants to help districts train *all* teachers who work with ELL students. These grants support activities to improve preservice and in-service professional development coursework to better reflect the instructional and assessment needs of ELL students. These grants also should support innovations to extend ELL-related training to key nonteaching staff, including counselors, administrators, and technology specialists.
- Grants to fund innovative career ladder programs designed to upgrade the qualifications and skills of existing educational personnel to meet certification and licensure requirements as language development teachers and other instructional personnel serving ELL students.
- Fellowships in bilingual education awarded to individual students for graduate studies related to the instruction of children and teens with limited English proficiency, as well as for the support of related research.

Additionally, a long-term shortage of teachers specially trained to work with language-minority students underscores the need for the OELA to become more involved in efforts to improve college preservice preparation programs in bilingual education and in funding grants or loan forgiveness programs that encourage more individuals to pursue careers in bilingual education.

FEDERAL GUIDELINES FOR INCLUDING ELLS IN TEST-BASED ACCOUNTABILITY SYSTEMS

Studies by the Citizens' Commission on Civil Rights have amply demonstrated that as states roll out new accountability systems, many have failed to provide the resources needed by schools to effectively educate ELL students to high standards (Citizens' Commission on Civil Rights, 2002, 2001, 1999). Despite these warnings, states such as Texas and New York have begun to use their assessments to visit high-stakes consequences on students (e.g., relying on test scores to determine student promotion and graduation). Such use of tests, especially where the curriculum and instruction are not aligned with standards, can violate both accepted professional guidelines and federal civil rights laws. In recognition of this danger, the Clinton administration issued *The Use of Tests as Part of High-Stakes Decision Making for Students* (U.S. Department of Education, 2000), a resource guide for state and district school leaders. The guidelines were compiled by the Office for Civil Rights with substantial input and support from the National Academy of Sciences, recognized test experts, major test publishers, education associations, and civil rights groups. Nevertheless, this guidance has been withdrawn— without explanation—by the Bush administration, and the Department of Education is no longer disseminating the guide to education officials. Given the increased emphasis on testing in the reauthorized Elementary and Secondary Education Act, the Bush administration ought to reaffirm and promulgate fair testing guidelines to schools and districts. A broader question for educators is whether it is appropriate to attach high-stakes consequences to ELL student test performance, given the school-level issues outlined earlier in this chapter.

ENSURING RECIPROCAL ACCOUNTABILITY: A FEDERAL RESPONSIBILITY

There remain great disparities across schools in the quality of education that our children receive. Too many schools cannot provide the resources and conditions necessary for teaching and learning to the highest standards. This is most painfully true in schools where English-language learners are concentrated. Yet, in every state, the bar for achievement is being raised. And, most state accountability systems hold students, teachers, and school leaders accountable for results without making state and district leaders reciprocally accountable to students, teachers, and school leaders. This must change. The federal government (or failing that, the individual states) should identify appropriate standards for delivering and measuring high-quality learning resources, conditions, and opportunities to learn in each public school. These standards would indicate the resources that states and districts must provide each school, and the performance of states and districts on these measures should be publicly available as part of each district's "report card." At a minimum, the required resources would include:

- An appropriately trained teacher for each classroom, and campus administrators who have the knowledge and skills to promote teaching and learning of the highest quality.
- Up-to-date textbooks and technology, and a curriculum that is aligned to state and district performance standards.

- A physical learning environment that is safe, well equipped, and well maintained.

States should also be required to set standards for measuring state and district-level efforts to support hard-to-staff or low-performing schools and to help students with special learning needs, including ELLs. At a minimum, these standards would include measurable indicators of how well schools have been supported to

- Provide additional instruction that supplements the general curricula.
- Provide appropriate support services for helping students address learning barriers.
- Provide teaching staff with the training and resources necessary for effective instruction.

The guiding principle is that accountability in a public system requires more than high standards for students and teachers. States and district leaders—and by extension, the communities they represent—must be held accountable for providing the resources and conditions necessary for students to meet high learning standards.

SUMMARY

The inclusion of ELL students in one-sided accountability reforms remains extremely problematic. Performance-based accountability measures, as implemented in states that attach high-stakes consequences to performance results, assume that classroom teachers have the expertise and resources needed to prepare students to meet new learning standards and that students are capable of learning the requisite material within a generally narrow time frame. Both assumptions are wrong with respect to ELL students and their teachers. A look into the "black box" of the classroom indicates that wide language, literacy, and skill diversity among students, and system capacity and organizational barriers facing teachers, leave educators unprepared to help all their students meet the same standards on the same timetable. Moreover, continuing knowledge gaps within the profession concerning how best to help ELL students meet new standards suggest that including ELL students in the same accountability regime designed for English speakers will remain problematic well into the next decade. These circumstances underscore the need to take a much more cautious approach to implementing high-stakes accountability systems for ELL students, as well as the need for reciprocal accountability provisions that hold state and district leaders accountable for providing all students with adequate resources and opportunities to meet high standards for learning. They also suggest that federal efforts to help state and local educators improve ELL education over the long term should focus on critical research, demonstration, and professional development needs.

NOTES

1. One recent example is an assessment by Stanford education historian Larry Cuban, who is concerned that the movement has strengthened traditional teacher-centered instructional practices at the expense of more progressive, student-centered, innovations. "[A]pproaches such as portfolios, project-based teaching, and performance-based testing that blossomed between the mid1980s and 1990s," writes Cuban, "have since shriveled under the unrelenting pressure for higher test scores." (Cuban, 2001, p.180)

2. Also limited-English proficient (LEP). The term "English-language learner" is used here throughout for consistency.

3. The National Commission on Excellence in Education, for example, was composed principally of business leaders, public officials, and leaders in schools of education.

4. In an influential article for the Politics of Education Association, Marshall Smith and Jennifer O'Day (1991) argued that a state or nationally based instructional guidance and accountability system would improve the overall quality of public education as well as equalize the quality of instruction offered to poor and minority students specifically.

5. *GI Forum v. Texas Education Agency*, Civil Action No. SA-97-CA-1278-EP (U.S District Court, Western District of Texas). For an analysis of this suit, see Horn (2001).

6. Although Title I contains language indicating that states are obligated to ensure that poor and disadvantaged students have the resources and assistance they need to meet new standards, the Citizens' Commission for Civil Rights (1999) has noted that these provisions are not enforced. Indeed, under the current Title I framework, states are required to direct additional help and resources to schools only *after* the accountability system has been implanted and *after* schools have demonstrated an inability to meet standards.

7. Although not all students are expected to meet the standards initially, the typical performance timetable suggests an expectation that all students who initially fail can be brought within the standards within a short period of time, usually one school year.

8. These issues are treated in greater depth in Ruiz de Velasco and Fix (2001).

9. In Texas, assessment exemption decisions regarding ELL students are made by a local Language Proficiency Assessment committee. The scope of authority exercised by these committees is substantially less than that available to committees that develop Individualized Education Plans (IEPs) for special education students. Nevertheless, these committees provide an infrastructure that could potentially function much like an IEP committee with the authority to determine an individual education plan for each ELL student.

10. Although Illinois has issued benchmarks for predicting how results from the state's language assessment test for ELLs (the Illinois Measure of Annual Growth in English test) might translate to scores on the grade-appropriate ISAT language arts tests, there is little guidance on how schools can help ELLs to meet the state standards in other subjects.

11. Illinois explicitly includes mainstream teachers, administrators, and special education teachers in its ELL staff development programs, and keeps track of their participation. Yet, while two-thirds of mainstream teachers in schools with bilingual education programs reported participating in multicultural awareness training, only about one-third of teachers in these high ELL-serving schools reported receiving training in language acquisition or other techniques for making their courses accessible to English-language learners. Illinois State Board of Education, *Evaluation Report: Transitional Bilingual Education and Transitional Program of Instruction, Fiscal Year 2000*, (ISBE Research Division, December 2000).

12. The issues raised in this section are treated in greater depth in Ruiz de Velasco and Fix (2001), *Overlooked and Underserved*, supra, at pp. 55–65.

13. It is unfortunate that dropout data are rarely reported on the basis of ELL status. As I argue later, this is one indicator of success to which state and district leaders ought to be held accountable.

14. Not inclusive of impact aid dollars administered through the Emergency Immigrant Education Act to school districts with large number of newcomer students. These funds, though administered by the Department of Education, were not restricted to use in language-development programs.

15. OELA, formerly the Office of Bilingual Education and Language Minority Affairs (OBEMLA), was created as part of the reauthorization of the Elementary and Secondary Education Act in 2001.

REFERENCES

Adger, C. T., & Peyton, J. (1999). Enhancing the education of immigrant students in secondary school: Structural challenges and directions. In C. Faltis and P. Wolfe (Eds),. *So much to say: Adolescents, bilingualism and ESL in the secondary school* (pp. 205–224). New York: Teachers College Press.

Anstrom, K. (1997). *Academic achievement for secondary language-minority students: Standards, measures, and promising practices.* Washington, D.C.: National Clearinghouse for Bilingual Education.

August, D., & Hakuta, K. (Eds.). (1997). *Improving schooling for language-minority children.* Washington, D.C.: National Academy Press.

Chaplin, D., & Hannaway, J. (1996). *High school employment: Meaningful connections for at-risk youth.* Paper presented at the Annual Meeting of the American Educational Research Association. New York, April, 1996.

Citizens' Commission on Civil Rights. (1999). *Title I in midstream: The fight to improve schools for poor kids.* Washington, D.C.: Author.

Citizens' Commission on Civil Rights. (2001). *Closing the deal: A preliminary report on state compliance with final assessment and accountability requirements under the Improving America's Schools Act of 1994.* Washington, D.C: Author.

Citizens' Commission on Civil Rights. (2002). *Title I in California: Will the state pass the test?* Washington, D.C: Author.

Cohen, D. (1996). Standards-based reform: Policy, practice, and performance. In H. Ladd (Ed.), *Holding schools accountable* (pp. 99–127). Washington, D.C.: The Brookings Institution.

Cuban, L. (2001). Introduction: The bottom line. In S. Mondale and S. Patton (Eds.)., *School: The story of American public education* (pp. 173–182). Boston: Beacon Press.

Fleishman, H., & Hopstock, P. (1993). *Descriptive study of services to limited english proficient students.* Arlington, VA: Development Associates.

García, O. (1999). Educating Latino high school students with limited formal schooling. In C. Faltis and P. Wolfe (Eds।., *So much to say: Adolescents, bilingualism, and ESL in secondary school* (pp. 61–82). New York: Teachers College Press.

Grasky, S. (1996). Exploring the effects of childhood family structure on teenage and young adult labor force participation. *IRB Discussion Papers.* 1111-96. Madison, WI: Institute for Research on Poverty.

Hakuta, K., Butler, Y., & Witt, D. (2000). *How long does it take English learners to attain proficiency?* Santa Barbara, CA: University of California, Linguistic Minority Research Institute. Retrieved March 1, 2004, from http://www.cde.ca.gov/el/hakutas.pdf

Haney, W. (2001). "Revisiting the Myth of the Texas Miracle in Education (p. 15). Paper prepared for the Harvard Civil Rights Project, January 13, 2001, Cambridge, MA.

Horn, R. A. (2001). Kids, the court, and the State of Texas: The legal challenge to the TAAS. In R. Horn and J. Kincheloe (Eds.), *American standards: Quality education in a complex world* (pp. 281–303). New York: Peter Lang.

Illinois State Board of Education, Research Division. (2000). *Educator supply and demand.* Chicago, IL: Author.

Jacob, B. (2001). Getting tough: The impact of high school graduation exams. *Educational Evaluation and Policy Analysis, 23*(2), 99–121.

Lillard, D., & DeCicca, P. (2001). Higher standards, more dropouts? Evidence within and across time. *Economics of Education Review, 20*(5), 459–473.

Lowery, S., & Buck, J. (2001). Three decades of educational reform in Texas: Putting the pieces together. In R. Horn and J. Kincheloe (Eds.), *American standards: Quality education in a complex world* (pp. 267–277). New York: Peter Lang.

Mace-Matluck, B., Alexander-Kasparik, R., & Queen, R. (1998). *Through the golden door: Educational approaches for immigrant adolescents with limited schooling.* Washington, D.C.: Center for Applied Linguistics.

McNeil, L. (2000). *Contradictions of School Reform.* New York: Routledge Press.

McNeil, L., & Valenzuela, A. (2000). The harmful impact of the TAAS system of testing in Texas: Beneath the accountability rhetoric. In G. Orfield and M. Kornhaber (Eds.), *Raising standards or raising barriers? Inequality and high-stakes testing in public education* (pp. 127–150). Cambridge, MA: Harvard Civil Rights Project.

Olsen, L. (1997). *Made in America: Immigrant students in our public schools.* New York: The New Press.

Reyes, P., Scribner, J., & Paredes Scribner, A. (1999). *Lessons from high-performing Hispanic schools: Creating learning communities.* New York: Teachers College Press.

Roderick, M., & Engel, M. (2001). The grasshopper and the ant: Motivational responses of low-achieving students to high-stakes testing. *Educational Evaluation and Policy Analysis, 23*(3), 197–227.

Ruiz de Velasco, J. & Fix, M. (2000). *Overlooked and underserved: Immigrant students in U.S. secondary schools.* Washington, D.C.: Urban Institute Press. Retrieved March 1, 2004, from http://www.urban.org/pdfs/overlooked.pdf

Smith, M. S., & O'Day, J. (1991). Systemic school reform and educational opportunity. In S. Fuhrman and B. Malen (Eds.), *The politics of curriculum and testing* (pp. 250–312). New York: Taylor and Francis.

Steinberg, L. D., Fegley, S., & Dornbusch, S. (1993). Negative impact of part-time work on adolescent adjustment: Evidence from a longitudinal study. *Developmental Psychology, 29*(2), 171–180.

Texas Education Agency, Office of Bilingual Education. (2001, April). *Test performance summary report, 10th grade exit level administered February, 2001.* Austin: Author.

Thomas, W., & Collier, V. (1997). *School effectiveness for language minority students.* Fairfax, VA: George Mason University.

U.S. Department of Education. (2000). *Fall 1999 elementary and secondary school civil rights compliance report.* Washington, D.C.: Author.

U.S. Department of Education. (2000). *The use of tests as part of high-stakes decisionmaking for students.* Washington, D.C.: Author.

U.S. Department of Education. National Center for Education Statistics. (1995). *Schools and staffing survey, 1993.* Washington, D.C.: Author.

Valenzuela, A. (1999). *Subtractive schooling: U.S.-Mexican youth and the politics of caring.* New York: State University of New York Press.

Wiley, T. (1996). *Literacy and language diversity in the United States.* Washington, D.C.: Urban Institute Press.

3

Faking Equity: High-Stakes Testing and the Education of Latino Youth

LINDA McSPADDEN McNEIL

Official education policy in the state of Texas is claimed by its advocates to be improving the overall quality of education. Its proponents also claim that under this system, the achievement gap that separates Anglo students from Latino and African American students is closing, thus making schooling more equitable. Both of these claims, sadly, are false. The irony of this education policy, based on high-stakes testing, is that it is driving down the quality of public education and driving significant numbers of students out of school. Most of the students who are leaving school without graduating are Latino and African American.

The state, for evidence that its test-based accountability system is improving achievement, points to students' scores on the mandated state test—scores that seem to be rising for all three cultural subgroups. What they do not discuss is that the state's standardized test is the *only indicator* of academic achievement on which Texas children are showing gains. *On every other indicator of academic achievement,* Texas children are not only showing weak academic performance, but also growing increasingly weak over time.

If this were merely a Texas story, it would be serious enough. The state is the second most populous in the United States In addition, its population previews the ethnic diversity that within the next decade, will characterize cities outside the Southwest, even in such unexpected places as Chicago. And within less than two decades, the diverse population of Texas will become the face of most of America.

Even more important to the immediate future, the Texas testing system has, by force of federal law, become the driving education policy for the entire nation. It was the model for the Elementary and Secondary Education Act of 2002, a law that dramatically shifts control over public schools to the federal government.

Anyone who knows the true picture of academic and student losses produced by the Texas version of this system will be unlikely to call the federal law by its slogan, the "No Child Left Behind" Act. As will be shown in this chapter, the Texas accountability system succeeds—that is, produces positive indicators—only when it loses a significant number of children. By far, the majority of those losses are among poor, Spanish-language-dominant, and other Latino children, with equally significant losses incurred by African American children as well. That 25% of the White (Anglo) children are also lost from public schools would be a crisis in many states, but in Texas that figure seems less urgent because it is barely half the percentage rates of those lost in the other ethnic categories. The record of losses incurred during the decade of experience under the Texas testing system provides a cautionary tale to those states that are only now beginning to adopt the Texas accountability system or where the federal law is imposing the Texas system on their schools. They will find that an accountability system based on standardized testing reduces educational quality, produces unnecessary failures, and fakes its claims to more equitable schooling.

How the testing and accountability system helps produce those damaging results is the message of this chapter. A close look at the wide gaps between the state's indicator of academic success, the Texas Assessment of Academic Skills (TAAS) test, and other more established measures of learning will show Texas students to be making few gains and even, by some measure, to be losing academic ground under this accountability system. I will also analyze the losses of children from the public schools under this system. Finally, I will analyze the ways these academic and child losses are the result of the accountability system itself.

First, a review of the nuts and bolts of the Texas system is necessary because it is easy for people in states where high-stakes testing has not long been implemented to interpret the Texas (and now, federal) system through their commonsense definitions of accountability or by whatever is familiar in their own state's education policies and, in doing so, to miss the ways the Texas model reduces academic quality and creates new inequities.

THE ACCOUNTABILITY SYSTEM AND ITS
INDICATORS OF SUCCESS

How could a legislature enact, and a state department of education implement and enforce, a public education policy that directly undermines the quality of schooling and which contributes to massive dropouts? How, once enacted, could such a policy be carried out by teachers? How can it be tolerated by children and their parents? And even more unlikely, how could such a policy be made a model to be copied by other states and directly and explicitly become the basis for the whole nation?

The Texas system became the model for the nation because this system was promoted as an accountability system, even though it has had demonstrable negative effects on the quality of public education and on the possibility that Latino and African American youth, in particular, will receive a full, high-quality education. It is the state's official system for evaluating schools and school districts. It is the state's official system for measuring children's academic performance.

Accountability as a System of Controls

The accountability system is an extreme form of centralization. It is a system of centralized controls governing virtually all aspects of public schooling in Texas. The controls hinge on a standardized test. Through a simple set of linkages, the centralized educational bureaucracy of the state has established a test that must be taken by all children, in key subjects and in key grades. The state then rates each school according to the test scores of the children in the school. School districts are rated by the scores of all their schools. Set up as a hierarchical system, each layer of the bureaucracy is held accountable to the one above it. The rules are set at the top and there can be no variations in their implementation, nor can schools or districts opt out if they prefer a different method of evaluating children's learning or assessing the quality of their schools.

No matter the strengths or weaknesses of a particular school (a thriving arts program, healthy sports for all students, a weak math curriculum, teachers unqualified in the subjects they are teaching), no aspect of the school enters into the rating system except the children's test scores. No one is held accountable for under-resourced classrooms, for dangerous school facilities, for exceptional literature collections, for significant and engaging student projects—or their absence, for enduring connections (or for deep cultural divides) between the school and the children's communities. School administrators and, by extension, teachers are held accountable to produce scores on the state test. Period.

Compliance comes from the mandatory nature of every facet of the system. High stakes are built into the system at every level. Stakes are high for school principals: their pay, and in many districts their entire job contract, is based on their school's test scores. Superintendent contracts are written to emphasize the importance of the district's test scores in determining the superintendent's job security, salary and substantial bonuses, and contract renewal.

The stakes are also high for children. No student may graduate from a Texas public high school without passing the high school version of the state test. Even a student with excellent grades in all required subjects, with more than the number of course credits needed to graduate, will not receive a diploma without passing the exit level of the state test. New legislation, going into effect as this book goes to press (spring, 2003), has made the stakes even higher. No child is to be permitted to promote from third to fourth grade without passing the reading section of the third-grade test. This retention policy does not permit the consideration of whether and how well a child may actually be reading. Only the score on the state test counts, under the accountability system, as evidence of the ability to read.[1] The legislation that produced the third-grade reading requirement calls for phasing in high-stakes in other grades, and in other subjects, in the coming years.

Under this closed system, what counts as learning and what matters as educational content are not left to individual teachers, to school faculties, to local communities, nor even to local school boards. The decisions are made centrally, and at the top of the bureaucracy. The lower levels of the bureaucracy, where teachers and children reside, are not invited to create variations or improvements on this system or to offer alternatives to it. They are, rather, intended merely to comply. They are to be accountable to those above them.

If the system is not appropriate for the differing ways that some children learn, if it does not encompass the subject content or values of a community, if it does not allow for more than one kind of evidence of learning, that is its design. Only in a generic, standardized system can large numbers of schools across dozens of jurisdictions be compared and rank-ordered by use of a single measure. The ratings and rankings under such a system displace other educational considerations, such as whether the lessons engage children's imaginations, whether lessons are meaningful, whether children's minds are enhanced by what they are doing at school. The ratings do not allow consideration for whether a neighborhood, a community, is enriched by what its children are learning. And there is no provision under this system for the intellectual and cultural assets that reside in teachers, in families, and in children to add to the knowledge base of the classroom.

The innocuous language of accountability is very misleading. "Accountability" sounds benign. It sounds like "responsibility." "Testing" sounds educational. It brings to mind "achievement" and "learning." "Standardization" is very close to "standards." And haven't we as a country been trying over the past two decades to raise academic standards?

This language is also misleading because it shifts the terms of educational policy away from a discussion of educating children toward producing test scores. The test scores are presumed to be—or advertised to be—indicators of learning. But in fact, to date, there have been no studies that show that a score on a state-mandated, standardized test is an accurate, or even valid, measure of whether a child has learned, or what he or she has learned. There have been no well-designed, longitudinal studies that demonstrate how and whether standardized test scores on state tests—on high-stakes state tests—correlate with achievement over time in any subject.

Rising TAAS Scores

The Texas state standardized testing system, which has been used as a model for the accountability systems in many other states and, most recently, the federal government's education policy, is the TAAS, the Texas Assessment of Academic Skills. In place for more than a decade, this multiple-choice, computer-scored test has been given in reading, mathematics, and writing in various grade levels. The shifts of grade level administration in the early years have made it difficult to track progress longitudinally. In recent years the tests have been given in grades three through eight and ten. The high school-level test, given at tenth grade up until the 2002–2003 school year, was the high-stakes exit test, the test all students had to pass to graduate from a Texas public high school regardless of their course grades and credits.[2]

Every year, there is great publicity surrounding the administration of the test and even greater publicity in the reporting of scores. School signboards proclaim the dates of the TAAS to passing motorists. Banners in hallways remind students to get a good night's sleep before the TAAS or rally their spirits with militaristic slogans such as "Make War on the TAAS" and "Conquer the TAAS." Because principals' pay, and often their

job contracts in this nonunion state, rest on the aggregate scores produced
by the children in their building, they devote many faculty meetings and
professional development days to providing teachers with techniques to
use in their classrooms to help students score higher on the TAAS.

Schools are ranked according to the overall scores and the scores
are disaggregated by ethnicity. In Texas, the formally designated groups
for purposes of school population decisions are Hispanic, African American, and White/Other.[3] The racial designations are of critical importance
because they create the impression that the testing system is addressing
the long history of educational inequality in the state. For a school to receive an "exemplary" or "recognized" rating, rather than a mere "acceptable" or worse, the accountability system requires that a certain
percentage of children in all three of the ethnic categories attain a certain
level of score on the TAAS. The assumption is that if the stakes are high
for administrators, they will have to assure that all children in the school
are being taught—because all will be tested.

The assumption that testing all children would lead to teaching all
children has proven not to be the case, as I will discuss. But it is true that
testing all children has led to preparing all children for the tests (Sloan,
this volume). And as a result, test scores on the TAAS have improved over
the years, and they have improved for all three racial groups.

Table 1 is an official Texas Education Agency report of scores on
the TAAS for all students in Texas public schools from the 1994 spring
semester to the 2002 spring semester. The "all students" category shows
that in 1994, only 53% of the school children of Texas passed the TAAS.
By 1999, 78% were passing the TAAS. And by 2002, fully 85% of Texas
children were passing the state test. This does seem to indicate remark-
able improvement.

Table 3.1[4] also shows racial gaps appearing to close. In 1994, for
example, only 31% of African American children passed the TAAS, as
compared to 66% of White children—a gap of 35 percentage points. By
1999, the gap was 24 percentage points between African American and
White children. The gap had shrunk to 16 percentage points by 2002.

The same table shows that in 1994, only 39% of Hispanic children
passed the TAAS as compared to 66% of White children—a gap of 27
percentage points. That gap decreased to 17 percentage points in 1999
and to 13 percentage points in 2002. The last line of the table, representing the scores of *Limited English Proficient* students, shows much lower
pass rates—from 22% in 1994 to 58% in 2002—a very telling set of
scores in light of the high pass rates for *Hispanics* (line 3) not designated
as *Limited English Proficient*. Most limited-English students in Texas are

TABLE 3.1

Percent Meeting Minimum Expectations, Texas Assessment of Academic Skills (All Students, Grades 3–8, 10)

All Tests Taken	1994	1995	1996	1997	1998	1999	2000	2001	2002	Gain/Loss 94–02
All Students	53%	58%	63%	69%	73%	78%	79%	82%	85%	32 pts.
African American	31%	36%	44%	52%	58%	63%	67%	71%	76%	45
Hispanic	39%	44%	50%	58%	63%	70%	72%	75%	79%	40
White	66%	71%	75%	80%	83%	87%	89%	90%	92%	26
Econom. Disadvantaged	37%	42%	48%	56%	61%	68%	70%	73%	78%	41
Limited English Proficient	22%	26%	30%	37%	42%	49%	49%	55%	58%	36

(TEA, 2003b).

native Spanish speakers; having those students disaggregated from the Hispanic cohort is the first clue that the much-touted increases in TAAS scores need to be more closely examined.

It may be difficult for anyone living outside a high-stakes-testing state to fully comprehend the public fuss made over these scores. Every year the major newspaper in each city publishes a special pullout section with rows and rows of boxes on each page. In each box is the report card for a school, with the number of students passing the TAAS shown in the school's overall score and then disaggregated by the ethnicity of the students. Improved school ratings based on student scores can earn principals up to a $10,000 annual bonus. Superintendents receive bonuses upward of $25,000 for having their school district's overall passing rate go up, or an increase in the number of schools listed as exemplary or recognized. Huge signs are posted outside exemplary and recognized schools so that all going by can see their school rating. These ratings are used by realtors to sell parents on the property values in neighborhoods where the local school is ranked exemplary or recognized.

Anyone who knows local schools well may be puzzled to see in the rankings that a very strong school can receive a mere "acceptable" ranking on the TAAS system, or that a very weak school suddenly has a spike in test scores. The report card provides no information about the instructional programs of a school, whether a school has a library (one high school in a major Texas city is only now, after decades of educating young people, getting a library), or whether the teachers are qualified.[5] The report card does not have any way to convey whether children at that school love learning. The TAAS school report card merely lists the scores on the state test, with the school building as the unit of analysis.

Thoughtful parents consider many aspects of a school when they think of their children spending their young years in its care: What will my child be learning? Are the teachers energetic and caring and attentive to the children? Do the teachers exhibit a love of learning? Do the teachers and children have what they need for learning? Do children leave this school well prepared for the next level of schooling? Is the school a safe and healthy place to be? Are the children thriving there? Am I as a parent welcome in this school? Does the school district care about this school? Are there adults in the school who speak my family's language? Is the school an asset to the community? Will my child find activities that grab his or her interest, that help the children make friends or help them find their own talents and gifts?

These parents seek a well-rounded education for their children. Instead, they find schools that focus on a single measure of success. That indicator is the score on a single test, the state's standardized, multiple-choice, computer-scored test. It is a test created far from classrooms, detached from the interactions of teachers and students, and overtly technical so as to invite no interpretation or independent thought on the part of the one being tested. The student's responses on the test are just that, responses to information provided. Children are not called on to show what they understand or to exhibit their own skills. The information in the questions is not intended to be explained, elaborated, connected to other ideas, or applied to a new situation. When seen against the universe of extraordinarily rich educational possibilities, the intellectual and moral impoverishment of a single indicator for learning brings its absurdity to light. What is important to note is that within this system, all major decisions—about ranking schools, rewarding or sanctioning administrators, even graduating students—hinge on a single indicator.

The single-indicator system is praised as being borrowed from business. As the disparities between the educational achievement shown by the accountability system's single indicator and other measures of academic achievement are examined, the reader may readily recognize the business model most closely paralleling the accountability system. That model is Enron.

According to press accounts, Enron stipulated a single indicator of success, the price of its stock. Unlike other potential indicators used to value corporations, including a valuation of assets, analysis of price-to-earnings ratios, or other complex measures, the stock price was an indicator that could be manipulated by management to move ever upward. Upward movement of the stock price lured banks, investors, politicians, and even Enron employees to believe the company was invincible. Enormous power accrued to Enron and its executives, both in the industry and in politics, because its stock kept rising.

But according to the authors of *What Went Wrong at Enron?* Enron's single-indicator system hid the company's weaknesses. Its profits and successes were reflected in its stock price. But its debts and losses were carried on a different set of ledgers. These were the bogus companies set up to borrow millions, to create the illusion of profitable trades, to bolster the official indicator by hiding the company's debt. Press accounts reveal, and the courts will have to judge, the entanglements between the official corporate statements of soaring stock values and these secret deals. There seems to be strong evidence that these bogus companies, and their deals with Enron, were central to the company's operations (Fusaro & Miller, 2001).

Enron's accounting firm, Arthur Andersen, signed off on the corporation's finances and corporate reports, apparently with knowledge that the official numbers were not the real ones; Arthur Andersen was found to be guilty in a criminal court for this abuse of accounting practices. Ironically, the immediate casualty of the disclosure of this fraud was the single indicator, the price of Enron stock: it plummeted to pennies per share, robbing shareholders, retirees, investors, and even Enron employees of their savings.

To adopt a single-indicator system to measure a complex enterprise, whether an energy trading company or the state's public schools, is to invite the temptation to hype that indicator, to do anything to keep it propped up, to make sure it carries an image of success. One way Enron kept its stock price high was to carry its losses on a separate set of ledgers. The Texas public school system, as we will see, placed so much importance on the TAAS that it began to shift its resources (including teachers and students) into the production of TAAS scores, even if the means used to produce higher and higher scores undermined the value of the education the indicator was meant to measure, and the losses were carried on a different set of books. In the case of the schools, these losses were the children themselves, the tens of thousands of young people who drop out of Texas public schools every year. Their numbers are staggering. Their existence belies the validity of the indicator, the rising TAAS scores. If they were ever counted in the equation, the public might come to feel as betrayed as the Enron stockholders. In fact, as will become clear in the analysis to follow, their leaving helps bolster the scores in the schools they left. Texas children and their families paid a high price when the state adopted a business model for the running of its schools.

DECLINING INDICATORS OF EDUCATIONAL ACHIEVEMENT

If TAAS scores were a reflection of real learning, Texas students should be doing better regardless of what measure is used. Yet the opposite turns out to be true. An examination of the scores of Texas students on the Scholastic Assessment Test (SAT I), the American College Test (ACT), and NAEP (the National Assessment of Educational Progress) shows Texas students actually declining in their performance on these national tests at the very same time TAAS scores have been rising. And even more seriously, the number of Texas students who complete school is also declining.

College Readiness: Weak Scores on the State's College
Readiness Test

The first interesting indicator is one that should, in theory, confirm the
TAAS figures. It is the state's own test of college readiness, the Texas Academic Skills Performance (TASP). A fairly low-level test of reading, writing, and mathematics, far less sophisticated than the SAT I or the ACT,
the TASP is required for all students applying to a Texas public university.
(Students with high SAT I, ACT, or TAAS scores are exempt from TASP).
Students who graduate from Texas high schools would have had to pass
the tenth-grade TAAS to graduate, so there should be a strong correlation
between the TASP scores and the passing rates on the tenth-grade TAAS.

According to the Texas Higher Education Coordinating Board
(THECB), the governing and budget board that oversees the state's systems of higher education, recent TASP scores show that increasing numbers of college applicants graduating from Texas high schools are not
college ready, having failed one or more sections on the TASP. The Coordinating Board finds these data troubling because of the cost to the university systems in having to provide summer and academic-year remedial
courses for students whose college admission is contingent on their erasing
these deficits (THECB, 2000; THECB, 2003c). The Higher Education Coordinating Board reported, for example, that 51.7% of the 73,270 students in the 1995 graduating class passed all three sections of the TASP,
whereas only 28.6 % of the 77,562 students in the 1999 graduating class
passed all sections. This same coordinating board report showed propor-
tionate drops among all ethnic groups: Blacks, Hispanics, Whites, Asians,
and Native Americans.[6] More than 60% of those taking the test needed
remediation in at least one section (reading, writing, and/or mathematics).

The percentage needing remediation has increased over a period of
years, even though the high-stakes testing accountability system has been
in place for almost a decade. Even when the approximately 17% of students who are exempt from TASP because of their high SAT, ACT, or
TAAS scores are factored into the totals, the percent of Texas young people graduating under the TAAS system and still failing to pass all sections
of the TASP presents an increasing financial burden to the higher education system for those who chose to take remedial prefreshman year
courses. It also presents a formidable barrier to students who thought, by
virtue of passing TAAS, that their high schools had educated them, only
to learn from the TASP scores that they are not prepared for even entry-
level college courses. To face the personal expense of extra, remedial

courses before enrolling in courses for college credit creates a hardship for many students and their families.

Many of these high school graduates never proceed to the remedial courses and college enrollment. In fact, the state has one of the lowest percentages of 19-year-olds enrolled in higher education in the nation (Mortenson, 2001). The Metropolitan Organization, an advocacy organization in Houston affiliated with the Industrial Areas Foundation, has reported on the number of high school graduates in several Texas school districts, comparing the number of graduates to the number designated "Texas College Ready" under the Texas Education Agency (TEA) criteria: passing TASP or exempt from TASP on the basis of SAT or ACT scores. They have also compared the number of graduates with the percentage of students who are actually college bound (Higgs, 2002). They report that of the students graduated from Texas high schools in 1999, only 28% were college ready and only 51% of that number were actually college bound (Higgs, 2002).

College Readiness: Declining Performance on SAT and ACT

It could be argued that the SAT and ACT tests are measuring indicators of college preparedness or of likely college success and therefore do not provide a persuasive comparison to student performance on the state TAAS test, which claims to measure more basic learning and academic skills. The rhetoric surrounding the accountability system based on the TAAS, however, is that it is improving academic achievement for all students. In the words of the State Board of Education, "All Texas students will be provided a quality education that enables them to achieve their potential and fully participate in the social, economic, and cultural activities of our state and nation."[7] Therefore, it follows that if the scores on the state's high-stakes TAAS test are a valid indication of its schoolchildren's academic performance toward these goals, they should approximately parallel Texas students' scores on the College Board's SAT I and the ACT college admissions tests.

Certainly, if overall academic improvement is, as claimed, represented in the state's school ratings, then under the accountability system, more students should be more qualified to aspire to higher education. In particular, those who have attended accountability-driven schools for virtually their whole K–12 experience should be increasing both in the numbers sitting for precollege exams and in performance on those and other nationally normed tests. If this system were improving educational quality for all students, the trends in the SAT and ACT scores should *exceed* the TAAS pattern of scores because the students taking the SAT and ACT are among the most academically accomplished and personally motivated to pursue university studies.

An analysis of scores on these tests, however, shows that Texas students' performance on these national examinations does not match the increases in performance as measured by the TAAS. Over a ten-year period, Texas students have shown only modest gains (5 points on the SAT I verbal and 8 points on the SAT I math section), gains that mirror—but do not exceed—national trends (Haney, 2000, part 7, p. 12). A report by the College Board shows that Texas students continue to score near the bottom of the 50 states on the SAT I, scoring even with North Carolina and above only Georgia, South Carolina, and the District of Columbia (College Board, 2001) with a combined verbal and math score of 992.

Although it is difficult to compare SAT scores, or any other single indicator, across states because participation rates differ, the lack of any significant rise in the SAT scores shows that on tests that help enhance opportunity for higher education, the accountability system has not added value to Texas children's education. The state's low ranking among the 50 states also calls into serious question the adoption of the Texas accountability system as a model for the nation, when almost every other state had higher SAT scores, with upward trends in SAT scores during this time period, and many had far higher (and increasing) participation rates among their students.

The Texas Education Agency, in its Academic Excellence Indicator System Report (AEIS), reports that 62.9% of Texas public school students (seniors) in 2001 took the SAT I or ACT (TEA, 2002a). TEA has established a score of 1110 on the SAT I and 24 on the ACT as minimum criterion scores for these tests in determining college readiness. The College Board report for 2001 shows Texas SAT scores to be 493 in verbal and 499 for math, for a total of 992 (TEA reports 987), substantially below 1110 (College Board, 2001). According to the report by The Metropolitan Organization in Houston, only 27% of Texas students taking the SAT or ACT met the criterion score. "Those figures indicate that 1999 Texas graduates fared even worse in meeting the minimum criterion score on the SAT or ACT than they did passing the TASP, the state's indicator of college readiness" (Higgs, 2002). These figures generally describe seniors, students still in school in twelfth grade, likely to graduate and motivated to plan for college. And, it must be remembered that this group, which met the minimum criterion is the 27% of the students who are still in school by senior year—a small fraction of those who began in that grade cohort, particularly among Latinos and African Americans.

Scores from a large, fairly typical comprehensive high school in the Houston metropolitan area provide an example of the gaps between TAAS performance and SAT and ACT performance in a multiracial high school. The student body at Longview High (a pseudonym) is culturally and economically diverse, with a dedicated faculty, strong ties to the community, a wide range of student activities, and a reputation as a "good" school. The school qualified for a grant as a lead school in a large-scale urban school reform effort because of its reputation and the commitment of its principal to further improving the school. The rate of Longview students passing the reading section of the tenth-grade TAAS, the test required for graduation, rose from 66.6% in the first year of the grant (three years into the state's attachment of high-stakes consequences to school administrators and to school rankings) to 86.1% in the third year, to 94.5% in the fourth year of the grant. Math scores similarly rose dramatically, from 49.6% passing in the first year of the grant to 87.6% during the fourth year. Overall pass rates went from 60% percent in the first year of the grant to 78.1% passing in the fourth year. Certainly by the criteria of the state's accountability system, Longview High students made significant progress during this period—a 50% increase in reading scores, around 55% improvement in math, and a 30% improvement overall (Coppola, 2002).

Did high TAAS scores mean more learning, higher academic performance? Other indicators provide less basis for optimism. During the time of this dramatic rise in TAAS scores, the number of students at Longview High taking the SAT declined, from 33% of the senior class at the beginning of the grant period to 28% in 2000. Of these, only 7% of those tested scored above 1000. The average score declined from 836 (combined math and verbal) to 772.

Did high TAAS scores mean all students were learning, and learning to a higher standard? The school, thought by the students, their families, the district, and people throughout the region as a fairly good high school, had an attrition rate of more than one-third of its freshman class before those students ever reached their senior year to take the SAT. If only 7% of the 28% *who were tested* scored 1000 or better, then the gap between TAAS and SAT scores is even more dramatic: In a year when 94.5% of Longview High students (sophomores, primarily) passed TAAS, slightly fewer than 2% of these seniors were scoring 1000 on the SAT I, still 110 points below what TEA itself lists as a college-ready score. And almost one-third of the class of 2000 had already left school without graduating. The high-stakes testing system had been driving educational practice in the state since these seniors were in elementary school. The experience of this school, by all accounts a *good* school with success in raising the TAAS scores, makes concrete the gaps outlined by Amrein and Berliner (2002b) between the TAAS and students' access to the academic currency that will open doors to future educational opportunities.

Statewide scores on the ACT college admissions test provide additional data counter to Texas students' progress indicated by rising TAAS scores. In their comprehensive comparison of states' indicators of public school children's academic performance in this era of high-stakes testing, Amrein and Berliner (2002a, 2002b) note that under high-stakes testing, participation in the ACT in Texas has increased slightly, but the scores have decreased. The ACT's own report of Texas students' scores for 2002 reveals that Texas students score slightly below the national average on the ACT. The average Texas score was 20.1; the national average was 20.8. Not a large difference but significantly less than the TEA's recommendation of a score of 24 as college ready (ACT, 2002). Although the Texas scores are only slightly below the national average, the scores demonstrate, and the Amrein and Berliner analysis confirms, that Texas students' performance on the ACT does not come close to paralleling the gains of students in the state on the TAAS. The ACT scores do not lend credence to the Texas system as a model for the nation. According to Amrein and Berliner, "If academic achievement did not change after stakes were attached to a state test or if achievement decreased, the effectiveness of the high-stakes policy as a means of improving student performance must be called into question" (2002b, p. 2).[8]

NAEP and TAAS: Smoke and Mirrors

The NAEP test provides another comparison on which we may examine whether the Texas accountability system is improving children's learning. State officials frequently justify gains on the TAAS as real gains by invoking comparisons with the NAEP, the National Assessment of Educational Progress. The NAEP has, up to the present, been a low-stakes test, a test that states may participate in voluntarily. The NAEP scores have not been reported out by student or by school. The exam provides information by state, based on a sample of students in each state.

Amrein and Berliner note that "when analyzing NAEP data it is important to pay attention to who is actually tested" (2002a, p. 24). In each state, districts are randomly sampled. Then, within districts, schools are to be randomly sampled. Finally, students within schools are randomly sampled. "Once the list of participants is drawn," according to Amrein and Berliner, "school personnel sift through the list and remove students who they have classified as Limited English Proficient (LEP) or who have Individualized Education Plans (IEPs) as part of their special education programs . . . . In short, although the NAEP uses random sampling techniques, not all students sampled are actually tested. The exclusion of these students biases NAEP results." The percentage of students included or excluded from the cohort is left to local discretion and not made transparent in the publication of state-to-state or year-to-year NAEP score comparisons.

According to Walter Haney, a researcher who has analyzed the "myth of the Texas miracle in education" (2000), Texas students have made some gains on the NAEP, especially at the fourth-grade level because the high-stakes testing accountability system has been in place. However, when Haney looked behind the numbers, he found that Texas excludes from NAEP more students and more categories of students than most other states. In fact, Haney found that the percentages of Texas students who were being excluded from NAEP testing increased during the period that Texas NAEP scores were going up (2000, part 7, pp. 21–22). As cited by Amrein and Berliner (2002a, p. 24), "Exclusion rates increased at both grade levels (4 and 8) escalating from 8% to 11% at grade 4 and from 7% to 8% at grade 8 (in Texas) from 1992–1996. Meanwhile, in contrast, *exclusion rates declined* at both grade levels at the national level, decreasing from 8% to 6% at grade 4 and from 7% to 5% at grade 8." [emphasis mine] They quote Haney, who termed the NAEP score gains in Texas an "illusion arising from exclusion."

This pattern of making *school and district scores* appear to go up by excluding increasingly large numbers of *students* creates the appearance that each year Texas students are improving over past Texas performance and improving relative to children in other states. It exploits parents' and other lay citizens' lack of technical knowledge about testing, sampling, cross-site comparisons, and the inherent limitations of indicators. The failure to make transparent the fact that some, if not all, of the increase in scores is due to excluding children not expected to do well on the tests is just one example of faking educational improvement. It is also a way of faking educational equity because, as Haney found, the students most likely to be excluded from the tested sample are, of course, the Limited English Proficient, not the English-fluent, gifted and talented students. The appearance of gains ignores whether schools are serving those children well.

A compelling study by Linton and Kester (2003) provides an additional caution for using NAEP scores to bolster claims that the Texas accountability system is improving achievement and closing the achievement gap between White and minority students in the state. Their detailed analysis of Texas eighth graders' mathematics scores on NAEP and TAAS show that the appearance of a narrowing of the gap between ethnic groups may stem less from improved equity and more from the ceiling effect that artificially caps scores at the upper end, in this case the scores of White students. They point out that in 2000, 60.4% of the White students "had TAAS scores that fell in the top 10% of the score range. In contrast, there was no evidence of a ceiling effect for the NAEP" (p. 2). By looking at TAAS score distributions for all three ethnic groups in 1996 and again in 2000, they noted that the percentage gains among African American and Latino students (more than 30% in each case) far exceeded the percentage gains made by White students (17.1%) during the same period. But because more White students were clustered near the top of the scale, they were being tested on a scale that left little room for upward movement reflecting their true achievement. "There is a strong possibility that a ceiling effect artificially restricted the 2000 TAAS scores for white students and created the illusion that the achievement gap between minority and white students had been narrowed" (p. 2). Their analysis further shows that student gains on both NAEP-Texas and NAEP-National have been primarily at the lower range of the test (from *below basic* to *basic*), with "little change in the percentage of students achieving the *advanced* range." The authors consider the possibility of test-score inflation due to teaching to the test and related factors. Their primary findings, however, are based on their statistical analysis of NAEP and TAAS scores. They conclude that "a more reasonable interpretation of the available data is that because the test ceiling has differentially affected the scores for white, Hispanic, and African American students, TAAS results cannot be used to determine whether or not the achievement gap has been narrowed." This study carries added weight because Linton has served in an advisory capacity to the student assessment division of the Texas Education Agency. The study directly challenges the state's claims, often cited in the drafting and lobbying for passage of the accountability sections of the "No Child Left Behind Act," that the Texas accountability system is making Texas schools more equitable.

To reiterate, the gains on TAAS, used to justify an extreme form of centralization and standardization, evaporate when compared with other established measures of academic performance: Texas students—even those passing the TAAS and making it to their senior year—fail in large numbers to do well on tests of college readiness. Clearly, the accountability system has failed to hold anyone accountable for providing a high-quality learning experience for Texas children.

HOW THE ACCOUNTABILITY SYSTEM PRODUCES EDUCATIONAL LOSSES AND NEW INEQUALITIES

Raising Scores by Losing Kids

Rising scores on the TAAS test, as we have seen, cannot be validated as reliable measures of student learning by comparison with other, more established, tests nor with the state's own college readiness test. We know that for those Texas students who make it to their senior year, having passed the TAAS will have little correlation with their ability to do well on the ACT, the SAT or even the TASP.

But many students in Texas, in fact most of the students in our urban districts, never make it to their senior year. They never have a chance to try for a good score on a college admissions test. Who are the students being lost from the system? If the accountability system is so dramatically improving the schools, then why are so many students leaving school before graduating? It is in examining the dropout rates, school completion rates, that the harmful effects of the accountability system become most clear. A close examination of the data on school enrollments and school completion will provide a clearer picture of the educational and the racial impact of this system. The accountability system itself is creating incentives for principals to "lose" their low-performing students, more frequently their Latino, African American, Limited English Proficient, and immigrant children to make sure the *school's* scores are high. Losing low-achieving students automatically raises the school's average scores, a practice that should be illegal, but in fact is invited and rewarded.

Official statistics on dropouts and school completion in this state are notably unreliable. In September 2002, the *Dallas Morning News* reported that the federal government was threatening to withhold money for dropout prevention because the state's formulas for calculating dropouts was so completely inaccurate (Stewart, 2002).[9]

The official dropout numbers reported by the state and districts have tended to be in the single-digit range. The *Profiles* handbook and the website for the Houston Independent School District (HISD), for example, have in recent years listed the district's dropout rate as low as 3.2% and 2.8%, with similar numbers being posted by the state. The public relations director of the Houston School system told a reporter in October 2001 that the district's dropout rate, as certified by the state, was 1.9% (Downing, 2001). The *Profiles* page for each high school lists its dropout rate, with the figures typically between 1.8 and 3.2 for the city's thirty high schools (HISD, 2000). In 2001, with literally thousands of students exiting school, the TEA announced that it had reduced the overall dropout rate from 1.6% to 1.3%, with the Hispanic dropout rate down to 1.9% from 2.3% the year before.

The way these numbers are calculated is not explained. But a walk through almost any high school in any city in the state will reveal the inaccuracy of these percentages: there are often two to four times as many freshman homerooms as senior homerooms. It is clear that huge numbers of freshmen students never make it through to graduation.

The Intercultural Development Research Association (IDRA) in San Antonio, a research organization that has tracked statewide dropouts since 1986, put the dropout rate in 2001 conservatively at 40%. IDRA Director Maria Montecel sees the state's official figures as "camouflage"; IDRA calculates that Texas public high schools lose between 90,000 and 95,000 students every year. State Senator Carlos Truan told a reporter for the *Houston Press* that he believes the TEA figures to be "treasonous" (Downing, 2001).

Their claims seem less extreme in light of a study of urban districts conducted by Balfanz and Legters (2001) at Johns Hopkins. Balfanz and Legters wanted to study what they termed "promotion power." They wanted to find out which districts across the nation were holding onto their students and which ones were losing students. In a paper analyzing the fourteen districts with the worst dropout rates, it is noteworthy to mention that six of the fourteen are Texas cities. The baseline year for their study was the 1993–94 school year. In that year, approximately half the high schools in the Dallas Independant School District and Houston ISD graduated at least half of their students, a dire picture by anyone's standards. Four years later, they show that only one in four of the high schools in Dallas and Houston graduated at least half their students.

Balfanz and Legters were looking at cities across the United States; their analysis was not tied to any particular policy. But anyone who has been following Texas schools knows that Balfanz and Legters's baseline year was the first year in which the accountability system carried high stakes for administrators. Four years into that system, according to the Balfanz study, Texas urban districts were graduating dramatically fewer students than before the tests of the children were tied to the performance contracts of the adults in the system.

The Manhattan Institute showed similar findings on the matter of dropout rates in urban districts. Their report by Jay Greene (2002) puts the Houston Independent School District's school completion rate at 52%.

A single district's enrollment figures paint a stark picture of the losses of students from that district. The Houston Independent School District, held up in the Elementary and Secondary Education Act (No Child

TABLE 3.2
Houston Independent School District Student Enrollment Grade

| | HISD 1993–1994 | | HISD 2001–2002* | |
	Count	Percent	Count	Percent
Total Students	200,445	100.0%	210,993	100.0%
Students by Grade				
Early Childhood Education	549	0.3%	832	0.4%
Prekindergarten	9,258	4.6%	13,502	6.4%
Kindergarten	16,612	8.3%	16,741	7.9%
Grade 1	19,019	9.5%	19,079	9.0%
Grade 2	17,311	8.6%	18,565	8.8%
Grade 3	16,834	8.4%	18,490	8.8%
Grade 4	16,118	8.0%	17,511	8.3%
Grade 5	15,637	7.8%	16,545	7.8%
Grade 6	15,340	7.7%	14,427	6.8%
Grade 7	14,800	7.4%	14,088	6.7%
Grade 8	13,542	6.8%	13,501	6.4%
Grade 9	18,758	9.4%	19,386	9.2%
Grade 10	10,367	5.2%	10,924	5.2%
Grade 11	8,642	4.3%	9,627	4.6%
Grade 12	7,658	3.8%	7,775	3.7%

Note. *These figures for 2001–2002 show that the loss of students has persisted, even worsened, after seven years of the "accountability" system that tied students' graduation and principals' job contracts to students' scores on the TAAS. Houston Independent School District *Profiles*, 1994, 2002.

Left Behind) legislation as the model for the nation, has had a consistent pattern of attrition during the years since school ratings, administrator pay, and students' graduation were tied to the school-level scores on TAAS.

Table 3.2 shows enrollment by grade in the state's largest district across two years: the year principals went on a TAAS-based performance contract (1993–94) and the 2001–2002 school year, about the time President Bush was holding Texas, and Houston, up as the basis for federal education policy. The key figures are the ninth and tenth grade numbers and the twelfth grade. Every year at least half the freshmen never make it to tenth grade. In many Texas high schools, freshmen constitute fully half the enrollment of the school.[10]

It would be easy to see this rate of losses as perhaps a national problem, or a universal problem in city schools, not merely a Texas or Houston problem. But a ranking of the 94 largest U.S. school districts, based on district enrollment and data on school completers from the U.S. Department of Education, shows that the Texas problem is serious even in comparison to other cities (see Table 3.3 following). Calculating high school graduates in 2000–2001 as a percentage of average enrollment in grades seven to nine, the table shows Dallas as having a 47.61% graduation rate (ranked 87th among the cities), Houston with a 49.02% graduation rate (ranked 84th)—below the District of Columbia (ranked 54th), Philadelphia (ranked 63rd), and the New York City public schools (ranked 83rd). Austin, with only a 57.69% graduation rate, ranked 67th, and San Antonio ranks 79th, with slightly more than 54% graduating. This means of calculating graduation rates using U.S. Department of Education data confirms the Balfanz and Legters study. And it shows that six years into the Texas Accountability System and its high-stakes tests, the system is not providing to Texas children the kind of education that would prepare them for successful school completion, much less a post–high school education.

The state has more than 20 categories of reasons for leaving school prior to graduation that do not fall within the official dropout count (TEA, 2003a). One expected reason would be transferring to another district or another school. From statewide studies done by IDRA (1999) and by Walter Haney, we know that these attrition rates, although the numbers may vary, hold up statewide, so cross-district transfers do not account for these sharp drops in enrollment. The state has many designations that allow districts to *exclude from dropout counts* many of the students they lose—being incarcerated or put in juvenile detention and never returning to school, having no follow-up transfer address, or even completing the General Educational Development certificate

TABLE 3.3

High School Graduates 2000–2001
as a Percentage of Average Enrollment Grades 7–9 1997–1998

Names of Reporting District	State	Enrollment 1997–98 Grades 7–9	Number of 2000–01 Graduates	Grads. 2000–01 as % of Grades 7–9 enroll. 97–8 ÷ 3
1 Davis School District	UT	13,501	4,567	101.48%
2 Jordan School District	UT	16,687	5,509	99.04%
3 Fairfax County Public Schools	VA	32,126	10,187	95.13%
4 Cleveland City School District	OH	19,269	5,784	90.05%
5 Alpine School District	UT	9,789	2,906	89.06%
6 Montgomery County Public Schools	MD	26,602	7,748	87.38%
7 Baltimore County Public Schools	MD	23,732	6,545	82.74%
8 Ysleta Independent School District	TX	11,192	3,052	81.81%
9 Chesterfield County Public Schools	VA	12,008	3,249	81.17%
10 San Juan Unified	CA	11,180	3,020	81.04%
11 Granite School District	UT	17,285	4,666	80.98%
12 Fort Bend Independent School District	TX	12,620	3,391	80.61%
13 Jefferson (CO) County R-1	CO	21,598	5,731	79.60%
14 Prince Georges County Public Schools	MD	28,095	7,435	79.39%
15 San Francisco Unified	CA	13,898	3,676	79.35%
16 Prince William County Public Schools	VA	11,573	3,044	78.91%
17 Cypress-Fairbanks ISD	TX	13,341	3,477	78.19%
18 Garden Grove Unified	CA	10,118	2,574	76.32%
19 North East Independent School District	TX	11,417	2,893	76.02%
20 Cobb County School District	GA	21,270	5,323	75.08%
21 Seattle	WA	9,956	2,482	74.79%
22 Northside Independent School District	TX	14,801	3,669	74.37%
23 Anne Arundel County Public Schools	MD	17,664	4,324	73.44%

TABLE 3.3 (continued)
High School Graduates 2000–2001
as a Percentage of Average Enrollment Grades 7–9 1997–1998

Names of Reporting District	State	Enrollment 1997–98 Grades 7–9	Number of 2000–01 Graduates	Grads. 2000–01 as % of Grades 7–9 enroll. 97–8 ÷ 3
24 Gwinnett County School District	GA	22,199	5,392	72.87%
25 Hawaii Department of Education	HI	44,157	10,666	72.46%
26 Shelby County School District	TN	11,076	2,633	71.32%
27 Fulton County School District	GA	13,761	3,245	70.74%
28 Long Beach Unified	CA	18,157	4,248	70.19%
29 Knox County School District	TN	12,266	2,861	69.97%
30 Clark County School District	NV	42,123	9,630	68.58%
31 Virginia Beach City Public Schools	VA	19,011	4,345	68.57%
32 Garland Independent School District	TX	10,941	2,500	68.55%
33 Wake County Schools	NC	21,127	4,825	68.51%
34 Portland School District 1J	OR	12,618	2,881	68.50%
35 Greenville County School District	SC	14,188	3,238	68.47%
36 Albuquerque Public Schools	NM	20,844	4,745	68.29%
37 Washoe County School District	NV	11,625	2,588	66.79%
38 Puerto Rico Dept of Education	PR	141,559	30,856	65.39%
39 Seminole County School District	FL	14,112	3,076	65.39%
40 Lee County School District	FL	12,694	2,760	65.23%
41 Guilford County Schools	NC	14,053	3,055	65.22%
42 Mobile County School District	AL	16,325	3,542	65.09%
43 San Diego City Unified	CA	29,811	6,449	64.90%
44 Boston School District	MA	14,198	3,059	64.64%

(Continued)

TABLE 3.3 (continued)
High School Graduates 2000–2001
as a Percentage of Average Enrollment Grades 7–9 1997–1998

Names of Reporting District	State	Enrollment 1997–98 Grades 7–9	Number of 2000–01 Graduates	Grads. 2000–01 as % of Grades 7–9 enroll. 97–8÷3
45 Charlotte-Mecklenburg Schools	NC	22,256	4,764	64.22%
46 Anchorage School District	AK	10,920	2,334	64.12%
47 Arlington Independent School District	TX	12,873	2,746	63.99%
48 Omaha Public Schools	NE	10,979	2,335	63.80%
49 Cumberland County Schools	NC	12,251	2,594	63.52%
50 Brevard County School District	FL	16,648	3,524	63.50%
51 De Kalb County School District	GA	22,105	4,637	62.93%
52 East Baton Rouge Parish School Board	LA	13,712	2,857	62.51%
53 El Paso Independent School District	TX	15,590	3,247	62.48%
54 District of Columbia Public Schools	DC	14,091	2,916	62.08%
55 Orleans Parish School Board	LA	18,469	3,813	61.94%
56 Jefferson (KY) County	KY	23,520	4,851	61.88%
57 Hillsborough County School District	FL	36,822	7,546	61.48%
58 Orange County School District	FL	33,055	6,700	60.81%
59 Broward County School District	FL	52,593	10,651	60.76%
60 Sacramento City Unified	CA	11,902	2,395	60.37%
61 Fresno Unified	CA	18,539	3,686	59.65%
62 Palm Beach County School District	FL	35,172	6,986	59.59%
63 Philadelphia City School District	PA	49,926	9,873	59.33%
64 Jefferson Parish School Board	LA	12,855	2,535	59.16%
65 Wichita	KS	10,958	2,148	58.81%

TABLE 3.3 (continued)
High School Graduates 2000–2001
as a Percentage of Average Enrollment Grades 7–9 1997–1998

Names of Reporting District	State	Enrollment 1997–98 Grades 7–9	Number of 2000–01 Graduates	Grads. 2000–01 as % of Grades 7–9 enroll. 97–8÷3
66 Volusia County School District	FL	14,987	2,898	58.01%
67 **Austin Independent School District**	**TX**	**18,179**	**3,496**	**57.69%**
68 Caddo Parish School Board	LA	12,135	2,327	57.53%
69 Pasco County School District	FL	10,734	2,057	57.49%
70 Buffalo City School District	NY	9,695	1,857	57.46%
71 Los Angeles Unified	CA	144,204	27,439	57.08%
72 Polk County School District	FL	19,025	3,617	57.04%
73 Fort Worth Independent School District	TX	17,435	3,291	56.63%
74 Pinellas County School District	FL	27,077	5,111	56.63%
75 Santa Ana Unified	CA	11,406	2,145	56.42%
76 Memphis City School District	TN	23,514	4,341	55.38%
77 Dade County School District	FL	85,570	15,750	55.22%
78 Nashville-Davidson County School District	TN	15,684	2,857	54.65%
79 **San Antonio Independent School District**	**TX**	**14,498**	**2,619**	**54.19%**
80 Aldine Independent School District	TX	11,435	2,024	53.10%
81 Denver County 1	CO	14,679	2,571	52.54%
82 San Bernardino City Unified	CA	11,445	1,984	52.01%
83 New York City Public Schools	NY	243,982	40,827	50.20%
84 **Houston Independent School District**	**TX**	**47,337**	**7,735**	**49.02%**

(*Continued*)

TABLE 3.3 (continued)
High School Graduates 2000–2001
as a Percentage of Average Enrollment Grades 7–9 1997–1998

Names of Reporting District	State	Enrollment 1997–98 Grades 7–9	Number of 2000–01 Graduates	Grads. 2000–01 as % of Grades 7–9 enroll. 97–8÷3
85 Minneapolis	MN	10,925	1,784	48.99%
86 City of Chicago School District 29	IL	93,221	14,875	47.87%
87 **Dallas Independent School District**	**TX**	**36,777**	**5,837**	**47.61%**
88 Duval County School District	FL	30,252	4,777	47.37%
89 Columbus City School District	OH	14,767	2,266	46.04%
90 Atlanta City School District	GA	13,456	2,056	45.84%
91 Baltimore City Public School System	MD	24,874	3,742	45.13%
92 Oakland Unified	CA	11,443	1,716	44.99%
93 Milwaukee School District	WI	22,343	3,279	44.03%
94 Cincinnati City School District	OH	11,750	1,273	32.50%
Detroit City School District	MI	36,733	N/A	N/A
Mesa Unified School District	AZ	15,671	N/A	N/A
Tucson Unified District	AZ	14,296	N/A	N/A
Elk Grove Unified	CA	N/A	2,405	N/A
Plano Independent School District	TX	N/A	2,571	N/A
Clayton County	GA	N/A	1,741	N/A
St. Louis City	MO	9,152	N/A	N/A
Escambia County School District	FL	10,969	N/A	N/A
St. Paul	MN	9,903	N/A	N/A

Note. N/A: Data not available or not applicable due to changes in which schools are in the Top 100.

Young, 1999, 2002, adapted from Haney, 2001.

(GED—formerly the General Equivalency Diploma). But no bureaucratic exclusions or exemptions from the count can provide an education for the students who are not in school. And there are not enough private schools in the state, nor home schoolers, to absorb the tens of thousands of students who are being lost from the system.

The claims by the proponents of the accountability system that high-stakes testing was helping close the achievement gap between Anglos and other ethnic groups have been touted so often that they seem to go un-

TABLE 3.4
Selected Enrollment Counts for Freshmen from Selected Districts
Who Graduated Four Years Later

Freshman Year 1992–93, Senior Year 1995–96

Ethnicity		Austin ISD	Dallas ISD	El Paso ISD	Fort Worth ISD	Houston ISD	San Antonio ISD
Native American	9th Gr.	14	60	9	44	16	1
	Grads	2	17	4	7	6	0
	% Grads	14.3%	28.3%	44.4%	15.9%	37.5%	0.0%
Asian	9th Gr.	108	249	53	199	464	19
	Grads	63	95	24	75	251	8
	% Grads	58.3%	38.2%	45.3%	37.7%	54.1%	42.1%
African American	9th Gr.	1323	6258	233	2142	6571	552
	Grads	381	2012	62	602	1991	135
	% Grads	28.8%	32.2%	26.6%	28.1%	30.3%	24.5%
Hispanic	9th Gr.	2199	4882	4555	1771	8397	3877
	Grads	601	1220	1369	373	2076	1155
	% Grads	27.3%	25.0%	30.1%	21.1%	24.7%	29.8%
White	9th Gr.	2262	1675	1095	1709	2029	268
	Grads	1258	634	528	749	1011	100
	% Grads	55.6%	37.9%	48.2%	43.8%	49.8%	37.3%
Totals	9th Gr.	5906	13124	5945	5865	17477	4717
	Grads	2305	3978	1987	1806	5335	1398
	% Grads	39.0%	30.3%	33.4%	30.8%	30.5%	29.6%

Note. The figures on these major urban districts were taken from a chart that also included 5 additional smaller districts with much smaller total number of students but similar graduation patterns.

TEA, 2000.

TABLE 3.5
Selected Enrollment Counts for Freshmen from Selected Districts
Who Graduated Four Years Later

Freshman Year 1996, Senior Year 1999

Ethnicity		Austin ISD	Dallas ISD	El Paso ISD	Fort Worth	Houston ISD	San Antonio ISD
Native American	9th Gr.	14	59	4	19	15	4
	Grads	5	15	3	7	7	1
	% Grads	35.7%	25.4%	75.0%	36.8%	46.7%	25.0%
Asian	9th Gr.	122	220	55	152	455	17
	Grads	81	97	29	77	278	9
	% Grads	66.4%	44.1%	52.7%	50.7%	61.1%	52.9%
African American	9th Gr.	1442	6193	302	2343	7236	552
	Grads	472	2299	113	892	2446	230
	% Grads	32.7%	37.1%	37.4%	38.1%	33.8%	41.7%
Hispanic	9th Gr.	2922	5762	4822	2317	9787	4439
	Grads	809	1695	1970	795	2731	1693
	% Grads	27.7%	29.4%	40.9%	34.3%	27.9%	38.1%
White	9th Gr.	2456	1527	1093	1670	1973	283
	Grads	1405	644	593	857	1080	105
	% Grads	57.2%	42.2%	54.3%	51.3%	54.7%	37.1%
Totals	9th Gr.	6956	13761	6276	6501	19466	5295
	Grads	2772	4750	2708	2628	6542	2038
	% Grads	39.9%	34.5%	43.1%	40.4%	33.6%	38.5%

Note: The figures on these major urban districts were taken from a chart that also included 5 additional smaller districts with much smaller total numbers of students but similar graduation patterns. TEA, 2000.

The Houston figures for this particular year are of significance not just for what they say about the gap between official claims of academic progress under the state accountability system and actual student performance. This dismal picture has severe national implications: These figures were available at the time the Houston Independent School District was held up as the model that other states and districts need to follow. It is mentioned more than 40 times in the Elementary and Secondary Education Act of 2001. This federal legislation, known as the "No Child Left Behind" Act, mandates the Texas-style accountability system *as the model on which other states and districts should be based*. Its superintendent (Roderick Paige) was named U.S. Secretary of Education on the basis of claimed gains in Houston students' learning, as represented by the district's TAAS scores. These figures show a district far from "model" stature.

questioned. The common wisdom is "well, at least kids who were getting nothing before are getting something now." That claim, that somehow Latino and African American students were faring better under this system because their test scores had to be disaggregated before being factored into school ratings, masks continuing—and growing—inequalities in the system. A look at graduation patterns of Latinos and African Americans, in comparison to those of White students, during the years of the accountability system provides a strong reality check.

Table 3.4 and Table 3.5 display the graduation rates for six of the largest school districts in the state; Table 3.4 shows the class of 1996, early in the accountability system, and Table 3.5 shows the class of 1999, several years after the system had been in place. Although there are some improvements in graduation rates, the figures show a system that continues to fail its children and its communities (TEA, 2000).

Table 3.4 shows that for freshmen who began high school in the 1992–93 school year, graduation rates across all ethnic groups were quite low: For example, no city graduated more than one-third of its African American students. Of 6,258 African American freshmen in Dallas in the spring of 1993, only 2,012, 32.3%, graduated in 1996. Houston graduated 30.3% of its African American students during this period, 1,991 of the 6,571 who had begun as freshmen four years before. The rates for Austin (28.8%) and Fort Worth (28.1%) are even worse.

The picture for Hispanic students of the class of 1996 was also bleak: El Paso had the highest graduation rate for Hispanics with 30.1% (1,369 of 4,555). Houston graduated only 24.7% of its Hispanics (2,076 of 8,397) and Dallas 25% (1,220 of 4,882).

White students were graduating at dismal rates, but still considerably higher than African American or Hispanic students. In El Paso, 48.2% of White students graduated. In Dallas the rate was 37.9%, in Austin 55.6%, and in Houston 49.8%.

If the TAAS tests and accountability system were improving the quality of a Texas education, graduation rates for all ethnic groups should have dramatically improved during this period when TAAS scores for all three groups were steadily rising. However, the class of 1999 (see Table 3.5) showed only slight improvement over 1996. Dallas graduated 37.1% of its African American students (up from 32.2%), and Houston graduated 33.8% of its African American students (up from 30.3%). White students in the two cities graduated at a rate of 42.4% (Dallas) and 54.7% (Houston).

Latino students continued to graduate at very low rates: 29.4% in Dallas (1,695 of 5762), 27.7% in Austin (809 of 2,922), 40.9% in El Paso (1,970 or 4822), and 27.9% in Houston (2,731 of 9,787).

These rates call to mind third-world conditions. Yet these are among the richest, most advanced cities in the world. Dallas is an important center of commerce; Houston is a major producer of science knowledge in a range of fields from medicine to computers, space physics to petrochemicals. Austin, the state capital, is a growing technology center. El Paso anchors the border in a tri-state, bicultural area of great manufacturing and transportation activity. All these cities are major arts centers. Yet from these charts it appears that success, even here, means graduating barely half of the White students and, quite commonly, fewer than one-third of Latinos.

The public relations spokespeople for the state and for the Houston district frequently answer the dropout question with "oh, they all go back to Mexico" (TEA spokeswoman to the education writer from a major Florida newspaper, Nov 2000; HISD spokesperson in conversation with McNeil, 2000). Teachers and principals know that most of their immigrant students are in the United States because their parents wanted them to have an American high school education. They know that friends may sometimes cover for peers who have left school by saying they went back to their home country. But that dismissive comment from the state and from the district sends the powerful message of official default, of abstention, of refusing to take responsibility—refusing, if you will, to be held accountable for the tens of thousands of students being lost under this system. And it stretches the imagination to think that they could be serious in suggesting that 40–45% of the African American teenagers in Texas, and 25% of the Anglos, have "gone to Mexico" when they disappear from school.

The phoniness of single-digit dropout figures posted by the Houston school district was exposed when an assistant principal questioned district administrators about his high school's official dropout rate of *zero percent*. The school of 1800 admits 800 freshmen but graduates only 250 students per year (Peabody, 2003). For his whistle-blowing, the assistant principal, Robert Kimball, received an official reprimand and a reassignment to an elementary school (Zuniga, 2004). But the problem was exposed. A front page story in the *New York Times* (Schemo, 2003), followed by a local television investigative reporter's interviews with school leavers not coded as dropouts (Werner, 2003) forced the state to audit the district's dropout policies. The state audit focused on record-keeping, that is, the way records of school leavers are kept and coded and reported, not on the factors leading thousands of young people to drop out or disappear, many as young as fifteen years of age. The discrepancy between the officially reported dropout numbers and the actual losses of students became difficult to maintain in light of continued national coverage of cracks in the fake story of educational success, the story that had served to justify making the Houston school district the model for the nation's policy governing schools.

Whether school leavers are even termed "dropouts" is a complex political and bureaucratic issue, even more than a methodological one. But getting figures out into the open is the first step in understanding the fraud being perpetrated under the guise of accountability. It will be harder for the state to fake equity when the full scope of the problem is made public.

Structuring Inequality: Inside the System

The test score comparisons and the tracking of dropouts by these varied methods show quite clearly that the system of high-stakes testing and accountability, now in place almost a decade, has not produced educational quality. And it has not made schools in Texas more equitable.

The question is whether the current conditions in Texas schools are merely the entrenched legacies from years of low teacher pay and scarce and unequal funding, or whether the system in place is further lowering educational quality and creating new inequalities. To know the answer, we must look inside classrooms, inside schools, and inside the workings of the state to see what mechanisms lie behind the numbers. What is there about this accountability system that it can produce increasingly high numbers on the state test when all the other indicators of educational attainment point in a negative direction? In the following section, we will consider how the state manages to fake educational quality and create the appearance of greater equity. We will look at the ways the accountability system itself is perpetuating old inequalities and generating new ones.

The low performance of Texas children on non-TAAS indicators of academic achievement and the high number of dropouts under this system are not unintended consequences or accidental side effects of the system. They are the result of the system when it is working as it is intended. In fact, the system only works—that is, only produces rising scores on the state's standardized tests—when these losses are occurring. To understand how the system itself is generating failures, and how it is shifting the burden of the accountability system increasingly to the weakest link in the system—children of color—it is necessary to see what schools and systems are doing to produce higher scores.

Curricular Losses

When the newspaper publishes test scores in reading, writing, and mathematics, test scores that are rising every year for all ethnic groups, the public may be forgiven for thinking that schools are improving their teaching and that more children are learning in these vital areas. A look inside classrooms reveals quite a different story.

The work of classrooms under the accountability system has shifted from learning content, ideas, and skills to learning how to take a standardized test. The first loss to become regularized under the accountability system has been the curriculum. Principals are under enormous pressure to make sure their *school* scores are high. This is not the same as having the goal of educating *children* to a high level of learning in their academic subjects.

In an earlier paper with Angela Valenzuela, "The Harmful Effects of the TAAS System of Testing in Texas: Beneath the Accountability Rhetoric" (2001), we presented what we were seeing as the direct, negative educational consequences of the Texas accountability system.[11] We documented its harmful effects on the quality of education available to disadvantaged Latino and African American children. In summarizing our findings, we noted that "under the TAAS system of testing, curriculum, instruction, school resources, and children, [have all been] adversely affected:

- The TAAS system of testing reduces the quality and quantity of curriculum. It trivializes the subjects being tested and displaces subjects not being tested to create more time for test-prep in the tested subjects.
- The TAAS system distorts educational expenditures, diverting scarce instructional dollars away from such high-quality curricular resources as laboratory supplies and books toward test-prep materials and activities of limited instructional value.
- TAAS provokes instruction that is aimed at the lowest level of skills and information, and it crowds out other forms of learning, particularly for poor and minority children.
- TAAS-based teaching and test-prep violate what is known about how children learn.
- The TAAS is divorced from children's experience and cultures.

- The test is imposing exit measures that are particularly inappropriate for LEP (Limited-English Proficient) students.
- TAAS is widening the gap between the education of children in Texas' poorest (historically low-performing) schools and that available to more privileged children." (McNeil & Valenzuela, 2001, pp. 129–130)

To that list we could have added the finding that the incentives built into the accountability system are the drivers behind these losses.

In that paper, we describe how classroom time, children's time with teachers, came to be test-prep time as the high-stakes component of the school rating system took effect. The first subjects to be affected were the subjects to be tested: reading, writing, and math. Because the reading and math tests are in computer-scored, multiple-choice formats and the writing test highly formulaic, it became clear that learning to read for meaning was not the same as learning to pass a multiple-choice test on an unfamiliar sample of text.

To meet the single indicator goal of producing a high pass rate on the TAAS test, many principals began to require that teachers use commercial test-practice materials, or even sample questions from previous TAAS tests downloaded from the TEA website, as the curriculum in their classrooms. Some principals required teachers to devote part of every class period to test practice; others dedicated one day a week to practice tests in every classroom. Some principals even began buying practice tests to be given every four or five weeks during the months leading up to the official test and would pay to send these off to testing companies to be computer scored. On the basis of these test results, they would write up teachers whose students were not showing month-to-month improvement. They would pressure teachers to pull aside students not scoring well on the practice test to give them more time for practice tests—and in the process, less time for learning the real curriculum.

Reading for the state test is not interpreting text, engaging with literature or coming to understand how ideas connect with a writer's words. TAAS reading-test questions presented students with very brief, random paragraphs they were to read and then answer three or four multiple-choice questions about. As many students soon learned, with the help of consultants coming into schools to coach them and their teachers to create quick spikes in the schools' pass rates, a student could successfully answer the question by skipping the reading passage and looking for key words in the answers. If a key word in an answer showed up in the text, that answer was likely the correct one. As a student told me, "Miss, you don't even have to read it to get the right answer."

Math under the TAAS is essentially multiple-choice math. Students are taught how to select among given answers and then given hours and hours of practice tests. They may manage to produce a decent math score without learning the math concepts, without being able to think through a math problem or apply a mathematical operation.

Writing for the test is producing a twenty-five-sentence essay, evenly divided into five paragraphs, each with a topic sentence, three sentences of supporting detail, and a concluding sentence. This artificial format rewards being able to count to twenty-five, but it fails to teach students that writing is having something to say, finding one's voice, learning to use words to connect with an audience, and experimenting to find the right structure for what you as the writer are trying to convey to that audience.

Angela Valenzuela and I found in our research that this pattern of substituting a bogus curriculum of test practice for a real, academically challenging, and instructionally productive curriculum was most prevalent in predominately Latino and African American schools and in the lower academic tracks of our large multiracial comprehensive schools, where students of color are typically segregated. Here we found the greatest pressure from principals to substitute test practice for the academic curriculum.

This is a direct result of the accountability system. In this state, schools in Latino and African American neighborhoods are historically the least well resourced, the most likely to have been assigned teachers unqualified in their subjects, the least likely to have community resources that enrich children's lives outside of school. They are the least likely to have had a record of high achievement on technical, objective measures. So it is the principals of these schools who felt the greatest pressure right from the beginning to find ways to boost their school scores, and thus their school ratings, quickly. They knew not to expect, except in a few rare instances, their districts or the state to provide their schools with the resources comparable to well-stocked schools in affluent neighborhoods. They knew they could not expect to be able to hire extra staff to reduce class size, to bring in teachers fluent in the children's home languages, to be able to purchase abundant and up-to-date instructional materials so that their students could learn to a higher level. If these had been forthcoming, if the communities and school districts could have been depended on to provide for these schools those things whose absence had dragged down educational achievement, these principals, like those in more affluent areas, could have counted on children's improved learning over time to be reflected in substantive assignments in the classroom and also in standardized test scores. But that vision of quality schooling, and that luxury to take the long view, is not possible under an accountability system that holds no one accountable for providing schools with what they need but then demands that even the most neglected schools show an instant spike in the scores on state tests or face dire consequences. For the principals, those consequences included losing their principalships.

In more privileged schools, where test scores are traditionally high in the regular and honors tracks but lower in the remedial and ESL tracks where students of color are concentrated, the capacity for the school to boost its ratings depends on "those students" having passing scores. The prevailing pattern, given that pressure, is to further reduce the quality of instruction in those tracks by using more and more test practice in place of a traditional curriculum.

The "Harmful Effects" paper documents these curricular losses, beginning with the subjects tested, as we observed, in Latino and African American–dominant schools and classrooms (McNeil & Valenzuela, 2001). We then noted that in these same schools, the subjects not being tested also began to suffer. Principals demanded that teachers in non-TAAS subjects set aside their teaching of science, art, social studies, and even physical education to spend class time on practice test materials. The curriculum, the real substantive content of schooling, was disappearing in these schools.

The first analysis of this disappearance necessarily focused on the content areas, the ways they are narrowed or trivialized or rendered completely unrecognizable, as in the reading samples children are intended to forget the minute they answer the questions. As we combined our data, however, we noted a more serious loss: The longer children stay in this system, the less they have to carry forward from year to year.

We saw this, again, as an equity issue. When we began our joint writing effort, suburban schools and schools in more affluent areas whose students traditionally do well on standardized tests were still able to do "real school" for most of the year, stopping just before the test to go over test-taking skills with their students.

A system that pressured Latino and African American students, immigrant children, and children in under-resourced schools to quickly produce high scores on a test, even to the extent of shifting their curriculum from school subjects to test prep and test practice, was creating even greater inequalities than had existed before. Not only did they rarely have the benefit of well-stocked classrooms, labs and libraries, and highly qualified teachers instead of long-term substitute teachers on emergency credentials—impediments which already kept them from achieving at the levels of children in more well-supported schools. They also spent less and less time during the school year studying their subjects at all. Thus, each year a child of color was in this system of schooling, the gap between his or her education and that of more affluent students was growing, not shrinking.

A longitudinal look at children's experience under this system also helps explain the declining performance of Texas children on the SAT, the ACT, the TASP, and the NAEP. If children are reading literature, there is the possibility that they will build a cumulative knowledge base individually and as a group of learners in the company of an adult who is also engaging with that literature. Each semester they will have something to carry forward to the next. Intellectual growth and academic skills development do not proceed linearly. But real reading connects text over time with the ideas the children bring to its interpretation and with the ideas that develop through writing and discussion in a classroom.

Test practice and drill in test-taking strategies such as "skip the paragraph and find the key word in the answer" do not foster the development of a cumulative body of knowledge and skills. In fact, Valenzuela has noted that children in such a system are building a cumulative deficit. The longer they are in a school system devoted to producing scores on a single test, the less opportunity they will have to learn the substantive ma-

TABLE 3.6
When Do Texas Students Leave School?

	African American	Latino	White	Total
After 9th grade:	5791 (15.81% of AfAm.)	14969 (16.85% of Lat.)	10705 (8.16% of White)	32356 (11.20%)
After 10th grade:	3504 (11.44%)	8984 (12.67%)	7767 (6.62%)	20573 (8.59%)
After 11th grade:	1679 (6.44%)	5375 (9.03%)	8038 (7.78%)	14964 (7.34%)
Total per year:	10974	29328	26510	67893 *

Note. *This figure does not include the approximately 10,000 additional students per year who drop out during the 12th grade year.

Haney, 2000, part 5, p.11; part 8, p. 4

terial being studied by their peers in more privileged public and private schools, the curriculum not easily reducible to multiple-choice items for computer scoring. It is little wonder that so many enter high school ill prepared. As the pressure to produce increases in scores has tightened, now even suburban, Anglo, college-track students are having to spend valuable class time practicing for TAAS. The early impact of harm, the impact that is showing up in the dramatic losses of Latino children from our schools (see Table 3.6), is in large part the result of turning classrooms into test-score production mills. The skills learned have very little value beyond the test, and so do not stick. And the skills the children do need have too often been shunted aside to boost the school's accountability rating to the next level.

The strict curricular losses (science concepts not learned, historical studies set aside, wonderful literature replaced by "reading" drills) began in our poorest schools and have now spread across the state to all our communities. It could nevertheless be argued that the greatest losses are continuing to accrue to Latino students. That is true because this technical approach to schooling is so alien to a culture that values raising children to become *bien educado*, a culture that affirms a more comprehensive definition of what it means to be fully educated. And it is true because, as Alamillo et al. point out in chapter 7 of this volume, high-stakes testing has consequences that fall most heavily on students whose first language is not English.

Angela Valenzuela has written eloquently and powerfully about the losses to children when schooling is culturally subtractive, when the nature of instruction, the content of instruction, and the very culture of the school are ignorant of, even oppositional to, the children's language and culture (Valenzuela, 1999). The rigidity and narrowness of test-practice and test-score production on a standardized test by definition structure out possibilities for the expression of and affirmation of cultural identities. Otherwise, it would not be a standardized test. By rendering the extraordinary, awe-inspiring diversities (developmental, cultural, personal, social) inherent in our children into a single indicator, a test score, the system can function as a control system. The minute any of these inherent qualities is even acknowledged, the system cannot standardize, and its powers of control will be lost.

The rhetoric of the testing system, whether in this state or now nationally as a result of the federal enactment of accountability, claims that "no child" will be left behind. The illusion that if all children are being tested alike, then we must be teaching all children the same thing, has been very successfully misleading. From inside classrooms we know that the system has to de-personalize, has to exclude, has to structure out personal and cultural identities to claim objectivity. It has to silence differences, whether cultural, developmental, or idiosyncratic, or it loses its potency. *The system has to be subtractive or it cannot function as a generic, standardized system.*

Alamillo et al. must be read very carefully for their depiction of what we can expect to happen when standardized assessment systems intersect with laws forcing schools to ignore, and to refuse to help further develop, children's fluency in their home languages. Although the California, Arizona, and Massachusetts "English only" laws have thankfully not been adopted widely in other states (and in many have been resisted), even without the "English only" directives, the standardization of assessments doubly handicaps Latino children and others whose home language is not English, the language of the tests. The standardization forces schools to speed up children's readiness for tests in English, in doing so subtracting from one of their most powerful learning tools, their home language and all the understandings it embodies. The standardization also forces them into a non-expressive version of English that is of little use: the capacity to use just enough English to choose among answers provided by a testing company on a very narrow and artificial set of information. The dropout figures for Latino children seen in the district-by-district figures (see Tables 3.4 and 3.5) cannot come as a surprise in light of the limitations placed on their learning when their schools have to focus on test-score production. These children have been set up to fail.

Using Dropouts and Waivers to Boost School Ratings

The idea that a statewide school reform, a highly touted accountability system, could be worsening the conditions and outcomes of schooling seems far-fetched. But it is clearly a central component of the Texas accountability system. Many do not believe the loss of students to be an unintended consequence.

To understand how the system produces dropouts, it is essential to understand that this system is first of all a management-control system, not an education reform. Unlike standards movements in other states that later got co-opted by standardization, the reforms in Texas that produced this accountability system never invoked academic standards. From the beginning, a series of politicians, education commissioners, and the business and corporate advocates of the system used the language of top-down management: "We have to hold these (teachers, principals, schools) accountable. We have to be able to identify failures." One White corporate executive told me personally while the system was in its early stages of implementation, "You know of course that we would not even need these control systems if it weren't for all these Black teachers and all those little brown children." I believe he spoke sincerely.

The accountability system was justified to lawmakers and the public on the basis of the perceived weakness of teachers, the low performance of minority children, and the need to hold schools accountable to the people whose taxes pay for them. Traditionally, Texas schools have been highly centralized and regulated since the days of Reconstruction just after the Civil War when the state decided to create an official list of textbooks that could be adopted by local districts. But up until this accountability system's high-stakes pieces were in place, the central state authority prescribed in great detail the *processes* of schooling, from teacher licensing to school finance formulas, to the square footage needed per vocational student. The accountability system put in place a prescription for the *outcomes*. It created a centralized mechanism for measuring those outcomes. And it put into place that final accountability piece: the use of children's test scores for the rating of principals, teachers, schools, and districts (McNeil, 2000).

This was a politically risky move in a state where hating big government—or at least talking about hating big government—is a favorite pastime. It was risky because teachers are a powerful voting bloc. It was risky because it shifted so much power over every component of local schools away from local communities and school boards. Centralized power can quickly become a liability unless the controlled system proves successful.

The backers of this system needed to show quick and measurable results. Without quick, positive outcomes, they would have a hard time justifying this extreme form of centralization. These politicians and business leaders sold the accountability system as an inexpensive and surefire fix for the public schools of Texas. They knew they could not expect all students to do well on the tests—there were too many schools without highly qualified teachers, without adequate resources, without the capacity to teach increasingly diverse students well. Many students in the upper grades had come up through these schools, and many more would do so even now. Such students were not likely to score high on a statewide standardized test. Yet the powers behind the testing did not want to make the investment to bring those schools up to capacity, to give them a genuine chance at a great education, one that would also be reflected in standardized tests.

Their response was to put in place high stakes at every level of the system. And then they created a back door, an escape route for those they wanted to protect: school administrators and, not unexpectedly, themselves. That back door was a waiver system that enabled high school principals to exclude from the tenth-grade exit-TAAS cohort any student who was a potential liability to the school's test scores. The plan did not exempt these students from the exit TAAS. The students would still have to take it to graduate. It merely excluded them during the immediate school year, a way of protecting the principal who now was on a very short-term performance contract contingent on the school's passing rate on the TAAS.

The waiver worked like this: a school that had applied for a waiver from the state could hold back as a ninth grader any student who had failed even one ninth-grade course. In some schools, these students had to retake their ninth-grade year, even classes they had passed. In other schools, they were pulled aside into courses that were labeled as *local credit* (no credit for graduation) to drill and practice day after day for the TAAS, so when they did take it, they would not be a liability to the school's ratings. Others of these "technical ninth-graders" were allowed to continue to take courses they were ready for but often discouraged from immediately taking the course they had failed; some were thus carried on the enrollment ledgers as ninth-graders for as long as three years. If they stayed in school.

The tragedy of the waiver system is that it labeled as failures many students who otherwise were doing fairly well in school. These were students who had every intention of graduating from high school. But for many of these students, the effect of this designation as a failure and being retained in ninth grade caused them to lose interest in school. They suddenly saw themselves as failures rather than as needing to retake biology or algebra I. Their relations with their peers changed. And if they were in a school that took generous advantage of the waiver, they came to see that their school is not a good school; that they would be foolish to stay there and keep trying.

Teachers first made me aware of the ninth-grade waiver and its effects. They kept saying "this waiver is killing our Black kids, " or "this waiver is just pushing our Latino kids out the door." Rod Paige, the Houston superintendent at that time, was making public announcements that "all our children are being tested, no one is being excluded." The superintendent's announcements sounded convincing. Children were either being tested or they weren't.

What the teachers and principals explained was that all the students in the *tenth-grade cohort* were being tested, but that at many schools, particularly the predominantly Latino high schools, the number retained as ninth graders under the waiver might often be as high as half the class. The teacher who first explained to me the way the waiver worked pointed out that her high school had received much attention from the district by dramatically raising test scores from a 35% pass rate to an 82% pass rate within just two or three years. The principal was widely praised, and the public got the impression that this high school, long neglected by the district, had finally been improved. What no one pointed out was that this school of more than 3,000 students would have been expected to have between 700 and 750 students in its sophomore class, the class that takes the exit-TAAS required for graduation. Only 296 of those students were tested. The rest were all excluded under the waiver (still designated as ninth graders) or counseled to stay home on test day so they wouldn't fail.

From time to time the press, or even prosecutors, call our attention to cheating on standardized tests, usually by teachers or school administrators somehow manipulating student identification numbers or answer sheets to give the school a better rating. Parents, teachers, and students complained to a local television reporter in Houston that the principal of a predominantly African American high school had asked teachers and counselors to counsel students not likely to pass TAAS to stay home from school during TAAS week. When families challenged him, he changed his instruction and said that they could come to school but go to a GED prep class rather than take the TAAS and jeopardize the school rating, a suggestion that is as inappropriate for 15-year-olds who want a high school education as directing them not to come to school at all. The ninth-grade waiver seems in its operation and its consequences to be another form of cheating. The difference is that it is legally permissible within this accountability system, and in fact encouraged to ensure that school scores will rise.

When Walter Haney (2000) began tracking student enrollments, dropouts, and completions, the data showed the state to be graduating a smaller percentage of students in all three ethnic groups than had been true in the early 1980s before centralized standardization. Texas educators then asked him to reanalyze the data to find out at what point in the system students were being lost. His grade-level analysis confirmed what the teachers were saying about the effects of the ninth-grade waiver.

Table 3.6 shows that for 1998, five years into the accountability system, the state was losing 67,893 students from its high schools every year; these students left before ever enrolling in twelfth grade, so the number of actual school leavers would be closer to 75,000 each year. Of special interest is the percentage of students who leave school sometime after enrolling in ninth grade and before ever enrolling in tenth, the high-stakes testing year, the year the student scores affect principals' pay and schools' ratings. According to the TEA data Haney analyzed, almost 16% of African American high school students who enroll in ninth grade in a Texas public high school never make it to tenth grade. Close to 17% of Latino ninth graders never make it to tenth grade. The numbers are more dramatic than the percentages: this represents (annually) 5,791 African American young people and just under 15,000 Latino youth. The percentages for Whites are about half what they are for the other students but the actual number is very high: 10,705.

The waiver system is not widely understood by parents and by many teachers outside the large high schools. It is certainly not made transparent in the reporting of test scores and official dropout rates. But the waiver system assured the political popularity of the system because it enabled the state to put in place a system that seemed to be totally standardized, encompassing of all children. It is true the students may not opt out of the TAAS graduation requirement. So the kids are fully obligated. But the system is not.

The waiver permits the single indicator system to show an increase in that indicator by doing nothing at all to improve the school. The increase comes when the lowest-achieving children are shown the door, their scores no longer a liability to the school. When I first heard that so many ninth graders were being held back, I asked "which teachers move back to ninth grade with them and which teachers will then move up to tenth grade as the kids move up?" I was met with blank stares. "You know, when that bulge in school enrollment goes up the grades, which teachers will be shifted up the grades with them?" "Those students don't go on up. They leave." There was literally no discussion among faculties and school administrators that I studied during the early years of the waiver regarding how the ninth grade would be made ready for these students' second try, how the teaching or the curriculum could be improved to ensure their readiness for the upper grades; and no discussion of how to shift teaching loads as this bulge in student population would move on toward their senior year. The schools knew even then these kids were not intended nor expected to stay in school. Nor would their scores on high-stakes tests show up in the school ratings. As discussed earlier, for Texas to be excluding students from the NAEP sample for the purpose of generating a continued rise in Texas NAEP scores is consistent with its exclusionary policies on its own exit-level test.

Playing Games with Passing Scores

One other structural manipulation assured a positive reputation for this accountability system. Again, it is a manipulation that is not discussed when the annual TAAS report card hits the newsstands: that is the systematic lowering of what counts as a passing score. On a criterion-referenced test like TAAS, students have to have a certain number of answers right to pass. A score of 70 is widely thought to be the passing score on TAAS; it is the publicly discussed passing score; it is the score students strive to surpass. And every year, the state (and the politicians and bureaucrats and business advocates of this system) say they are "raising the bar," requiring more of Texas students.

But if 70 were held as an actual numerical percentage of right answers needed to pass, many students would not pass, their principals would not receive bonuses, their schools would not get higher ratings, and their parents would begin to question the wisdom of this system. So the bar gets lowered: the state lowers the number of answers a child has to get right to get a 70 on the TAAS. When this practice came to light, then education commissioner Jim Nelson wrote a letter to "the administrator addressed" explaining that all tests need to be "re-equated" from time to time and that the lowering of the cut score, the lowering of the actual number needed to pass, was in fact merely a psychometric technicality (Nelson, 1999/2000).

In "Revisiting the Myth of the Texas Miracle in Education: Lessons about Dropout Research and Dropout Prevention," Haney (2001) explains the significance of this lowering of the cut score. The passing score of 70 had been set arbitrarily in 1991 as "sounding like" a passing score, a score that would be politically acceptable as high enough to appear rigorous but not so high as to generate large numbers of failures. According to Haney, during the 30 administrations of TAAS between 1991 and 1999, the passing scores were re-scaled so that passing scores would remain roughly equivalent from year to year, with variations in the passing score as slight as one or two items out of 48 on the exit-level TAAS.

By fall 2000, it had become known that the passing scores on TAAS had been lowered. The passing score on TAAS reading varied in one year from 31 to 27 answers needed, and the math passing score between the fall 1999 and fall 2000 administration of the test varied as much as nine points (from 39 to 30). According to Haney, "On the fall 2000 exit level TAAS math test, the passing score was set at 30 out of 60 items correct or 50%—dramatically lower than the roughly 70% correct that was the passing score until 1999" (2001, p. 6). Haney notes that Nelson uses the justification that the test now incorporated more of the state curricular items. He said in his letter, "I want to be very clear that this year's raw scores will be lower than last year's due to the rigor of the test" (Nelson, 1999/2000). The state, school districts, and the media continue to make year-to-year comparisons across schools and districts (and the state as a whole) as though the passing rate, or *cut score* had remained constant from year to year. In fact, the arbitrary lowering of the cut score by the state education agency has rendered year-to-year comparisons statistically invalid. Newspaper and district reports of annual scores do not note in public announcements of scores (and score increases) that the percentage passing in the current year may have in fact correctly answered fewer questions than their counterparts in previous years. For example, on the eighth-grade TAAS mathematics test in 2001, the raw score for a passing grade was 30 out of 60, whereas just three years earlier, a student needed to answer 40 out of 60 to pass (TEA, 2002b, 2002c).

The "Texas miracle" Haney writes about was the hype that the accountability system, and the TAAS system of testing, had magically transformed Texas public schools. TAAS scores were rising. The rising scores proved the merits of the system. They gave the governor a strong plank in his platform for his presidential race. And they gave to advocates of accountability the concrete evidence they needed (the earnings figures, so to speak) to take to other state legislatures and governors and to ensure the accountability system would stand as the model for national legislation if Bush won the presidency.

More immediately within the state, the rising numbers could be used to silence dissenters and reinforce arguments that the accountability system was working. Once again, they were faking it: faking educational improvement by lowering the number of questions students had to answer right—in the case of math, a drop from 70% to 50% of the right answers needed to pass.

The lowering of the scores, when combined with the amount of class time used to drill on the test, helps explain why so many Texas young people, having gone to public school most of their lives under this system, would reach their ninth-grade courses or their college admissions tests so ill prepared academically. The Texas Education Agency, the com-

missioner, the governor, the State Board of Education, local superintendents, and school board members were all saying that Texas schools were
improving, that the bar was being raised, that Texas children were performing better every year. Like an Olympic athlete whose coach secretly
lowers the high jump bar during practice to create the feeling of success,
a student who passed the TAAS would feel academically successful until
he or she stepped out into the real competition—the ACTs, the SATs, the
state's college readiness test. Only then would the system's hollow value
become apparent. Only then would the state's disrespect for that child
and his or her future be visible.

If enough people understood them, these fine-grained technical issues could perhaps be used to dismantle the system, to show that the em-
peror of standardized testing wears no clothes. But ordinary parents are
de-privileged in these discussions. They lack the technical vocabulary to
make public the falseness of the indicators. The indicators, and the system of adjusting them, remain opaque to parents without psychometric
degrees and to parents new to English. All the while the schools are
putting more pressure on the kids to do well on the test, to get the
school's scores up, to raise the school ranking on the sign out front.

SUMMARIZING THE DISCREPANCIES

The Texas accountability system has successfully entrenched an extreme
form of centralization and has imposed on children and schooling a rad-
ical form of standardization. The alignment of the system is tight and
with the reading-by-third-grade test, getting tighter. The image is that this
system has improved educational quality in Texas schools and made
schools more equitable. Rising test scores on the state test for all three
ethnic groups are the state's evidence.

Artificial Success

We have seen that the improvement is not real. The state is faking it. The
TAAS test scores are not good solid indicators of academic quality. They
have been artificially produced by test-taking drills in classrooms and the
manipulation of cut scores by state officials. They are also boosted by the
system's rewards to principals who, by losing thousands of students before the high-stakes tenth grade test, manage to increase their school's av-

erage score. This presents a huge ethical dilemma for principals, whose jobs depend on these scores. Students pay a high price for the phoniness of the system. They discover this when they find themselves unprepared for the next level of schooling.

The state is also faking its claims of improving equity. The huge investment in the testing system itself has created the appearance of sameness but in the process has masked the old inequalities in funding, teacher quality and classroom resources. The system has created new inequalities by linking adults' pay and job security to children's test scores, creating an urgency to shift out of the testable cohorts, or into intensive test drills, children deemed a liability to the school scores. Often these are children of color.

The system is flawed, fraudulent, and harmful to children. It is also harmful to communities in the way it closes off all the other ways of talking about children and what it means to be educated.

Ser Bien Educado

In his book *Hispanic Education in the United States: Raíces y Alas*, Professor Eugene García invokes the advice of his father: "*Nunca te pueden quitar la educación.*" (They can never take away your education—what you have learned) (García, 2001, p. 9).

The history of Latino education in the United States has been a history of struggle. As Professor García documents in his book, Latinos have had to struggle for access to an education, then for permission to speak their own language within the school. The struggle for equitable funding goes on today. There is struggle to have a voice in who teaches, and in what is taught to the children. There continues to be struggle against the labels that close off possibilities when they mask the identity of the child: *regular track, remedial track, Limited English Proficient, retained in grade*, the labels used to limit children's access to full participation in all that the school has to offer.

Decades, even centuries, of struggle for an education speak to a deep yearning for children to be educated, for them to be able to fulfill their potential and find their gifts. That longing is for an education that is inseparable from the person, an education that "they can never take away."

In *Subtractive Schooling: U.S.-Mexican Youth and the Politics of Caring*, Valenzuela distinguishes the technical mastery of schooling from Latino families' hopes that their children will become *bien educados*.

Bien educado does not connote merely the accumulation of course credits and degrees, but also knowing "how to live in the world as caring, responsible, well-mannered, and respectful human beings" (Valenzuela, 1999, p. 23). To receive an *educación*, in her words, "additionally refers to competence in the social world, wherein one respects the dignity and individuality of others."

A standardized system of schooling by definition omits individuality. It has no structure that values caring or fosters respect. If it were informed by and infused with the cultural values of the children and their families, it could not, by definition, be a standardized system. To standardize is to strip away variation, to redefine the object of standardization (in this instance, the child) by distilling it to one or two characteristics common to the larger universe of objects. The Texas accountability system has been seen to reduce children to numbers above and below a cut score, to see them as an asset to the school or a potential liability depending on their ability to correctly fill in bubbles on an answer sheet for a computer, not a person, to score.

The chasm between standardization and *bien educado* cannot be bridged. Standardization structures out the relational experiences of schooling. It is not a matter of adding multicultural content to the questions or making other adjustments to make the testing system more culturally relevant. Standardized systems cannot become culturally relevant without losing the uniformity upon which standardization is predicated. They cannot be inclusive except on their own terms, necessitating the reduction of the person to be included to a single and passive dimension. The flaws in standardized systems of education are not glitches that can be fixed. They are essential to standardization. And they require an extensive apparatus of maintenance and control, because standardization is so counter to learning and to children's development. The depersonalization, the lack of respect for the person and the culture, is essential for standardization to be standardizing.

We have seen that the Texas high-stakes testing system is phony, that its claims of educational improvement and increased equity cannot be substantiated by external measures. Mr. García's advice to his children was grounded in the faith that their education would have worth. The struggle to open up access to schooling for Latino youth has, on the intake side, been largely successful. However, these centralized testing systems are creating formidable barriers to receiving an education of substance once inside. Unfortunately, these systems are structured to succeed only if they can push out a significant number of Latino youth before they can complete their education. It is as if the system is set up to insure that an "education that can't be taken away" is kept just out of reach of Latino youth in the first place.

It is important that the flaws and damaging consequences of the system be made transparent. But if the critique remains focused on the components of and effects of the testing system, then it risks reifying that system and its definitions of children, learning, and the purposes of schooling. To give children an education that "they can't take away," an education carried within the person, we must rethink what it means to be educated. We must offer more than a reaction to or point-by-point rebuttal against standardization. The re-envisioning must arise out of the community and its deeply held beliefs. It must be born of the mutual respect among the *bien educados*. It has to start from the traditions of the people who love and care about the children and out of the dreams they have for those children's future. Such an education would ultimately not have to become exclusive or divisive, segregated from other communities' goals for their children. In this diverse nation, it is actually the basis for an education that would reach out to commonalities across divergent traditions. Valenzuela has written that schooling that subtracts from children's language and culture subtracts from their identity and leaves them disconnected. An education that begins with an affirmation of personal and cultural identities is the only education that has the potential to center children in their own possibilities and to connect them in productive ways to the larger world.

In a democracy, claiming a voice in children's schooling is ultimately a political act. It challenges a power structure that depends on compliance and silence for its survival. The critique of high-stakes testing can begin with making public the fraud behind the numbers. Then it must move quickly beyond reaction. It must actively, and with urgency, claim the authority to redefine and assert the rich and complex purposes of public schooling our children are eager to believe in. To do less is to risk losing more of our children and to put democracy itself at risk.

NOTES

1. A child will have three chances to pass the test. The scheduled second administration of the reading test comes only days after the child receives notice of having failed the first time, a considerable pressure to be placing on eight-year-olds. In response to strong criticism, the state instituted an appeals process by which a parent, the child's teacher, and a school administrator may be convened after a child has failed the reading test twice to review whether the child should

be permitted to promote to fourth grade. Against the advice of educators, the presumption or the default position is retention, not promotion, and the committee's recommendation must be unanimous.

2. Beginning in the 2002–2003 school year, the TAKS test replaced the TAAS; TAKS stands for "Texas Assessment of Knowledge and Skills." It is advertised as a tougher test; it will be given in more subjects, with higher stakes for children in key grade levels. The high school exit test will be given in the eleventh grade instead of the tenth.

3. Asian and Native American students and immigrants from beyond the Spanish-speaking countries (including European, Middle Eastern and African) also fall within the "White" category by virtue of not being Hispanic or African American. (It was these two groups, in conjunction with the Mexican American Legal Defense and Education Fund, the National Association for the Advancement of Colored People and other organizations, that brought desegregation lawsuits more than thirty years ago; the designations of ethnic and racial groups by the courts ensuing from these legal challenges have persisted in the official categorizations used by school districts although the school populations have dramatically changed in the intervening years. Now more than 150 home languages are represented in the public schools of the major metropolitan areas.)

4. I am indebted to Laurie Hammons of the Rice University Center for Education for her invaluable assistance in organizing the data and data presentation for this chapter.

5. Texas ranks among the worst of the 50 states in the percentage of adults who are hired as teachers without the necessary qualifications for their subject. Education Week reports that one in four of the state's secondary school students is taught by someone who does not have even a minor in the subject (State of the states, 2003).

Rather than recruiting and adequately compensating highly educated teachers or investing in upgrading the knowledge of current teachers, the state has responded to the problem of non-certified teachers by substantially relaxing the qualifications for a teaching certificate. Beginning in May 2004, adults with a college degree and no professional preparation in pedagogy, curriculum, child development, culture, learning theory, or professional practicum courses may be deemed "certified" if they teach in a public school for two years (Elliott, 2004). The certificate as credential essentially displaces the need for actual qualifications to teach knowledge and skills to children.

6. Precise year-to-year comparisons of the passing rates of Texas high school graduates on the TASP is difficult because of what THECB calls "program changes" effective 1993 (prior to the years cited here), and the exempting from TASP, for the purpose of college admissions, students who score high on the ACT or SAT I. However, as this paper discusses, a declining number of Texas students are taking these tests, and the scores of those students have remained relatively low. Therefore, the sharp decline in TASP scores during the first five years of the accountability system has to be taken seriously as an educational quality indica-

tor, one which calls into question the validity of the steadily rising TAAS scores during the same period.

7. Texas State Board of Education, Long Range Planning 1996–2000, submitted December 1995 by Jack Christie, Chair (frontispiece and mission statement, unpaged).

8. On the basis of their review of state test scores in those states with high-stakes testing, as compared with those states' students' scores on major national tests, Amrein and Berliner conclude that "Although states may demonstrate increases in scores on their own high-stakes tests, transfer of learning is not a typical outcome of their high-stakes testing policy" (Amrein & Berliner, 2002a, p. 36).

9. As Eileen Coppola notes in her analysis of dropout rates, cohort attrition, and persistence to graduation in an urban high school participating in a national school reform effort, "Drop out and school completion rates in Texas are the subject of considerable controversy" (Coppola, 2002). Students may be individually tracked at the school, district, or state level through enrollment data, or student cohorts may be tracked to verify persistence to graduation. Dropout rates may be calculated as the ratio of freshmen to the remaining seniors or graduates four years later. Districts may count as dropouts only those students who withdrew notifying the school they were dropping out, not transferring. States write regulations specifying categories of school leavers not to be counted as "dropping out"; Texas excludes students in juvenile detention, students whose whereabouts are unknown, and more than two dozen other categories of non-school attenders who should not be counted as dropping out but neither can they be counted as persisting to graduation. Texas is one of the few states that counts individuals who pass the GED as having graduated from high school. For a thorough discussion of the methodologies they employ in their research and of their assessment of official state means for calculating school persistence/school leaving, see Carnoy, Loeb, and Smith (2000), Haney (2000, 2001), Balfanz and Legters (2001), and the reports of the Intercultural Development Research Association of San Antonio, at http://www.idra.org/. It should be noted that none of these researchers to date has factored in the continual in-migration (into Texas from other countries and from other states in the United States), even at the high school level, in the comparison of enrollment from grade to grade. When these numbers are not separated out, they inflate the numbers of students in the upper grades, giving the appearance that more of the original freshmen are persisting through to graduation. See also the TEA website listing the categories of students to be excluded when calculating the official dropouts in this state (TEA, 2003a). The Houston Press article by Margaret Downing cited in the references section of this chapter exemplifies the complexity, high degree of emotion, and competing definitions of dropouts and of research on dropouts in a particular state (Downing, 2001).

10. Traditionally, ninth grade enrollments tend to exceed both eighth and tenth enrollments for the same cohort because overage eighth graders are in some

districts "placed" up into ninth grade when they age out of middle school. In addition, there will be some ninth graders who fail enough of their subjects that they are retained as ninth graders for a second year. On top of these added numbers, the state waiver system has created an incentive for principals to retain on the rolls, as ninth graders, students who have failed only one of their ninth-grade subjects, particularly if the principal in reviewing the child's record anticipates that the child will not pass the tenth-grade TAAS. As discussed in this chapter, retentions under the waiver tend to serve the purposes of the principal's performance evaluation and the school's rating under the accountability system rather than an educational purpose related to the child's development. Whatever the reason for the large number of ninth graders, a test of a school-reform policy should be whether all of the children learn and thrive in their current grade so that they can successfully move to the next grade and on to graduation. The persistence of a bulge in the ninth-grade population, a bulge that does not move up the grades in successive years, throughout the period the accountability system has been governing Texas schools, is another indicator that this system is not fostering a high level of learning for Texas youth.

11. The McNeil/Valenzuela analysis, and the discussion of instructional losses, to follow, draw on emerging research on high-stakes testing and on our individual investigations. These include a longitudinal analysis of instruction when test-prep materials become the curriculum, a multiyear study of Latino children's high school experiences, investigations of Latino elementary schools, and research in urban schools with predominantly Mexican American and African American children (Valenzuela, 1999). Our investigations have entailed the documentation of the effects of centralized testing in Texas beginning with the Perot reforms of the 1980s and on through the 1990s, when such tests were increasingly tied to "high stakes" for children and school personnel (McNeil, 2000). Our investigations have included interactions over the past fifteen years with literally hundreds of public school teachers, representing all subjects and grades and a wide mix of urban and suburban districts, whom we have encountered through research projects and the teacher enhancement and school reform programs at the Rice University Center for Education. Our research required fieldwork in schools and classrooms and frequent interactions with students, teachers, and administrators, whose voices and experiences are vital to capture. In essence, our investigations have permitted us to gather and triangulate data from a variety of sources over a multiyear period. From these investigations, we understand that there is a wide variety of responses to the TAAS. However, those we report in our paper, and what I report here, are the most characteristic among the many schools, teachers, and students included in our research. The effects of the TAAS, which we describe herein, represent strong, persistent trends emerging from the data. We are not describing isolated or aberrant cases. To the contrary, we have unavoidably encountered this evidence in overabundance, and we have encountered this evidence even in the course of pursuing other research topics. For additional analysis of the ways compliance

with the accountability system can result in reduced academic quality, see also Sloan, chapter 5, and Hampton, chapter 6, herein.

REFERENCES

ACT, Inc. (2002). *ACT average composite scores by state, 2002 ACT-tested graduates. 2002 ACT national and state scores.* Retrieved January 27, 2003, from http://www.act.org/news/data/02/states.html

Amrein, A. L., & Berliner, D. C. (2002a, March 28). High-stakes testing, uncertainty, and student learning. *Education Policy Analysis Archives, 10(18).* Retrieved January 7, 2003, from http://epaa.asu.edu/epaa/v10n18/

Amrein, A. L., & Berliner, D. C. (2002b, December). *The impact of high-stakes tests on student academic performance: An analysis of NAEP results in states with high-stakes tests and ACT, SAT, and AP test results in states with high school graduation exams.* Retrieved January 6, 2003, from Arizona State University, Education Policy Studies Laboratory website: http://www.asu.edu/educ/epsl/EPRU/epru_2002_Research_Writing. htm

Balfanz, R., & Letgers, N. (2001). *How many central city high schools have a severe dropout problem, where are they located, and who attends them? Initial estimates using the Common Core of Data.* Paper presented at the 2001 Achieve and the Harvard Civil Rights Project Conference on Dropout Research: Accurate Counts and Positive Interventions. Retrieved July 19, 2002 from http://www.law.harvard.edu/groups/civilrights/publications/dropouts/dropout/balfanz.html

Carnoy, M., Loeb, S., & Smith, T. L. (2000). *Do higher state test scores in Texas make for better high school outcomes?* Paper presented at the 2001 Achieve and the Harvard Civil Rights Project Conference on Dropout Research: Accurate Counts and Positive Interventions, January 13, 2001, Cambridge, MA.

Christie, J. (1995). Long range planning, 1996–2000. Texas State Board of Education.

College Board (2001). *Mean SAT I verbal and math scores by state, with changes for selected years.* Retrieved January 23, 2003 from http://www.collegeboard.com/press/senior01/html/pdf/table3.pdf

Coppola, E. (August, 2002). Longview High School: Internal logic and external frameworks: Understanding the forces that shape school reform. In L. McNeil, et al. (Eds.), *Forming and reforming urban schools: An assessment of the effects of the Houston Annenberg Challenge on the quality of teaching and learning in four case study schools* (pp. 28–84). Report to the board of the Houston Annenberg Challenge, Houston, TX.

Dorn, S. (2003, January 1). High-stakes testing and the history of graduation. *Education Policy Analysis Archives, 11(1).* Retrieved January 7, 2003, from http://epaa.asu.edu/epaa/v11n1/

Downing, M. (2001, October 18). But who's counting: Thousand of students disappear from our schools yearly, but the TEA insists they're not dropouts. *Houston Press,* pp. 20, 22.

Elliot, J., Spencer, J., & Zuniga, J. A. (2004, February 28). State looks to install 'temporary' teachers: Plan lets college grads instruct for 2 years. *Houston Chronicle,* p. 1A.

Fusaro, P. C., & Miller, R. M. (2001). *What went wrong at Enron: Everyone's guide to the largest bankruptcy in U.S. history.* New York: John Wiley and Sons.

García, E. (2001). *Hispanic education in the United States: Raíces y Alas.* New York: Roman and Littlefield Publishers, Inc.

Greene, J. P. (2002). *High school graduation rates in the United States.* Retrieved February 11, 2003, from the Manhattan Institute website: http://www.manhattan-institute.org/html/cr_baeo.htm

Haney, W. (2000, August 19). The myth of the Texas miracle in education. *Education Policy Analysis Archives, 8*(41) Retrieved September 13, 2000, from http://epaa.asu.edu/epaa/v8n41

Haney, W. (2001). *Revisiting the myth of the Texas miracle in education: Lessons about dropout research and dropout prevention.* Paper presented at the 2001 Achieve and Harvard Civil Rights Project Conference on Dropout Research: Accurate Counts and Positive Interventions. Retrieved March 31, 2001 from http://www.civilrightsproject.harvard.edu/research/dropouts/haney.pdf

Higgs, J. (2002). *Creating a pathway to college.* Houston, TX: The Metropolitan Organization.

Houston Independent School District. (1994). *Profiles.* Houston, TX: Author.

Houston Independent School District. (2000). *Profiles.* Houston, TX: Author.

Intercultural Development Research Association. (1999). *Missing: Texas youth—dropout and attrition in Texas public high schools.* Retrieved March 20, 2002, from http://www/idra.org/Research/dropout.htm#Dropout.

Linton, T., & Kester, D. (2003). Exploring the achievement gap between White and minority students in Texas: A comparison of the 1996 and 2000 NAEP and TAAS eighth grade mathematics test results. *Education Policy Analysis Archives, 11*(10). Retrieved March 14, 2003, from http://epaa.asu.edu/epaa/v11n10/

McNeil, L. M. (2000). *Contradictions of school reform: Educational costs of standardized testing.* New York: Routledge.

McNeil, L. M., & Valenzuela, A. (2001). The harmful effects of the TAAS system of testing in Texas: Beneath the accountability rhetoric. In G. Orfield & M. Kornhaber (Eds.), *Raising standards or raising barriers? Inequality and high-stakes testing in public schooling* (pp. 127–150). New York: The Century Press.

McNeil, L. M., Coppola, E., Harcombe, E., Radigan, J., Sexton, A., & Silva, R. (2002). *Forming and re-forming urban schools: An assessment of the effects of the Houston Annenberg Challenge on the quality of teaching and learning in four case study schools.* Report to the board of the Houston Annenberg Challenge, Houston, TX.

Meier, D. (2002). *In schools we trust: Creating communities of learning in an era of testing and standardization.* Boston: Beacon Press.

Mortenson, T. G. (2001). Chance for college by age 19. Mortenson Research Seminar on Public Policy Analysis of Opportunity for Postsecondary Education. Retrieved January 27, 2003, from http://www.downstreet-magazine.com/archives/V2N3/learning/learning2.htm

Nelson, J. (1999/2000). *Memo to the administrator addressed.* Austin: Texas Education Agency. (Memo dated October 25, 1999, but likely misdated because the attachments include data from tests administered in 2000 in tables dated October 12, 2000).

Peabody, Z. (2003, July 6). Numbers game doesn't add up: Sharpstown High statistics should have spurred inquiry, officials say. *Houston Chronicle,* p. 1A.

Schemo, D. J. (2003, July 11). Questions on data cloud luster of Houston schools. *New York Times,* p. A1.

Sirotnik, K. A. (2002, May). Promoting responsible accountability in schools and education. *Phi Delta Kappan, 83*(9), 662–673.

State of the states: Texas. (2003, January 9). *Education Week,* p. 169.

Stewart, T. L. (2002, September 13). After-school programs scaled back: Some junior highs eliminate activities after funding cut. *Dallas Morning News,* p. 1Y.

Texas Education Agency. (2000). Selected enrollment counts for freshmen from selected districts who graduated four years later, Austin, TX. (Secured by former state Representative Domingo García as part of an open records request, June 9.)

Texas Education Agency. (2002a). Academic Excellence Indicator System 2001–02 state performance report. Austin, TX. Retrieved October 22, 2003, from http://www.tea.state.tx.us/perfreport/aeis/2002/state.html

Texas Education Agency. (2002b). Spring 1998 performance standards—English version. Retrieved August 27, 2002, from http://www.tea.state.tx.us/student/assessment/scoring/pstandards/perfst98.html

Texas Education Agency. (2002c). Spring 2001 performance standards—English version. Retrieved August 27, 2002, from http://www.tea.state.tx.us/student/assessment/scoring/pstandards/perfst01.html

Texas Education Agency. (2003a). Leaver reason codes: Public Education Information Management System data standards, 2002–2003. Retrieved January 28, 2003, from http://www.tea.state.tx.us/peims/standards/weds/index.html?app_leaver_reason_codes_and_documentation_requirements

Texas Education Agency. (2003b). Texas Assessment of Academic Skills: Percent meeting minimum expectations, all students, spring 1994–spring 2002, grades 3–8, 10. Retrieved January 24, 2003, from http://www.tea.state.tx.us/student.assessment/reporting/results/swresults/august/g310all_au.pdf

Texas Higher Education Coordinating Board. (2000). TASP results 1993–98. Interview with Richard Hamner, office of Senator Gonzalo Barrientos, senate of the state of Texas, October 24, 2000, from personal communication with Chris Patterson, Lone Star Foundation, March 22, 2000.

Texas Higher Education Coordinating Board. (2003a). Annual Texas Academic Skills Program/Alternative test report of student performance: Pass rates by race/ethnicity and test area, 1995–1999 high school graduating classes. Retrieved January 31, 2003, from http://www.thecb.state.tx.us/reports/PDF/0418.pdf

Texas Higher Education Coordinating Board. (2003b). Texas Academic Skills Program: Summary of TASP/alternative test results, academic year 1999–2000. Retrieved January 31, 2003, from http://www.thecb.state.tx.us/reports/PDF/0451.pdf

Texas Higher Education Coordinating Board and National Evaluation Systems, Incorporated. (2003c, February). TASP® technical summary 1998–1999. Retrieved February 10, 2003, from http://www.tasp.nesinc.com/techrpt.htm

Valenzuela, A. (1999). *Subtractive schooling: U.S.-Mexican youth and the politics of caring*. Albany: State University of New York Press.

Werner, A. (2003, November 25). HISD: Lesson in deception? Retrieved March 19, 2004, from http://www.khou.com/topstories/stories/khou031120_jt_defenders.25a6b0df.html (Part I), http://www.khou.com/news/defenders/investigate/stories/khou031123_ds_DefendersHISD.34747744.html (Part II).

Young, B. A. (1999). Characteristics of the 100 largest public elementary and secondary school districts in the United States: 1997–1998. U.S. Department of Education, National Center for Education Statistics, Washington, D.C. (Table 5). Retrieved January 7, 2003, from http://nces.ed.gov/pubs99/1999318/table5.html

Young, B. A. (2002). Characteristics of the 100 largest public elementary and secondary school districts in the United States: 2000–2001. U.S. Department of Education, National Center for Education Statistics, Washington, D.C. (Table 1) Retrieved January 7, 2003, from http://nces.ed.gov/pubs2002/100_largest/table_01_1.asp#f2

Zuniga, J. A. (2004, January 16). Retaliation allegations denied by school board: Lawsuit planned by whistle-blower. *Houston Chronicle*, p. 21A.

4

—

Texas' Second Wave of High-Stakes Testing: Anti–Social Promotion Legislation, Grade Retention, and Adverse Impact on Minorities

RICHARD R. VALENCIA AND BRUNO J. VILLARREAL

This chapter is concerned with the standards-based school reform movement that is sweeping across the landscape of U.S. public kindergarten through twelfth-grade (K–12) education. Our focus is on the use of high-stakes testing to control promotion from one grade to another. More specifically, our interest here is to examine the relations between anti–social promotion legislation, grade retention, and possible adverse impact on the educational progress of racial/ethnic minority students. In light of its bureaucratic leadership in high-stakes testing, interest in curbing social promotion, and diverse racial/ethnic K–12 population, the state of Texas provides an ideal locale for investigating the utility of high-stakes testing in promoting school reform (Valencia & Villarreal, 2003). The first wave of high-stakes testing in Texas, which began in 1993, was the use of the Texas Assessment of Academic Skills (TAAS) exit-level test to award or deny the high school diploma. Based on profound racial/ethnic group differences in TAAS exit-level pass rates, African American and Mexican American students experienced disproportionate denials of high school diplomas. Such denials prompted a group of Mexican American and African American students—accompanied by two Mexican American advocacy organizations—to file a lawsuit against the state of Texas (see Valencia & Bernal, 2000). This federal lawsuit—*GI Forum et al. v. Texas Education Agency et al.* (2000)—began on September 20, 1999, and was litigated by the Mexican American Legal Defense and Education Fund (MALDEF). As noted by Valencia and Bernal (2000):

After 200 hours of testimony by numerous witnesses and the showing of many exhibits, Judge Prado handed down his decision on January 7, 2000. He ruled that the TAAS test *did* result in adverse
impact against the plaintiffs, but he also found that the use of TAAS
to deny student diplomas was not illegal, as it served an educational
necessity for Texas' accountability system. In sum, Judge Prado ruled
in favor of the defendants—the State. (p. 407)

What lessons can be learned from the first wave of high-stakes testing in Texas? First, it is extremely difficult for minority groups to gain equity through the litigative process. As Fassold (2000), an expert for the
plaintiffs in the *GI Forum* case, concluded:

In the end, although Judge Prado ruled for the State, he did find that
TAAS exit-level test did result in disparate impact against African
American and Mexican American students. To plaintiffs this is a
mixed ruling. It acknowledges their plight, but at the same time allows the State's inequitable accountability system to prevail. (p. 478)

A second lesson that is learned from Texas' first wave of high-stakes testing is that for minority students and parents to continue to struggle for
equity in the assessment process, it is important to mount an offensive at
the locus from which high-stakes testing school reform emanated—the
Texas Legislature (see Valenzuela, chapter 1, this volume).

Texas' second wave of high-stakes testing that is being used to reform education stems from Senate Bill 4 (SB 4), an educational statute
that went into effect in the 2002–2003 school year. This new law requires
that all third graders pass a reading test (the English or Spanish version)
to be promoted to the fourth grade. The present chapter is an extension
of Valencia and Villarreal's (2003) article in *The Reading Teacher*, which
is a critique of SB 4. The following discussions are organized around (a)
the importance of the grade retention/promotion issue; (b) major research
findings on the grade retention/promotion issue: a glimpse of the literature; (c) racial/ethnic comparisons of grade retention, academic achievement, and dropouts in Texas: historical/contemporary sketch; (d) SB 4: an
overview; (e) adverse impact of SB 4; (f) conclusions.

IMPORTANCE OF THE GRADE
RETENTION/PROMOTION ISSUE

Grade retention, a euphemism for "flunking," is a long-standing educational practice and concern.[1] In *Laggards in Our Schools*, Ayres (1909)

reported that a little over 16% of the nation's students were "repeating" class. His conclusion was that "slow progress" was the major reason why repeaters were being retained; late entrance to school was a small factor. He also commented that ". . . we are annually spending about $27,000,000 in this wasteful process of repetition in our cities alone" (p. 5). The rationale behind retention is that an extra year at the same grade will serve as a powerful remedy for the student who is experiencing school failure (e.g., reading significantly below grade level). More contemporary scholars (e.g., King, 1984; cited in Campbell & Bowman, 1993) have perceived the repetition of a school year for the immature student as a "gift of time."

Although the retention of students has been practiced for decades, the rates of retention have varied—shaped, in part, by the politics of school reform. As reported by Shepard and Smith (1989a), based on modal grade data gathered by the U.S. Bureau of the Census, grade retentions hit an all-time low in the beginning of the 1970s, and then climbed in the late 1970s and through the mid-1980s.[2] The policy of retaining academically weak students has come to occupy a central position in the standards-based school reform movement of the 1990s and the present (Heubert & Hauser, 1999; Valencia, 2000a; Valencia & Villarreal, 2003). The escalation of grade retention rates over the last 25 years is likely related to the momentum brought forth by school accountability movements as expressed in back-to-basic skills (Rich, 1985), minimum competency testing (Jaeger, 1987), the notion of "excellence" (National Commission on Excellence in Education, 1983), and the Governors' Task Force on Education (U.S. Department of Education, 1991).

Why is retention/promotion a serious concern for students, parents, teachers, and school administrators? On one side of the issue are advocates who call for an end to "social promotion"—the practice of promoting students (with their same-age classmates) before they are deemed to have the requisite skills and knowledge to succeed in the next grade. During the late 1990s, even President Bill Clinton entered the discourse. In a memorandum directed to the Secretary of Education, Clinton wrote that he had

> . . . repeatedly challenged States and school districts to end social promotions—to require students to meet rigorous academic standards at key transition points in their schooling career, and to end the practice of promoting students without regard to how much they have learned. . . . Students should not be promoted past the fourth grade if they cannot read independently and well, and should not enter high school without a solid foundation in math. They should get the help

they need to meet the standards before moving on. (Clinton, 1998, pp. 1–2; quoted in Heubert & Hauser, 1999, pp. 114–115)

Calls by politicians, policy makers, and others have had some influence on the implementation of test-based requirements in controlling grade promotion. The American Federation of Teachers (AFT) has provided comprehensive national information on states that have passed policies for ending social promotion. When the AFT first began to monitor such policies in 1996, only 3 states used test data, in part, to decide a student's promotion or retention. In its most recent report (2001), the AFT noted that 16 states and the District of Columbia have institutionalized promotion policies at the elementary level. The 16 states are: Arkansas, California, Connecticut, Delaware, Florida, Georgia, Hawaii, Louisiana, Mississippi, New Mexico, North Carolina, Oklahoma, South Carolina, Texas, Virginia, and Wisconsin (see American Federation of Teachers, 2001, p. 33, Table 12). Of these 16 states, all but Arkansas, Georgia, and Hawaii have promotion policies at the middle school level (D.C. also does not have a promotion policy at this level).

Another major perspective on the grade retention/promotion issue stems from research findings. There is a voluminous amount of research that concludes, with very few exceptions, that retained students—compared to matched students who were not retained—typically fall behind in their academic achievement (e.g., reading), make few or no academic gains, seldom or never catch up, and have a higher probability of dropping out. In the next section, we provide a glimpse of these research findings.

MAJOR RESEARCH FINDINGS ON THE GRADE RETENTION/PROMOTION ISSUE: A GLIMPSE OF THE LITERATURE

The literature on the issue of grade retention/promotion—in both empirical studies and expository writings—is immense. It is not our intent here to review this literature in any detail. Rather, we present a very brief listing of the major findings we were able to cull from the literature on the grade retention/promotion controversy. The interested reader who wants to learn more about the issues surrounding retention/promotion may want to consult the more well-known literature reviews on the topic (e.g., Holmes, 1989; Holmes & Matthews, 1984; Jackson, 1975; Jimerson, 2001a, 2001b; Shepard, 1989; Shepard & Smith, 1990). Also, there is a prominent book on grade retention by Shepard and Smith (1989b), *Flunking Grades: Research and Policies on Retention.*

In this section we briefly discuss the following: (a) demographic characteristics of retainees; (b) retained students versus promoted students: academic achievement comparisons; (c) retained students versus promoted students: socioemotional and behavioral comparisons; (d) impact of grade retention on dropping out.

Demographic Characteristics of Retainees

There are considerable findings reported in the literature that certain demographic characteristics are associated with students who are retained. Students younger than their class peers, males, racial/ethnic minorities (particularly African American and Latino), language minorities, and students of low-socioeconomic status (SES) backgrounds have higher probabilities of being retained. (For examples of studies that have found one or more of these characteristics in the retained samples investigated, see: Abidin, Golladay, & Howerton, 1971; Dauber, Alexander, & Entwisle, 1993; Fowler & Cross, 1986; Hauser, Pager, & Simmons, 2001; Jackson, 1975; Jimerson, 1999; Jimerson, Carlson, Rotert, Egeland, & Sroufe, 1997; Jimerson & Kaufman, 2003; Langer, Kalk, & Searls, 1984; McCoy & Reynolds, 1999; Meisels & Liaw, 1993; Shepard, 1997; Zepeda, 1993). Regarding the association between race/ethnicity and grade retention, a powerful example demonstrating this linkage is the national investigation by Meisels and Liaw, who used data from the National Education Longitudinal Study of 1988 (National Center for Education Statistics, 1989). Of the total data file (N = 16,223 students), 19.3% of the students were retained at least once during their K–8 grade schooling. When this rate was disaggregated by race/ethnicity, Meisels and Liaw found that 29.9% of Blacks and 25.2% of Hispanics in the sample repeated a grade at least once. By contrast, 17.2% of White students were retained at least once. The frequent finding that minority students, compared to their White peers, are more likely to be retained is especially germane to the present paper.

Retained versus Promoted Students:
Academic Achievement Comparisons

A number of empirical studies and literature reviews have reported that students who are retained—compared to matched students who were promoted—typically fall behind in their academic achievement (e.g., reading and mathematics), make fewer or no gains, and seldom or never catch up (e.g., Gredler, 1984; Hagborg, Masella, Palladino, & Shepardson, 1991;

Holmes, 1983, 1989; Holmes & Matthews, 1984; Jimerson, 1999, 2001a; Jimerson et al., 1997; Jimerson & Kaufman, 2003; Jimerson & Schuder, 1996; Mantzicopoulos & Morrison, 1992; McCoy & Reynolds, 1999; Meisels & Liaw, 1993; Reynolds, 1992; Rose, Medway, Cantrell, & Marus, 1983; Shepard, 2001; Shepard & Smith, 1987; Temple, Reynolds, & Ou, 2001). In one of the most comprehensive reviews of literature to date, Holmes (1989) conducted a meta-analysis of 63 studies. His conclusion was consistent with earlier reviews of research findings (including his earlier coauthored meta-analysis [Holmes & Matthews, 1984]) that retention led to negative effects.

Retained versus Promoted Students: Socioemotional and Behavioral Comparisons

The socioemotional and behavioral aspects of retaining pupils have been less researched than has academic achievement. There are, however, some studies that have found retained students, in comparison to promoted peers, to have greater emotional and adjustment problems, peer rejection, negative attitudes toward school, diminishment of self-esteem, disengagement from school, and delinquency infractions (e.g., Byrnes, 1989; Hagborg et al., 1991; Holmes, 1989; Jimerson, 1999, 2001a; Jimerson et al., 1997; Jimerson & Kaufman, 2003; Meisels & Liaw, 1993; Pierson & Connell, 1992; Roderick, 1994; Smith & Shepard, 1989). Walters and Borgers (1995) have reviewed several empirical studies in which they discussed conflicting findings in this area. In sum, it appears that retention as a predictor of socioemotional and behavioral concern is somewhat more difficult to interpret, compared to the criterion of academic achievement.

Impact of Grade Retention on Dropping Out

Given that our focus in this chapter is on racial/ethnic minority students in Texas' public schools and these students' higher probabilities of being retained and dropping out of school, this body of literature is particularly relevant to our analysis of the SB 4 anti–social promotion legislation. There are ample and consistent findings from the literature that strongly link grade retention of students with an increased likelihood that they will drop out of school (e.g., Brooks-Gunn, Guo, & Furstenberg, 1993; Byrnes, 1989; Cairns, Cairns, & Neckerman, 1989; Dawson, 1991; Deridder, 1988; Ekstrom, Goertz, Pollack, & Rock, 1986; Fernández,

Paulsen, & Hirano-Nakanishi, 1989; Grissom & Shepard, 1989; Hammack, 1987; Hirano-Nakanishi, 1986; Jimerson, 1999; Jimerson & Kaufman, 2003; Lloyd, 1978; Mann, 1987; Neill & Medina, 1989; Roderick, 1994; Rumberger, 1987, 1995; Shepard, 2001; Temple et al., 2001; Wehlage & Rutter, 1986).

The preponderance of research findings on the relation between grade retention and subsequent dropping out are correlational in nature. The problem with correlational analysis is that one cannot infer causality. As such, one needs to be open to different interpretations of how the variables are associated. Perhaps a major hypothesis could be advanced that the repeating of a grade might directly increase the probability of dropping out. Or, a "competing hypothesis is that poor achievement explains both retention and dropping out" (Grissom & Shepard, 1989, p. 39). To explore this important explanatory issue, Grissom and Shepard—using path analysis (sometimes referred to as causal modeling or structural equation models)—reanalyzed data from schools in Austin, Texas and Chicago, Illinois. Controlling for differences in achievement scores, sex, and race/ethnicity, the authors found that grade retention significantly increased the likelihood of students dropping out of school—27% increase for Austin students and 18% for Chicago students.

Does the practice of grade retention, as it is intended, lead to school success for the low-achieving student? The existing literature on grade retention, though not unequivocal, shows, quite strongly, that this policy has not fulfilled its promise.[3] It is not uncommon to hear research conclusions as follows:

- ". . . The practice of retaining students in education is absolutely contrary to the best research evidence" (House, 1989, p. 204).
- ". . . Reviews of the literature . . . show little to no academic achievement benefits from retention. . . . On average, retained children are worse off than their promoted counterparts on both personal adjustment and academic outcomes" (Holmes, 1989, pp. 17, 27).
- "This literature [the impact of retention on school performance] almost unanimously concludes that retention is not as effective as promotion in improving school performance" (Roderick, 1994, p. 732).
- "Advocates for the practice of grade retention often refer to 'evidence' that students may do better during the following year. Yet, research consistently indicates that the short-term gains are not maintained over time (Jimerson & Kaufman, 2003, p. 632).

RACIAL/ETHNIC COMPARISONS OF GRADE RETENTION,
ACADEMIC ACHIEVEMENT, AND DROPOUTS IN TEXAS:
HISTORICAL/CONTEMPORARY SKETCH

In the scholarly literature, grade retention is typically viewed as a predictor variable, and diminished academic achievement (e.g., reading) and
dropping out are conceived as criterion variables. As we have discussed in
the previous section, many policy makers have ignored the importance of
these statistical connections. When SB 4 was passed in Texas in 1999, policy makers paid no attention to the historical and contemporary evidence
regarding the adverse impact of grade retention, particularly on certain
minority student populations. When bills are passed that do not consider
available scientific evidence regarding adverse impact, such bills are "bad
laws." Had the Texas House and Senate—as well as Governor George W.
Bush, who signed the bill—been cognizant of the long-standing evidence
regarding racial/ethnic comparisons in retention, achievement, and
dropouts in Texas, then perhaps SB 4 would have undergone serious, pro-
longed debate and never passed. If these policymakers and Governor Bush
had reviewed the evidence, the following is what they would have read.

Retention

There are overwhelming current data (which we present later) showing
clear differences in grade retention rates in Texas in which African American, Mexican American and other Latino students have higher rates than
do White students, and these contemporary differences have historical
roots.[4] In the case of Mexican American students, for example, a number
of investigations from decades past found that these students—compared
to their White peers—were more frequently overage for their grade level
(e.g., Coan, 1936) and were retained more frequently (e.g., Calderón,
1950; McLean, 1950). As a case in point, in a study more than a half-
century ago, McLean undertook a longitudinal investigation of Austin,
Texas public schools. As part of his study, McLean reported grade pro-
motions and failures for "Anglo-American" (i.e., White) and "Spanish-
name" (i.e., Mexican American) students at the elementary, junior high,
and high school levels. His findings are shown in Table 4.1. McLean's data
from more than 5 decades ago show that Mexican American students in
the Austin public schools were, in comparison to their White counterparts,
4 times more likely to be retained at the elementary school level, and 1.5
times more likely to be retained at the junior high and high school levels.[5]

TABLE 4.1
Grade Promotion and Failure Percentages by Race/Ethnicity in Austin Public
Schools: 1942–1943 School Year

School Level	Anglo American		Spanish Name	
	Promotion %	Failure %	Promotion %	Failure %
Elementary	94	6	76	24
Junior high	92	8	88	12
Senior high	80	20	70	30

Adapted from McLean (1950, p. 41, Figure 15).

Historically, the most comprehensive investigation of racial/ethnic differences in grade retention germane to the present discussion was the landmark Mexican American Education Study (MAES) conducted by the U.S. Commission on Civil Rights a little more than 3 decades ago. The massive MAES investigated a number of Mexican American (and at times, African American) schooling conditions and outcomes in the five southwestern states (Arizona, California, Colorado, New Mexico, and Texas); six reports on various educational issues (e.g., segregation, school financing) were published in the early 1970s.[6] In report no. 2 of the MAES (U.S. Commission on Civil Rights, 1971), data are presented for grade repetition by race/ethnicity for the southwestern states. Two major points can be gleaned from these revealing historical data reported over 30 years ago. First, despite a few exceptions, Mexican American and Black students—in comparison to their White peers—experienced higher rates of first- and fourth-grade repetition in all five states in the Southwest. Second, of the five southwestern states, Texas showed the highest grade repetition rates (first and fourth grades) for Mexican American and Black students. In first grade, for example, 22.3% of Mexican American students were retained—three times the White retention rate (7.3%); 20.9% of Black first graders repeated—also three times the rate of their White peers.[7] Regarding Mexican American students—the focal group of the MAES—the U.S. Commission on Civil Rights (1971) drew this conclusion between grade repetition and academic achievement:

There appears to be a strong relationship between grade repetition and low student achievement. *Thus, the State of Texas, which has the highest proportion of grade repetition in the first and fourth grades, also has 74 percent, the highest proportion of Mexican American eighth graders reading below grade level.* By contrast, in California, where fewer Mexican Americans repeat a grade, a smaller percentage of Mexican American eighth graders are reading below grade level. (p. 36) (Emphasis in original)

The most current data on grade retention at the elementary level (K–6) in Texas can be seen in the *2002 Comprehensive Annual Report on Texas Public Schools* (hereafter referred to as the *2002 Annual Report*; Texas Education Agency, 2002a).[8] For the 2000–2001 academic year, the number of K–6 students retained totaled 59,317 (Texas Education Agency, 2002a, p. 70, Table 6.2), at an aggregated retention rate of 2.8%. It is important to keep in mind, however, that the average retention rate of 2.8% is for the aggregate—all racial/ethnic groups combined. When the data are disaggregated by race/ethnicity, however, a distinct pattern is observed (Texas Education Agency, 2002a, p. 70, Table 6.2). The retention rate for White students was 1.8%. In sharp contrast, for African American and Hispanic students (i.e., overwhelmingly Mexican American students), the retention rates were 3.5% and 3.6%, respectively. This comparative analysis shows that Mexican American, other Latino, and African American K–6 students were *2.0 times more likely than their White peers to be retained during the 2000–2001 school year.*

The current higher retention rates experienced by Mexican American, other Latino, and African American students (Texas Education Agency, 2002a)—compared to their White counterparts in Texas—are not new developments. These differences are part of a continuous pattern as evidenced by data observed in reports going back more than 50 years.

Academic Achievement

There are numerous national, regional, state, and local reports and studies that have documented an unequivocal pattern: On the average, Mexican American, other Latino, and African American students—in comparison to their White peers—perform lower on measures of academic achievement (such as reading and mathematics).[9] Regarding this pattern in Texas, there are historical data as evidenced by the U.S. Commission on Civil Rights (1971) MAES report. Table 4.2 presents these data. What is particularly disturbing about these racial/ethnic comparisons from more than 30 years ago is that at the targeted grades of 4,

TABLE 4.2
Estimated Percentages of Students Reading Below Grade
Level: Texas, 1969

| | Grade | | |
Race/Ethnicity	4	8	12
White	21.0	27.5	30.9
Mexican American	51.8	73.5	64.7
Black	59.0	63.9	71.7

Adapted from U.S. Commission on Civil Rights (1971, p. 33,
Figure 12).

8, and 12, the majority of Mexican American and African American students were reading below grade level in Texas public schools. By sharp contrast, approximately one fifth to one third of White students in these three grades performed below grade level in reading.

The most current data on academic achievement for Texas students is based on the 2001–2002 Texas Assessment of Academic Skills (TAAS) test, a state-mandated test (reading, mathematics, and writing) taken by students in grades 3 to 8, and 10.[10] Using the TAAS Reading test as a case in point, Table 4.3 contains racial/ethnic comparisons (i.e., White; Hispanic; African American) of pass rates for TAAS Reading in English (grades 3–8 and 10) for the 2001–2002 school year (Texas Education Agency, 2002b).[11] The cross-sectional data presented in Table 4.3 confirm this unwavering pattern in Texas public schools: African American and Mexican American (and other Latino) students—compared to their White peers—perform, on the average, lower on TAAS reading.[12] The pass rate gaps between White and minority students are substantial. The gaps between White and Hispanic students range from a low of 6.5 percentage points (grade 8) to a high of 12.3 percentage points (grade 6). For the White/African American gaps, they range from a low of 5.4 (grades 8 and 10) to a high of 13.4 (grade 3).

Dropouts

The issue of very high dropout rates among minority youths in Texas, particularly Mexican Americans, has been a long-standing concern (e.g.,

TABLE 4.3
Percent Passing TAAS Reading by Race/Ethnicity for Grades 3–8 and 10: Texas, 2001–2002

Race/Ethnicity	Grade						
	3	4	5	6	7	8	10
All[a]	88.0	92.5	92.7	88.2	91.3	94.3	94.5
White	94.0	96.5	96.6	94.8	96.3	97.5	97.9
Hispanic	83.5	89.7	89.9	82.5	86.5	91.0	90.5
African American	80.6	86.8	87.5	81.7	87.1	92.1	92.5

Note. [a]"All" refers to combination of White, Hispanic, African American, Native American, and Asian/Pacific Islander students. Texas Education Agency (2002b).

see Cromack, 1949; Wilson, 1953; also, San Miguel & Valencia, 1998).[13] The dropout problem among Mexican American and African American students in Texas (and the other Southwestern states) first received national attention more than 30 years ago with the publication of report no. 2 of the MAES (U.S. Commission on Civil Rights, 1971). The study concluded: "The Texas survey area demonstrates the poorest record of any of the Southwestern States in its ability to hold minority students in school" (p. 17). The MAES found that the White dropout rate in Texas was 15%. By sharp contrast, the Mexican American and African American dropout rates were reported to be 47% and 36%, respectively.

These historical patterns of higher dropout rates among Mexican American (and other Latino) and African American students continue today in Texas. Contemporary data are presented in Figure 4.1. In the *2002 Annual Report* (Texas Education Agency, 2002a), data from 2000–2001 show that Hispanic students comprised 37.4% of all students in the seventh- to twelfth-grade total enrollment, yet were 54.0% of all seventh- to twelfth-grade dropouts. African American students were 14.3% of the seventh- to twelfth-grade total enrollment, but were 18.7% of the total seventh- to twelfth-grade dropouts. By contrast, Whites comprised 45.3% of the seventh- to twelfth-grade cohort, and only 25.5% of the seventh- to twelfth-grade dropouts (Texas Education Agency, 2002a, p. 61, Table 5.3).[14]

Based on research reports and other sources, there are unequivocal historical and contemporary data that Mexican American (and other Latino) and African American students in Texas public schools are

Racial/Ethnic Percentages of Total Grade 7-12 Student

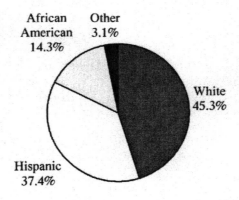

Racial/Ethnic Percentages of Total Grade 7-12 Dropout

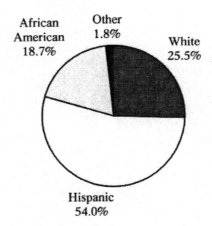

Figure 4.1. Comparisons of Racial/Ethnic Percentages of Total Grade 7–12 Students to Total Grade 7–12 Dropouts: Texas, 2000–2001.
(Texas Education Agency, 2002a, p. 61, table 5.3)

retained at higher rates, perform more poorly on achievement tests, and drop out at higher rates than their White peers. These facts, coupled with the voluminous research base showing that grade retention is a solid statistical predictor of school failure, point to the inevitable conclusion that SB 4 is a bad law in that it will exacerbate an already grave situation for minority students.

Furthermore, it needs to be understood that SB 4 was passed alongside SB 1, which calls for a more difficult, newly developed generation of tests that are to be implemented simultaneously with the new promotion standards in 2002–2003 (see Valenzuela, chapter 1, current volume). If Mexican American, other Latino, and African American students are already disproportionately failing an "easier" state-mandated test, one is hard-pressed to understand how an institutionalized retention policy set in tandem with a more difficult examination—an examination that controls retention/promotion—is in the best interests of these minority students. In a later section, we discuss the adverse impact the new retention policy in Texas will have on students of color.

SB 4: AN OVERVIEW

In this section, we provide an overview of SB 4 by briefly discussing the following: (a) origins, (b) requirements of the law, (c) instrumentation, and (d) implementation and intervention.

Origins

The origins of SB 4 stem from Governor George W. Bush's 1998 reelection bid in which he launched ". . . a get-tough pledge to make it harder for public school students to advance to the next grade before mastering basic skills" (Johnston, 1998, p. 1).[15] During his campaign, Governor Bush apprised the staff of the Texas Education Agency (TEA) at the 1998 Midwinter Conference of his views and plans about ending social promotion (Bush, 1998). In his speech, he asserted:

> The defenders of the status quo are alarmed. I recently saw a headline that read: Thousands of students would fail under Bush plan. With all due respect to the headline writer, it should have read: Tens of thousands are failing today and Gov. Bush has a plan to save them. . . . Social promotion creates false hopes, fuels the drop-out rate, and

destroys the dreams of too many Texas children. Social promotion undermines the integrity of our entire education system, because it pushes students from grade to grade even though they are not prepared to do the work—it hides the reason for their failures: poor reading skills. . . . The voices of the status quo will say, Let's continue to ignore the problem. I say, Let's fix it. Let's heed the reading research that says the window of opportunity is grades K through 3. Let's put our hearts and our souls into teaching programs that work. And let's fix reading problems so every child has the building block skills to succeed. . . . My plan says a child who does not pass the reading portion of the TAAS in the third grade must receive appropriate intervention and instruction before moving to regular classes in the fourth grade. The voices of the status quo will say, We can't hold back third graders—it will make them feel like failures. I say, They are failing today—let's stop pretending and start helping them. The best way to boost our children's self-esteem is teach them to read. . . . Later, our children will be required to pass reading and math tests in fifth grade—and reading, math, and writing tests in eighth grade. But by that time only third graders with good skills will be promoted, ensuring greater success in the fifth and eighth grades. The voices of the status quo will say, Too much is riding on one test. And I say, Stop the excuses. We are asking children to score a 70—a minimum passing grade on a basic skills test—because if they have a problem learning, we want to help them correct it. Some say tests should not matter. But I say our children are not with us long enough before they have to face the real world. And in the real world, tests are a reality. . . . My dream is for every child to read. And I know we will succeed. Because in Texas we care about our children. We care about their future. And we will settle for nothing less than opportunity and excellence for every single Texas child. I ask for your help and your support. God bless you all. And God bless Texas.

After sailing through the Senate and House of the Texas Legislature, the anti–social promotion bill (SB 4) was signed into law by Governor Bush on June 8, 1999.

Requirements of the Law

The new state law (described in Texas Education Code §28.0211) has promotion requirements for the kindergarten class of 1999–2000 and later cohorts.[16] The key elements of SB 4 are as follows:

- A reading test (English or Spanish version) will be administered to all third graders beginning in the 2002–2003 school year.[17]
- The phasing in of two more promotion gates for the 2002–2003 cohort will be as follows:
  —Fifth grade (2004–2005), reading and mathematics tests (English or Spanish version).
  —Eighth grade (2007–2008), reading and mathematics (English version).
- A student who initially fails to perform satisfactorily on the designated test will be given two additional opportunities to take the assessment instrument. If a student fails a second time, a "grade placement committee" will be formed consisting of the principal (or principal's designee), the student's parent or guardian, and the teacher of the subject of an instrument on which the student failed. If the student fails a third time, he/she will be retained at the same grade level.[18]
- Each time a student fails the test, he/she will be provided "accelerated instruction" in the applicable subject area (such instruction is decided by the grade placement committee).[19] The accelerated instruction group may not have a ratio of more than 10 students for each teacher.
- The student's parent or guardian may appeal the retention decision to the grade placement committee.
- All of the above applies to students who are limited English proficient (LEP) or are in special education.
- The law will stay in force only if there is sufficient state money to fund the program every year.

Instrumentation

As noted in this chapter, and elsewhere in the present volume, the TAAS will be replaced by the Texas Assessment of Knowledge and Skills (TAKS) beginning in the 2002–2003 school year. According to the TEA, the TAKS ". . . is a completely reconceived testing program. It includes more of the

Texas Essential Knowledge and Skills (TEKS) than the . . . TAAS did and attempts to ask questions in more authentic ways. . . . The TAKS tests will become more rigorous as students move from grade to grade" (Texas Education Agency, 2002c, p. 1). What is being heard in news accounts reflects the TEA's characterization: The TAKS is completely new, and is more comprehensive and difficult than its predecessor, the TAAS (Fikac, 2002). In a January 31, 2002 commentary in the *Austin American-Statesman*, Jim Nelson—then Texas Commissioner of Education—wrote:

> Texas launches a new era of student testing this week when it begins field testing the new state exam called the Texas Assessment of Knowledge and Skills. Make no mistake about it—the TAKS is not a recycled version of the Texas Assessment of Academic Skills. It is a new test from top to bottom and, like its predecessor, is expected to spur academic achievement. The TAKS, which will be given in third through eleventh grades, is broader and deeper than TAAS. (p. A15)

The reading test of the TAKS was selected as the measure of achievement when SB 4 kicked in for third graders in 2002–2003. Commissioner Nelson noted: "The reading passages on the exams will be longer and more complex" (p. A15).

Implementation and Intervention

According to the 2002–2003 Student Assessment Calendar (hereafter referred to as the Calendar) prepared in 2001 by the Student Assessment Division of the TEA (Texas Education Agency, 2001), a fall study (September 16–20, 2002) was scheduled to provide test data to the State Board of Education in November, 2002 so it could set performance standards for TAKS (more on this later). Following further field testing, the grade three TAKS Reading test was ready for its first administration on March 4, 2003 (Texas Education Agency, 2001). Figure 4.2 presents a flow chart of the pursuant dates and outcomes (the flow chart was developed by the authors based on information provided in the Calendar). As shown in Figure 4.2, the report date for initial test results was set for March 20, 2003 (according to the Calendar, the report date is 10 working days after National Computer Systems Pearson, scoring contractor, receives the scorable booklets). If a student failed, there would be an intervention (Intervention No. 1; see the Figure 4.2 flow chart). Following the Intervention No. 1 period (which we calculated to be 28 school days), there would be Retest No. 1, scheduled

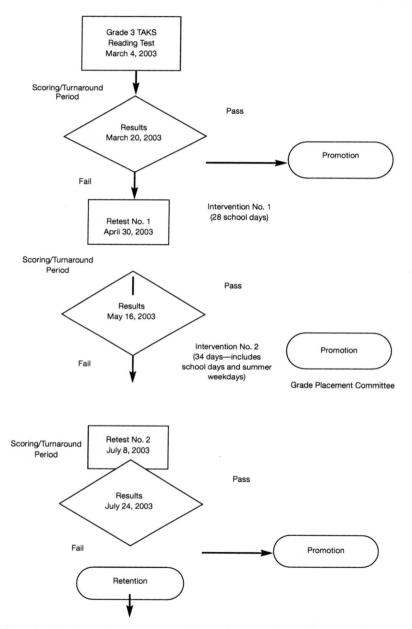

Figure 4.2. Student Assessment Calendar for Grade 3 TAKS Reading Test: 2003. Authors Valencia and Villarreal developed this flow chart based on information provided in the Student Assessment Calendar (Texas Education Agency, 2001).

for April 30, 2003. Reporting of results of the second administration would be scheduled for May 16, 2003. If the student failed the grade three TAKS Reading test the second time, Intervention No. 2 would follow (we calculated this to consist of 34 school days). Upon the student's failure of the Reading test the second time, the Grade Placement Committee would be constituted. As shown in Figure 4.2, the third and final administration of the Reading test (Retest No. 2) was scheduled for July 8, 2003. Test results were scheduled to be reported by July 24, 2003. If a student passed, he/she would be promoted to the fourth grade. If the student did not pass the TAKS Reading test, then he/she would be retained in the third grade (see footnote no. 19). It is this last scenario—retention—that is very likely to impact a disproportionate number of Mexican American, other Latino, and African American students. LEP Mexican American and other Latino students will very likely experience the greatest adverse impact.

We urge the reader to be mindful that our chapter was completed in May 2003, about two months before the initial (2002–2003) testing cycle of the third grade TAKS Reading test was completed. Given this time lag, some important questions come to mind. For example, will the allotted time for intervention be ample? Although there are general guidelines for the intervention (e.g., "accelerated instruction"), what will the specifics of the intervention be? What will be the actual role of the Grade Placement Committee? Most important, will SB 4 have adverse impact on minority students?

ADVERSE IMPACT OF SB 4

Earlier in this chapter, we examined historical and contemporary evidence regarding grade retention, academic achievement, and dropouts vis-à-vis Mexican American (and other Latino) and African American students in Texas. The literature informs us that many of these minority students—compared to their White peers—already experience higher grade retention and dropout rates, and poorer academic achievement. In this section, we ask: Will the effect of SB 4 have adverse impact on these minority students by increasing their already higher retention rates, which in turn increases the likelihood of school failure? Phillips (2000) has conceptualized adverse impact as follows:

> Differential performance occurs when passing rates for African-American and Hispanic students (minority groups) are lower than the passing rates for White students (majority group). When the differential performance between majority and minority groups be-

> comes too great, it is labeled *adverse impact*. An important issue in this context is determining when differential performance becomes large enough to qualify as adverse impact. (p. 363)

Adverse impact (sometimes referred to as "disparate impact") can be statistically investigated and measured using a variety of procedures (Fassold, 2000). In this chapter, our focus is on investigating the differential failure rates on the TAKS Reading test between minority and White third-grade students. As the following analyses indicate, the initial differences in failure rates are great enough, in our opinion, to qualify as "adverse impact." However, in the legal context, the final arbiter of deciding the existence of adverse impact would be a judge in a discrimination case (e.g., see Fassold, 2000; Saucedo, 2000).

To address the question of adverse impact, we examine the most recent TEA data on the TAKS Reading test failure rates across racial/ethnic groups. In addition to discussing the Texas data, we examine actual adverse impact (i.e., grade retention) on Louisiana African American students.

Adverse Impact in Texas

In the fall of 2002, the third-grade TAKS Reading test was subjected to a field test. This "predictor test" was used to identify the number of students who failed the test so the State Board of Education (SBOE) could set a reasonable passing standard (Copelin, 2002). The failure rates for African American and Hispanic students on the third-grade TAKS Reading predictor test were 25% and 19% respectively; White students failed at a considerably lower rate—7%. These failure rates of students of color were so grave that the SBOE, on November 15, 2002, voted (12–3) to set the passing standard on the new TAKS at a benchmark of 56% (Copelin). This passing standard is considerably lower than the 70% passing standard that has been used for TAAS. Once the TAKS passing rate is raised through a phasing-in process, adverse impact on minority students is very likely to intensify (more on this later).

On March 19, 2003 (one day earlier than anticipated; see Calendar, Figure 4.2), the results of the third-grade TAKS Reading test were reported by newspapers. In the *Austin American-Statesman*, reporter Kathy Blackwell, who reported statewide data, had her by-line read: "Students Rise to Challenge of Tougher Test in Reading; Third-Graders Breeze Through State's New Assessments Tests" (Blackwell, 2003). The re-

TABLE 4.4
Statewide Failure Rates on Third-Grade TAKS Reading Test by Race/Ethnicity

Group	First Administration of TAKS: March, 2003 (56% cut score)	Odds Factor
Aggregate	11%	
White	4%	
Hispanic		
English version	15%	3.8
Spanish version	23%	5.8
African American	18%	4.5

Note. "Odds Factor" is calculated as: Minority failure rate divided by White failure rate. Blackwell (2003).

porter's assertion is based on the aggregated results (89% pass rate). This reporting is misleading, however, and creates a false sense of security for the reader. When the data are disaggregated by race/ethnicity, they inform us that students of color did quite poorly compared to their White peers. Table 4.4 presents these data. The failure rate for the aggregate was 11%. Yet, the failure rate for Hispanic students who took the English TAKS Reading test was 15%, which was 3.8 times the failure rate for Whites (4%). The failure rate for African American students was 18%, 4.5 times the White rate. Finally, the failure rate for Hispanic students (23%) who were administered the Spanish version of the TAKS was 5.8 times the White failure rate.

Regarding the reporting of local TAKS results (e.g., Austin Independent School District [AISD]), reporter Michelle Martínez' (2003) by-line read: "Austin Schools Conquer New Test." Such reporting is also misleading because it fails to examine disaggregated data—which we have done, in a comprehensive manner. Table 4.5 lists the top 10 and bottom 10 of AISD's 74 elementary schools regarding percent failing the third-grade TAKS Reading test. Note that all the top 10 schools—which are predominantly high-enrollment White schools (73% to 92% White) had 0.0% failure rates. By striking contrast, the bottom 10 schools— predominantly minority (83% to 99% combined Hispanic and African American) had demonstrably higher TAKS failure rates (25% to 47%). We also conducted an analysis of the third-grade TAKS Reading test results for the entire AISD ($N = 74$ elementary schools). Figure 4.3 shows the results of a Pearson product-moment correlational analysis in which

TABLE 4.5

2003 Third-Grade TAKS Reading Failure Rates by Hispanic Plus African American Enrollment: Top Ten and Bottom Ten AISD Elementary Schools

School	% Hispanic + African American Enrollment[a]	% FailingTAKS[b]
1. Highland Park	8.3	0.0
2. Casis	10.7	0.0
3. Hill	12.7	0.0
4. Doss	13.1	0.0
5. Mills	15.6	0.0
6. Baranoff	16.9	0.0
7. Gullett	17.5	0.0
8. Barton Hills	19.4	0.0
9. Bryker Woods	20.3	0.0
10. Lee	27.0	0.0
65. Jordan	98.5	25.0
66. Andrews	96.4	26.0
67. Sims	98.1	26.0
68. Harris	97.0	29.0
69. Cook	82.8	30.0
70. Winn	96.9	31.0
71. Oak Springs	98.3	41.0
72. Allan	98.9	41.0
73. Pickle	99.0	42.0
74. Govalle	99.0	47.0

[a]Enrollment rates derived from Texas Education Agency (2003). Available online at: http://www.tea.state.tx.us/adhocrpt/. [b]Failure rates were calculated from data by Martínez (2003; database available online at: http://www.statesman.com/metro/schools).

percentage of students failing the TAKS Reading test is correlated with the percentage of Hispanic plus African American enrollment. The observed r of .70 is quite strong.

In sum, the data presented in Tables 4.4 and 4.5 and Figure 4.3 indicate that students of color fared considerably poorer (hence, adverse impact) than their White peers on the March 4, 2003 (first administration) of the third-grade TAKS Reading test. Unfortunately, due to the time lag issue previously discussed, we are unable to report the TAKS Reading test results of the second and third administrations, which were scheduled for April 30 and July 8, 2003, respectively. However, based on the results of the first TAKS administration—plus projections (see Valencia, 2000a; Valencia & Villarreal, 2003)—it is very likely that SB 4 will have a significant

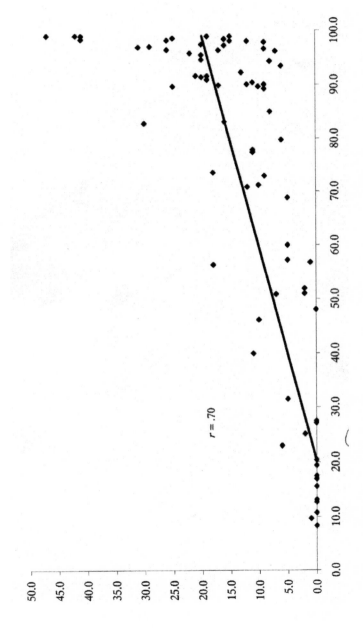

Figure 4.3. Scatterplot of 2003 TAKS Reading Third-Grade Failure Rates by Hispanic Plus African American Enrollment in AISD (N = 74 schools).
Enrollment rates derived from Texas Education Agency (2003). Available online at: http://www.tea.state.tx.us/adhocropt/. Failure rates were calculated from data by Martinez (2003; database available online at: http://www.statesman.com/metro/schools).

adverse impact (increased retention) on Mexican American, other Latino, and African American students. Given the dire consequences associated with grade retention that have been reported in the scholarly literature (e.g., failure to catch up; dropping out), the educational prospects for those minority students who comprise the first cohort (2002–2003) subject to SB 4 appear rather bleak.

Adverse Impact in Louisiana

As previously discussed, Texas is 1 of 16 states that has an institutionalized policy that uses state-mandated testing, in part to control grade promotion. Some of these states (e.g., California) have had their promotion policies in place for a number of years now. In these states, the ideal methodology to examine adverse impact would be to compare retention rates prior to the policy implementation to retention rates after the assessment program has been implemented. In educational research, this is similar to the useful and ubiquitous pretest/posttest design. Based on our review of the state education agency websites of those states (with high-minority school enrollments) that now have a brief history of having implemented retention policies, it is unfortunate to report that only one state provides the necessary pre-policy and post-policy test data to study the possibility of adverse impact.[20] This notable exception is Texas' neighboring state, Louisiana.

In 2000–2001, Louisiana implemented a policy using standardized test scores to make grade retention/promotion decisions similar to Texas' SB 4. Louisiana students in grades 4 and 8 must take the "Louisiana Educational Assessment Program for the 21st Century," or LEAP 21. All fourth-grade and eighth-grade students are required to pass the English Language Arts and Mathematics tests of the LEAP 21 to be promoted to the next grade. The 2001 Louisiana Department of Education report, entitled *Grade Level Retention in Louisiana Public Schools 1997–98 to 2000–01* (hereafter referred to as the *2001 GLR*), provides a rich source of retention data to examine the effects of Louisiana's grade retention policy on minority students.

For the three school years before LEAP 21 (1997–1998 to 1999–2000), the number of retained students in K–12 totaled 166,863, for an aggregated retention rate of 7.9% (based on our calculations from p. 11, Table 2 in Louisiana Department of Education, 2001). The average number of retained students was 55,621 per year. Bear in mind, however, that the average retention rate of 7.9% (for the three-year period) is for

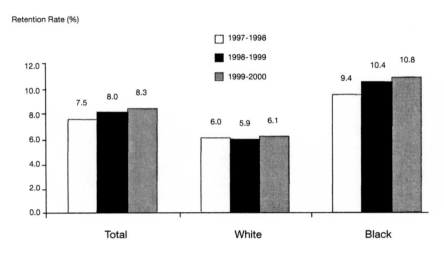

Figure 4.4. K–12 Retention Rates by Race/Ethnicity: Louisiana, 1997–1998 to 1999–2000.
Adapted from Louisiana Department of Education (20001, 0. 11, Table 2).

the aggregate—all racial/ethnic groups combined. When the data are disaggregated by race/ethnicity, however, a distinct pattern emerges (Louisiana Department of Education, 2001). Figure 4.4 shows average grade retention percentages by race/ethnicity for academic years 1997–1998 through 1999–2000. These data in the *2001 GLR* show that overall retention rates (K–12) range from 5.9% to 6.1% for White students, and 9.4% to 10.8% for African American students. This comparative analysis informs us that African American K–12 students were about *1.7 times more likely than their White peers to be retained during the 1997–2000 period.*

    Although the retention data shown in Figure 4.4 for African Americans in the Louisiana K–12 population clearly indicate that they are experiencing higher retention rates compared to their White peers, it is important to analyze data at the two promotional gates—grades 4 and 8—to observe the degree of current adverse impact. We obtained retention data from the *2001 GLR* for the academic years from 1997–1998 to 2000–2001 for grades 4 and 8, disaggregated by race/ethnicity. From these data, a clear pattern is observed (Louisiana

Retention Rate (%)

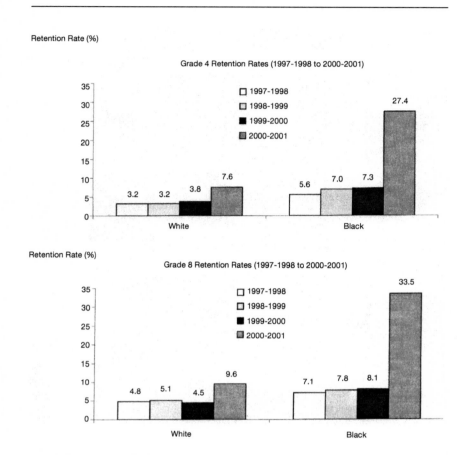

Figure 4.5. Retention Rates by Race/Ethnicity for Grades 4 and 8: Louisiana, 1997–1998 to 2000–2001.
Top panel (grade 4 data) is adopted from Valencia and Villarreal (2003, Figure 2). Both top and bottom panels adapted from Louisiana Department of Education (2001, p. 12, Tables 3 and 4).

Department of Education, 2001, p. 12, Tables 3 and 4). Figure 4.5 shows average grade retention percentages by race/ethnicity for academic years 1997–1998 through 2000–2001 for grades 4 and 8. Let us first examine grade 4 retention data (the top panel of Figure 4.5). These data in the *2001 GLR* show that retention rates ranged from 3.2% to 3.8% for White students prior to LEAP 21 implementation, and then rose to 7.6% in 2000–2001 after LEAP 21 became policy. Valencia and Villarreal (2003) reported:

For African American [fourth-grade] students, retention rates ranged from 5.6% to 7.3% before LEAP 21, then rose to a staggering 27.4% in 2000–2001 after LEAP 21 was implemented. In a more direct way of describing such adverse impact, we note the following:

- For African American fourth-grade students, about *1 in 15* students was retained during the pre–LEAP 21 years. During this same period, about *1 in 29* White fourth graders was retained.
- After LEAP 21 was implemented, about *1 in 4* African American fourth-grade students was retained, compared to *1 in 13* White fourth graders.

The above comparison informs us that African American fourth graders were *2.0* times more likely to be retained than White students prior to LEAP 21. However, after LEAP 21, African American fourth graders were *3.6* times more likely to be retained than their White counterparts. This increase in odds factor from 2.0 to 3.6 is substantial, and clearly indicates an adverse impact on African American students. (p. 616)

For eighth-grade students (bottom panel of Figure 4.5), the pattern is quite similar to the findings of the fourth-grade student analyses. For White eighth-grade students, the retention rates ranged from 4.5% to 5.1% before LEAP 21, and increased to 9.6% in 2000–2001. The retention rates for African American eighth graders ranged from 7.1% to 8.1% before LEAP 21, and increased to an enormous 33.5% in 2000–2001 (Valencia & Villarreal, 2003). Regarding adverse impact, note that:

- During the years before LEAP 21, *1 in 13* African American eighth-grade students was retained, compared to *1 in 21* White eighth graders.
- For African American eighth graders, about *1 in 3* students was retained after LEAP 21 was implemented. During this same period, about *1 in 10* White eighth-grade students was retained.

Prior to LEAP 21, African American eighth graders were 1.6 times more likely to be retained than White eighth-grade students. After LEAP 21, however, the odds factor for African American eighth grade students being retained increased to 3.5 times that of their White counterparts, clearly indicating adverse impact on African American eighth graders.[21]

The data from Louisiana informs us that African American students are adversely impacted by grade retention policies based on performance on high-stakes tests. It is important to keep in mind that the adverse impact (i.e., disproportionate retention rates) we have discussed is *not* presented in the context of *projected* disparate impact in Louisiana. Our analysis is based on real data derived from the pre– and post–LEAP 21 periods. In sum, the voluminous amount of scholarly literature on grade retention and the negative consequences associated with it shows that racial/ethnic minority students in Louisiana, Texas, and other states that have implemented retention policies, are likely to suffer the negative educational effects of such adverse impact—diminished academic achievement and the increased likelihood of dropping out. In the concluding section, we offer a critical appraisal of the current standards-based school reform climate.

CONCLUSIONS

The data presented in this chapter—much derived from the TEA itself—demonstrate three indisputable facts.[22] On the average, Mexican American, other Latino, and African American students in Texas public schools—in comparison to their White peers—experience higher rates of (a) *grade retention*, (b) *failure on the state mandated test*, and (c) *dropouts*. These persistent and pervasive findings showing that such schooling outcomes are not independent of the demographic characteristic of race/ethnicity should be of major concern to us. One major explanation of this trinity of undesirable schooling outcomes is the perspective that such school failure is endogenous in root and branch. This deficit thinking framework for explaining school failure among minority students locates the student's inability to succeed academically in his/her (alleged) limited cognitive abilities, poor motivation, low-SES background, and inadequate family socialization for academic competence (Valencia, 1997). The characteristics of the student's school—for instance, degree of segregation; curricular offerings; teacher certification status (see Valencia, 2002)—are very seldom considered by policy makers and educators as factors that help to shape school failure.

There is, of course, another major perspective on minority school failure—one that we believe has more credibility and evidential power in explaining why some minority students in Texas have greater odds at being flunked, failing TAAS (the predecessor), and the TAKS (the successor), and dropping out. This view interprets these schooling outcomes as symptoms, not pathologies located within the students. Flunking grades, failing high-stakes tests, and dropping out are events much more probable in segregated, high-minority enrollment schools with a disproportionate number of noncertified teachers. Such tight connections between school characteristics and schooling outcomes point to an exogenous account of school failure—away from the presumed shortcomings of the student, and toward the systemic and structural ways in which schools are organized that make it difficult for minority students to attain school success (see Pearl, 1997, 2002; Valencia, 2000b, 2002).

Without acknowledging the divide between the deficit thinking verses systemic perspectives on minority school failure, it becomes extremely difficult, if not impossible, to have genuine discourse on standards-based school reform. If policy makers and educators in Texas are indeed serious about workable school reform, they must undergo paradigmatic shifts in their ways of viewing minority school failure—away from a deficit thinking model to a systemic, structural model of understanding variability in students' academic performance in which race/ethnicity has a central position.

Senate Bill 4—Texas' most recent response to standards-based school reform—is bound to fail by creating adverse impact on many Mexican American, other Latino, and African American students. There are three major reasons SB 4, an anti–social promotion measure, will not do what it seeks to do: improve the academic performance of low-achieving minority students. First, it is important to underscore that the failure rates of students of color are likely to intensify in the next two cycles of testing as the higher passing standards on the third-grade TAKS Reading test are phased in as follows (SEM refers to standard error of measurement):

2003:	56%	(2 SEM below SBOE panel's recommendation)
2004:	61%	(1 SEM below SBOE panel's recommendation)
2005:	67%	(Nov., 2000 SBOE panel's recommendation)[23]

As the passing bar rises from 56% in 2003, to 61% in 2004, and then to 67% in 2005, will equal educational opportunities for Mexican American, other Latino, and African American students commensurately increase? Given the entrenched schooling inequalities in Texas schools (Valencia, 2000b), the answer to this critical question is, very likely, "no."

Second, SB 4 is inherently flawed when placed in the context of school reform. As noted by Valencia, Valenzuela, Sloan, and Foley

(2001, p. 319): "The standards-based school reform misses the mark. It is structurally misdirected because it treats the symptoms of school failure (e.g., poor achievement), rather than the cause (i.e., inferior schools)." As such, we expect that SB 4 will have the same invidious effect that Texas' first wave of standards-based school reform has had (i.e., by increasing school failure for students of color; see: Haney, 2000; Valencia & Bernal, 2000).

Third, SB 4 will not succeed in its mission because the law's originators and supporters have failed to consider over 50 years of research evidence that grade retention demonstrates little to no academic improvement among low-achieving students, is not effective as grade promotion (with intensive remediation) in enhancing the academic performance of low-achieving students, and is a statistical predictor of dropping out. To place the retention/promotion controversy and standards-based school reform in its broadest context, the words of Smith and Shepard (1989) are important to consider:

> To some, retention is a way of demonstrating rigorous standards. To children, retention is flunking, an indication that they themselves are deficient. For the system of public schools, retention functions as a way to preserve the structure of efficient, grade-level production while enhancing the meritocratic image. But because retentions do nothing to promote the achievement of the affected individuals or the average of the group as a whole, and because the disadvantaged and minority children are most apt to be affected, retention should best be thought of as educational waste and denial of life chances to those who most need the benefits of education. Retention has high cost and virtually no value, save the public relations advantages for the schools. Those children who are retained or otherwise failed by public schools are thereby deprived of rightful learning opportunities and, more important, opportunities to succeed in life beyond school. (pp. 234–235)

On a final note, we must underscore that one can be critical of the notion of accountability, yet agree that it is necessary for the public school system to have a system of accountability. Valencia et al. (2001, p. 321) have commented:

> We argue that accountability is vital to public education. However, it must be implemented with care. We need to shape our accountability system in accordance with principles such as (1) parents' involvement

in their children's schoolwork; (2) the allowance for teachers not to be fettered to rote, unchallenging, and measurement-driven instruction; (3) comprehensive diagnostic testing; and (4) multiple indicators of academic performance.[24]

NOTES

The section headed "Major Research Findings on the Grade Retention/Promotion Issue" is excerpted, with revisions, from Valencia (2000a, pp. 7–10).

1. This section is excerpted, with revisions, from Valencia (2000a, pp. 2–5, 44).

2. It is important to note that accurate data on national trends in grade retention are difficult to obtain. As such, researchers rely on "modal grade" data reported by the U.S. Bureau of the Census. Shepard and Smith (1989a) explained:

> Despite its salience, rates of promotion and retention are not kept by government agencies. Instead, retention rates are inferred from the proportion of pupils of a given age who are not in the appropriate (or modal) grade. For example, third grade is the normal grade for eight-year-olds. Therefore, most eight-year-olds enrolled in second grade or first grade are likely to have been retained. This indicator has been used since the turn of the century (Thorndike, 1908). (p. 6)

3. Although there is a strong consensus in the literature that retention is mostly ineffective in enhancing or sustaining the achievement of low-performing students, there are a few scholars who are cautious in drawing this conclusion. Jimerson et al. (1997) observed: "while evidence supporting retention has been in short supply, the issue is not fully resolved" (p. 6). Furthermore, there are methodological criticisms that have been raised by some authors about the retention/promotion research (e.g., Alexander, Entwisle & Dauber, 1994; Jimerson, 1999; Jimerson et al., 1997; Pierson & Connell, 1992; Reynolds, 1992; Tanner & Gallis, 1997). For example, Jimerson (1999) commented that these methodological concerns include:

> comparing pre- and posttest scores of retained students rather than a comparison group; characteristics of comparison groups are rarely delineated; data collected 30–40 years ago may be outdated; most studies do not consider socioemotional outcomes; and most studies are unable to examine the long-term outcomes associated with grade retention. (p. 244)

4. This section is excerpted, with revisions, from Valencia (2000a, pp. 11–13, 45).

5. McLean (1950) also reported similar trends in racial/ethnic grade retention differences for academic years 1943–1944, 1944–1945, 1945–1946, 1946–1947, and 1947–1948.

6. For a discussion and listing of these six MAES reports by the U.S. Commission on Civil Rights, see Valencia (2002).

7. The U.S. Commission on Civil Rights (1971) also reported student data on "severe overageness" (two or more years overage for his/her grade level) by grade (1, 4, 8, and 12), race/ethnicity (Anglo, Mexican American, and Black), and the five southwestern states. The study's findings (see p. 37, Table 3) were:

> At the first grade level [total Southwestern states], Mexican American children are four times more likely to be two or more years overage than Anglo or black students. By eighth grade, the proportion who are overage (9.4 percent) is almost eight times as high for Mexican Americans as for Anglos, and more than four times as high for black students. (p. 36)

As was the case for grade repetitions, Texas ranked first of the southwestern states in having the highest percentages of Mexican American students characterized as being severely overage in the studied grade levels (1, 4, 8, and 12). Texas also had the most pronounced rates of severe overageness for Blacks in the investigated grades, except the twelfth.

8. For a discussion of cross-racial/ethnic retention data from 1994–1995 to 1998–1999 in Texas, see Valencia (2002, p. 16).

9. For a brief discussion and citations of references for the persistent and pervasive nature of this pattern of lower academic achievement performance regarding Mexican American students, see Valencia (2002). A number of the reports cited by Valencia are also applicable to African Americans.

10. The TAAS test was phased out in 2002. The current data we report here are based on the last administration of the TAAS. Test results for the TAAS successor, the TAKS test, were not available for any grade (except grade 3) at the time of writing this chapter.

11. We present achievement test data only for White, Hispanic, and African American students because the ns for Asian/Pacific Islanders and Native Americans are quite small. For grades Early Childhood Education to 12, the percentages of Asian/Pacific Islanders and Native Americans were 2.8% and 0.3%, respectively, in the 2001–2002 school year (Texas Education Agency, 2002b).

12. Mexican American (and other Latino) and African Americans also demonstrated lower pass rates on the other TAAS tests (i.e., mathematics, writing, science, social studies; see Texas Education Agency, 2002b).

13. This section is excerpted, with slight revisions, from Valencia (2000a, p. 17) and Valencia (2002, p. 18).

14. For the "Other" population (Asian/Pacific Islander; Native American), it comprised 3.1% of all students enrolled in grades 7–12, and only 1.8% of the seventh- to twelfth-grade dropouts.

15. This section on "Origins" and the following section, "Requirements of the Law," are excerpted, with minor revisions, from Valencia (2000a, pp. 21–23).

16. SB 4 can be accessed and downloaded from the Texas Legislature Online search engine at http://www.capitol.state.tx.us/tlo/billnbr.htm

17. According to SB 4, a school district may—if it wishes—administer a state-approved alternative instrument.

18. In May of 2002, language was added by the Commissioner of Education to Rule §101.2007 ("Role of Grade Placement Committee") of the Texas Administrative Code. Existing language allows the parent, guardian, or designee the opportunity to appeal the automatic retention after a student's third failure on the third-grade TAKS Reading test. The new language pertains to the appellate process, in which the grade placement committee may decide to promote the student, despite failing the TAKS. As noted in the code:

> These standards may include but are not limited to the following:
>
> (1) evidence of satisfactory student performance, including grades, portfolios, work samples, local assessments, and individual reading and mathematics diagnostic tests or inventories;
> (2) improvement in student test performance over the three testing opportunities; and
> (3) extenuating circumstances that have adversely affected the student's participation in either the required assessments or accelerated instruction. (Texas Administrative Code, 2002, Rule §101.2007f)

19. It appears that local districts will have some flexibility on how "accelerated instruction" is designed. In the case of a child who fails the reading test:

> That child will be given accelerated, research-based, phonics-driven reading instruction so he or she can catch up. Each district's strategy for delivering the accelerated instruction will be decided by local parents, educators and school boards. Possible strategies could include: after-school programs, individual tutoring, summer school, or reading academies—intensive reading programs within public schools. . . . (Office of the Governor, n.d., p. 5)

20. We identified the states for investigation using two criteria: (a) the state is one of the top 10 states with the largest combined minority school enrollments as described in Valencia and Suzuki (2001, p. 319, footnote 38); (b) the state has a retention policy in place, as listed in the American Federation of Teachers (2001) report. These two criteria limited the number of states to seven: California, Florida, Georgia, Louisiana, North Carolina, Texas, and Virginia.

21. Hispanics and American Indians, though only a very small percentage of the fourth- and eighth-grade populations, show similar patterns to African Americans of higher retention rates before LEAP 21, and substantial retention increases in 2000–2001 (post–LEAP 21), indicating adverse impact for these groups as well.

22. This section is excerpted, with revisions, from Valencia, (2000a, pp. 41–43).

23. Personal communication (Gean Wilkerson, Curriculum, Assessment, and Technology, TEA, March 20, 2003).

24. For concrete suggestions directed to test developers and policy makers about improving high-stakes testing and accountability, see Bernal and Valencia (2000).

REFERENCES

Abidin, R. R., Golladay, W. M., & Howerton, A. L. (1971). Elementary school retention: An unjustifiable, discriminatory, and noxious educational policy. *Journal of School Psychology, 9*, 410–417.

Alexander, K. L., Entwisle, D. S., & Dauber, S. L. (1994). *On the success of failure*. New York: Cambridge University Press.

American Federation of Teachers. (2001). *Making standards matter 2001: A fifty-state report on efforts to implement a standards-based system*. Washington, D.C.: Author.

Ayres, L. P. (1909). *Laggards in our schools: A study of retardation and elimination in city school systems*. New York: Russell Sage.

Bernal, E. M., & Valencia, R. R. (2000). The TAAS case: A recapitulation and beyond. *Hispanic Journal of Behavioral Sciences, 22*, 540–556.

Blackwell, K. (2003, March 19). Students rise to challenge of tougher test in reading. *Austin American-Statesman*, pp. B1, B6.

Brooks-Gunn, J., Guo, G., & Furstenberg, F. F. Jr. (1993). Who drops out of and who continues beyond high school? A 20-year follow-up of Black youth. *Journal of Adolescent Research, 3*, 271–294.

Bush, G. W. (1998, January 22). Remarks at TEA Midwinter Conference. Austin, TX.

Byrnes, D. A. (1989). Attitudes of students, parents and educators toward repeating a grade. In L. A. Shepard & M. L. Smith (Eds.), *Flunking grades: Research and policies on retention* (pp. 108–131). London: Falmer.

Cairns, R. B., Cairns, B. D., & Neckerman, H. J. (1989). Early school dropout: Configuration and determinants. *Child Development, 60*, 1437–1452.

Calderón, C. I. (1950). *The education of Spanish-speaking children in Edcouch-Elsa, Texas*. Unpublished master's thesis, The University of Texas at Austin.

Campbell, C., & Bowman, R. P. (1993). The "fresh start" support club: Small group counseling for academically retained students. *Elementary School Guidance & Counseling, 27*, 172–185.

Clinton, W. J. (1998). Memorandum to the Secretary of Education. Press release. Washington, D.C.: The White House.

Coan, B. E. (1936). *A comparative study of the American and Mexican children of the "Big Bend" area for 1935–1936*. Unpublished master's thesis, The University of Texas at Austin.

Copelin, L. (2002, November 16). Board lowers 3rd-graders' benchmark. *Austin American-Statesman*, pp. B1, B7.

Cromack, I. W. (1949). *Latin-Americans: A minority group in the Austin public schools*. Unpublished master's thesis, The University of Texas at Austin.

Dauber, S. L., Alexander, K. L., & Entwisle, D. R. (1993). Characteristics of retainees and early precursors of retention in grade. *Merrill Palmer Quarterly, 39,* 326–343.

Dawson, D. A. (1991). Family structure and children's health and well-being: Data from the 1988 National Health Interview Survey on children's health. *Journal of Marriage and the Family, 53,* 573–584.

Deridder, L. M. (1988). School dropout prevention begins in the elementary years. *Education, 108,* 488–492.

Ekstrom, R. B., Goertz, M. E., Pollack, J. M., & Rock, D. A. (1986). Who drops out of high school and why? Findings from a national study. *Teachers College Record, 87,* 356–373.

Fassold, M. A. J. (2000). Disparate impact analyses of TAAS scores and school quality. *Hispanic Journal of Behavioral Sciences, 22,* 460–480.

Fernández, R. M., Paulsen, R., & Hirano-Nakanishi, M. (1989). Dropping out among Hispanic youth. *Social Science Research, 18,* 21–52.

Fikac, P. (2002, June 25). Educators warn TAKS will be tough; Report says public support needed for reforms to work as new test introduced. *San Antonio Express-News,* p. 1B.

Fowler, M., & Cross, A. (1986). Preschool risk factors are predictors of early school performance. *Journal of Developmental and Behavioral Pediatrics, 7,* 327–341.

Gredler, G. R. (1984). Transition classes: A viable alternative for the at-risk child? *Psychology in the Schools, 21,* 463–470.

Grissom, J. B., & Shepard, L. A. (1989). Repeating and dropping out of school. In L. A. Shepard & M. L. Smith (Eds.), *Flunking grades: Research and policies on retention* (pp. 34–63). London: Falmer.

Hagborg, W. J., Masella, G., Palladino, P., & Shepardson, J. (1991). A follow-up study of high school students with a history of grade retention. *Psychology in the Schools, 28,* 310–317.

Hammack, F. M. (1987). Large school systems' dropout reports: An analysis of definitions, procedures, and findings. In G. Natriello (Ed.), *School dropouts: Patterns and policies* (pp. 20–37). New York: Teachers College Press.

Haney, W. M. (2000). The myth of the Texas miracle in education. *Education Policy Analysis Archives.* Available: http://epaa.asu.edu/v8n41/

Hauser, R. M, Pager, D. I., & Simmons, S. J. (2001). Race-ethnicity, social background, and grade retention: An analysis of the last thirty years. *CEIC Review, 10,* 11–12.

Heubert, J. P., & Hauser, R. M. (Eds.). (1999). *High stakes: Testing for tracking, promotion, and graduation.* Committee on Appropriate Test Use, Board on Testing and Assessment, Commission on Behavioral and Social Sciences and Education, National Research Council. Washington, D.C.: National Academy Press.

Hirano-Nakanishi, M. (1986). The extent and prevalence of pre–high school attrition and delayed education for Hispanics. *Hispanic Journal of Behavioral Sciences, 8,* 61–76.

Holmes, C. T. (1983). The fourth r: Retention. *Journal of Research and Development in Education, 17,* 1–6.

Holmes, C. T. (1989). Grade level retention effects: A meta-analysis of research studies. In L. A. Shepard & M. L. Smith (Eds.), *Flunking grades: Research and policies on retention* (pp. 16–33). London: Falmer.

Holmes, C. T., & Matthews, K. M. (1984). The effects of nonpromotion on elementary and junior high school pupils: A meta-analysis. *Review of Educational Research, 54,* 225–236.

House, E. R. (1989). Policy implications for retention research. In L. A. Shepard & M. L. Smith (Eds.), *Flunking grades: Research and policies on retention* (pp. 202–213). London: Falmer.

Jackson, G. B. (1975). The research evidence on the effects of grade retention. *Review of Educational Research, 45,* 613–635.

Jaeger, C. (1987). *Minority and low income high schools: Evidence of educational inequality in metro Los Angeles* (Report No. 8). Chicago: Metropolitan Opportunity Project, University of Chicago.

Jimerson, S. R. (1999). On the failure of failure: Examining the association between early grade retention and education and employment outcomes during late adolescence. *Journal of School Psychology, 37,* 243–272.

Jimerson, S. R. (2001a). Meta-analysis of grade retention research: Implications for practice in the 21st century. *School Psychology Review, 30,* 420–437.

Jimerson, S. R. (2001b). A synthesis of grade retention research: Looking backward and moving forward. *The California School Psychologist, 6,* 46–59.

Jimerson, S., Carlson, E., Rotert, M., Egeland, B., & Sroufe, L. A. (1997). A prospective, longitudinal study of the correlates and consequences of early grade retention. *Journal of School Psychology, 35,* 3–25.

Jimerson, S. R., & Kaufman, A. M. (2003). Reading, writing, and retention: A primer on grade retention research. *The Reading Teacher, 56,* 622–635.

Jimerson, S. R., & Schuder, M. R. (1996, June). *Is grade retention an appropriate academic intervention? Longitudinal data provide further insights.* Paper presented at Head Start's Third National Research Conference, Washington, D.C.

Johnston, R. C. (1998). The governor has social promotion in his sights. *Education Week,* February 11, p. 1 (*Education Week on the Web*). Available: www.edweek.org

King, M. J. (1984). *"Ready or not, here they come": A sourcebook on developmental readiness for parents, teachers, and school boards.* Unpublished master's thesis, California State University at Fresno.

Langer, P., Kalk, J. M., & Searls, D. T. (1984). Age of admission and trends in achievement: A comparison of Blacks and Caucasians. *American Educational Research Journal, 21,* 61–78.

Lloyd, D. N. (1978). Prediction of school failure from third-grade data. *Educational and Psychological Measurement, 38,* 1193–1200.

Louisiana Department of Education. (2001). *Grade level retention in Louisiana public schools 1997–98 to 2000–1.* Baton Rouge, LA: Author. Available: http://www.doe.state.la.us

Mann, D. (1987). Can we help dropouts? Thinking about the undoable. In G. Natriello (Ed.), *School dropouts: Patterns and policies* (pp. 3–19). New York: Teachers College Press.

Mantzicopoulos, P., & Morrison, D. (1992). Kindergarten retention: Academic and behavioral outcomes through the end of second grade. *American Educational Research Journal, 29,* 182–198.

Martínez, M. N. (2003, March 22). Austin's schools conquer new test. *Austin American-Statesman,* pp. B1, B7.

McCoy, A. R., & Reynolds, A. J. (1999). Grade retention and school performance: An extended investigation. *Journal of School Psychology, 37,* 273–298.

McLean, R. J. (1950). *A comparative study of Anglo-American and Spanish-name children in the Austin public schools over a seven-year period.* Unpublished master's thesis, The University of Texas at Austin.

Meisels, S. J., & Liaw, F-R. (1993). Failure in schools: Do retained students catch up? *Journal of Educational Research, 87,* 69–77.

National Center for Education Statistics. (1989). *National education longitudinal study of 1988—Base tear student component file user's manual.* U.S. Department of Education, Office of Educational Research and Development (NCES 90-464). Washington, D.C.: Author.

National Commission on Excellence in Education. (1983). *A nation at risk: The imperatives for educational reform.* Washington, D.C.: Government Printing Office.

Nelson, J. (2002, January 31). Testing the TAKS test. *Austin American-Statesman,* p. A15.

Neill, M. D., & Medina, N. J. (1989). Standardized testing: Harmful to educational health. *Phi Delta Kappan, 70,* 688–697.

Office of the Governor. (n.d.). Questions and answers about social promotion. Austin, TX.

Pearl, A. (1997). Democratic education as an alternative to deficit thinking. In R. R. Valencia (Ed.), *The evolution of deficit thinking: Educational thought and practice* (pp. 211–241). Stanford Series on Education and Public Policy. London: Falmer.

Pearl, A. (2002). The big picture: Systemic and institutional factors in Chicano school failure and success. In R. R. Valencia (Ed.), *Chicano school failure and success: Past, present, and future* (2nd ed., pp. 335–364). London: RoutledgeFalmer.

Phillips, S. E. (2000). *GI Forum v. Texas Education Agency*: Psychometric evidence. *Applied Measurement in Education, 13,* 343–385.

Pierson, L. H., & Connell, J. P. (1992). Effect of grade retention on self-system processes, school engagement, and academic performance. *Journal of Educational Psychology, 84,* 300–307.

Reynolds, A. J. (1992). Grade retention and school adjustment. *Educational Evaluation and Policy Analysis, 14*, 101–112.

Rich, J. M. (1985). Back to basics: A reappraisal. In J. M. Rich (Ed.), *Innovations in education: Reformers and their critics* (4th ed., pp. 295–300). Boston: Allyn & Bacon.

Roderick, M. (1994). Grade retention and school dropout: Investigating the association. *American Educational Research Journal, 31*, 729–759.

Rose, J. C., Medway, F. J., Cantrell, V. L., & Marus, S. H. (1983). A fresh look at the retention-promotion controversy. *Journal of School Psychology, 21*, 201–211.

Rumberger, R. W. (1987). High school dropouts: A review of issues and evidence. *Review of Educational Research, 57*, 101–121.

Rumberger, R. W. (1995). Dropping out of school: A multilevel analysis of students and schools. *American Educational Research Journal, 32*, 583–625.

San Miguel, G. Jr., & Valencia, R. R. (1998). From the Treaty of Guadalupe Hidalgo to *Hopwood*: The educational plight and struggle of Mexican Americans in the Southwest. *Harvard Educational Review, 68*, 353–412.

Saucedo, L. M. (2000). The legal issues surrounding the TAAS case. *Hispanic Journal of Behavioral Sciences, 22*, 411–422.

Shepard, L. A. (1989). A review of the research on grade retention. In L. A. Shepard & M. L. Smith (Eds.), *Flunking grades: Research and policies on retention* (pp. 64–78). London: Falmer.

Shepard, L. A. (1997). Children not ready to learn? The invalidity of school readiness testing. *Psychology in the Schools, 34*, 85–97.

Shepard, L. A. (2001). Understanding research on the consequences of retention: An overview of the research. *CEIC Review, 10*, 19–20.

Shepard, L. A., & Smith, M. L. (1987). Effects of kindergarten retention at the end of first grade. *Psychology in the Schools, 24*, 346–357.

Shepard, L. A., & Smith, M. L. (1989a). Introduction and overview. In L. A. Shepard & M. L. Smith (Eds.), *Flunking grades: Research and policies on retention* (pp. 1–15). London: Falmer.

Shepard, L. A., & Smith, M. L. (Eds.). (1989b). *Flunking grades: Research and policies on retention*. London: Falmer.

Shepard, L. A., & Smith, M. L. (1990). Synthesis of research on grade retention. *Educational Leadership, 47*, 84–88.

Smith, M. L., & Shepard, L. A. (1989). Flunking grades: A recapitulation. In L. A. Shepard & M. L. Smith (Eds.), *Flunking grades: Research and policies on retention* (pp. 214–236). London: Falmer.

Tanner, C. K., & Gallis, S. A. (1997). Student retention: Why is there a gap between the majority of research and school practice? *Psychology in the Schools, 34*, 107–114.

Temple, J., Reynolds, A., & Ou, S-R. (2001). Grade retention and school dropout: Another look at the evidence. *CEIC Review, 10*, 5–6, 21.

Texas Administrative Code. (2002). *Rule §101.2007: Role of grade placement committee*. Austin, TX: Office of the Secretary of State. Available: http:www.tea.state.tx.us/rules/tac/chapter101/ch101bb.html#101.2007

Texas Education Agency. (2001). *Student assessment calendar, 2002–2003 school year*. Austin, TX: Author. Available: http://www.tea.state.tx.us/student. assessment/admin/calendar/calnd03.html

Texas Education Agency. (2002a). *2002 comprehensive annual report on Texas public schools*. Austin, TX: Author.

Texas Education Agency. (2002b). *Academic Excellence Indicator System*. Austin, TX: Author. Available: http://www.tea.state.tx.us/perfreport/aeis/

Texas Education Agency. (2002c). *Texas Assessment of Knowledge and Skills information booklet: Reading, grade 3*. Austin, TX: Author.

Texas Education Agency. (2003). *2002–2003 student enrollment: Austin Independent School District totals*. Austin, TX: Author. Available online using Public Education Information Management System (PEIMS) search engine at: http://www.tea.state.tx.us/adhocrpt/

Thorndike, E. L. (1908). *Elimination of pupils from schools*. U.S. Bureau of Education Bulletin, No. 4. Washington, D.C.: Government Printing Office.

U.S. Commission on Civil Rights. (1971). *Mexican American education study, report 2: The unfinished education. Outcomes for minorities in five southwestern states*. Washington, D.C.: Government Printing Office.

U.S. Department of Education. (1991). *America 2000*. Washington, D.C.: Author.

Valencia, R. R. (Ed.). (1997). *The evolution of deficit thinking: Educational thought and practice*. The Stanford Series on Education and Public Policy. London: Falmer.

Valencia, R. R. (2000a, July). *Legislated school reform via high-stakes testing: The case of pending anti–social promotion legislation in Texas and its likely adverse impact on racial/ethnic minority students*. Commissioned paper for the National Academy of Sciences Committee on Educational Excellence and Testing Equity. Paper presented at the workshop on School Completion in Standards-Based Reform, Washington, D.C.

Valencia, R. R. (2000b). Inequalities and the schooling of minority students in Texas: Historical and contemporary conditions. *Hispanic Journal of Behavioral Sciences, 22*, 445–459.

Valencia, R. R. (2002). The plight of Chicano students: An overview of schooling conditions and outcomes. In R. R. Valencia (Ed.), *Chicano school failure and success: Past, present, and future* (2nd ed., pp. 3–51). London: RoutledgeFalmer.

Valencia, R. R., & Bernal, E. M. (Eds.). (2000). The Texas Assessment of Academic Skills (TAAS) case: Perspectives of plaintiffs' experts [Special issue]. *Hispanic Journal of Behavioral Sciences, 22*(4).

Valencia, R. R., & Suzuki, L. A. (2001). *Intelligence testing and minority students: Foundations, performance factors, and assessment issues*. Thousand Oaks, CA: Sage.

Valencia, R. R., Valenzuela, A., Sloan, K., & Foley, D. E. (2001). At odds—Let's treat the cause, not the symptoms: Equity and accountability in Texas revisited. *Phi Delta Kappan, 83*, 318–321, 326.

Valencia, R. R., & Villarreal, B. J. (2003). Improving students' reading performance via standards-based school reform: A critique. *The Reading Teacher, 56*, 612–621.

Walters, D. M., & Borgers, S. B. (1995). Student retention: Is it effective? *School Counselor, 42*, 300–310.

Wehlage, C. G., & Rutter, R. A. (1986). Dropping out: How much do schools contribute to the problem? *Teachers College Record, 87*, 374–392.

Wilson, J. H. (1953). *Secondary school dropouts, with special reference to Spanish-speaking youth in Texas*. Unpublished doctoral dissertation, The University of Texas at Austin.

Zepeda, M. (1993). An exploratory study of demographic characteristics, retention, and developmentally appropriate practice in kindergarten. *Child Study Journal, 23*, 57–78.

5

Playing to the Logic of the Texas Accountability System: How Focusing on "Ratings"—Not Children—Undermines Quality and Equity

KRIS SLOAN

As its promoters hoped it would, the Texas Accountability System (TAS) put in place in the 1990s has spurred teachers and administrators across the state to embrace significant curricular and pedagogical change (e.g., see McNeil, 2000a; Skrla, Scheurich, & Johnson, 2000b). However, as the old adage "Be careful what you wish for . . ." warns, change has not always led to the improvement in educational quality and equity that is the underlying premise of the accountability movement. This chapter reports results from my ethnographic investigation of Glendale Elementary School in the Twin Oaks (Texas) Independent School District (ISD).[1] There, an initially positive response to the TAS, one that emphasized teacher development and child-centered, activity-based learning, recently was supplanted by a district-mandated focus on school ratings that compels teachers to dedicate large amounts of classroom instructional time to preparing their students for the annual Texas Assessment of Academic Skills (TAAS) exam. My ongoing research at Glendale, which serves a largely low-income Latino student population, documents how the shift from a "reform-focused response" to the TAS to a "ratings-focused response" has adversely impacted the overall educational quality at the school level—even though TAAS scores have risen at each grade level.

153

DIFFERING RESEARCH FOCI, DIFFERING VIEWS OF EFFECTS

Over the past two years, I have been engaged in two projects at Glendale Elementary School: I have been conducting an ethnographic research study of my own, and I have been assisting in a large-scale evaluation of the Annenberg systemic reform project, collecting data and assessing the impact of this nationally-known reform effort.[2] Glendale was selected for the evaluation research project because it offers a particularly robust site for examining how schools respond to systems of accountability. The school has shown promise in meeting the imperatives of the reform effort *and* in improving student achievement on the TAAS, Texas' high-stakes assessment instrument.

Conducting research at sites like Glendale Elementary is especially important because efforts to independently evaluate systems of accountability such as the TAS have proven surprisingly challenging and controversial. Some studies insist that the TAS is successfully "leveraging" higher quality and more equitable education for low-income children of color (Scheurich, Skrla, & Johnson, 2000; Skrla, Scheurich, & Johnson, 2000a). Others charge that the TAS is reducing the quality and quantity of curricula delivered to low-income children of color (McNeil, 2000a; McNeil & Valenzuela, 2000). At professional conferences and in leading educational journals, researchers present dramatically contradictory findings. Which are we to conclude—that the TAS is forcing out the very best teachers and "de-skilling" those left behind (Hoffman, Pennington, Assaf, & Paris, 2000; McNeil, 2000a), or that it has diminished turnover among teachers and increased professional satisfaction (Scheurich et al., 2000)? How can researchers, each of whom is committed to promoting equity and fighting racism, come to such divergent views of the TAS?

I see two possible causes for the deep differences in reported findings. The first, simply put, is that in a state as large and diverse as Texas, *any* multifaceted assessment scheme, when combined with factors such as increased preschool education funding, class-size reduction legislation, more equitable statewide funding of schools, and complex local conditions, will produce a range of results. The second, and perhaps more important reason for the divergent views of the TAS involves research orientation, even paradigmatic orientation. Although it is true, as Scheurich and colleagues (2000) point out, that "each side in this debate . . . can legitimately quote real and accurate data to support its conclusions" (p. 294), there are some significant differences in the foci of the research that has generated these data. Skrla, Scheurich, and Johnson (2000b) focus on district-level administrative practices related to "systemic school success" (p. 1) and rely most heavily on "outputs" (e.g., TAAS scores, high school end-of-course test scores, enrollment in Advanced Placement courses) to support their conclusions. They buttress these statistics with testimonials from district-level administrators and other "central office personnel." Drawing on the "effective schools" paradigm introduced by the late Ronald Edmonds, Scheurich, Skrla, and Johnson generate their results from the outside in, asserting that in the districts they have studied, gains are attributable largely to strong administrative leadership and high expectations for all students.

Critics of the TAS tend to focus their research on curricular and pedagogical practices related to the creation of productive and inclusive classrooms. Drawing on an educational/teacher-quality paradigm, these researchers use an inside-out approach, making teachers and teachers' work central to their investigations. They assert that the TAS has undermined the work of teachers and has telescoped the products and processes of education around a narrow skill range that can be more easily assessed by simplified, standardized means (McNeil, 2000a). They also note that the TAS contributes to "subtractive schooling," whereby students' culture is removed from classroom contexts (Valenzuela, 1999).

In framing my ethnography, I took an inside-out approach. I went to Glendale Elementary hoping to show how a state-level policy such as the TAS shapes the day-to-day lives of teachers and children. Based on my past statewide research in Texas' bilingual education classrooms (Guerrero & Sloan, 2001), I am skeptical of the linear logic that equates high TAAS scores with high-quality, more equitable education. My research and my experiences as a teacher in elementary classrooms in the United States and abroad lead me to define quality curricula and pedagogy as involving the following mutually reinforcing components: authentic engagements with subject matter, a developmental-constructivist understanding of the learning process, and a commitment to providing frequent opportunities for activity-based learning.

THEORETICAL FRAMEWORK

The concept of authentic approaches to disciplinary knowledge grew out of the work of curriculum developers in the 1960s who advocated giving children multiple opportunities to emulate the actions of more knowledgeable adults, even experts, in their efforts to solve everyday problems (Bruner, 1960; Schwab, 1964). Authentic approaches to curricula and pedagogy are championed through educational standards established by national curriculum organizations such as the National Council of Teachers of Mathematics (NCTM) (1989, 1991) and the National Research Council (NRC). In *National Science Education Standards* (1996), for example, the NRC asserts that " inquiry into authentic questions generated from student experiences is the central strategy for teaching" (p. 32). A similar commitment to an authentic approach to subject matter is clear at the local level in the Twin Oaks ISD. The district's mathematics curriculum information states that "knowing mathematics means being able to use it in purposeful ways . . . in a wide variety of real-world situations."[3]

A constructivist orientation toward learning holds that knowledge acquisition, or understanding, is achieved when a learner is able to relate a new idea, concept, principle, or experience to previously acquired knowledge. Moreover, this connection between new and previously acquired knowledge *must be evident to the learner* (Cary, Fennema, Carpenter, & Franke, 1995). Thus, "simply covering topics, vocabulary, or information in textbooks is in direct conflict with the central goal of having students learn knowledge with understanding" (NRC, 1996, p. 78). Again, the Twin Oaks ISD seems to embrace a similar philosophy, as evidenced by the district's description of children as "active individuals who construct, modify, and integrate ideas by interacting with the physical world, materials, and other children."

Activity-based learning involves students taking part in what the NRC (1996) terms "minds-on experiences." The NCTM maintains that "Students' ability to reason, solve problems, and use mathematics to communicate their ideas will develop only if they actively and frequently engage in these processes" (1989, p. 13). Consistent with these and other nationally recognized educational standards (e.g., NCTM, 1991), the Twin Oaks guidelines state that successful instruction "requires a classroom environment that stimulates activity, creativity, innovation, and discovery."

In addition to these aspects of curriculum and pedagogy, my framework for assessing educational quality includes the relational aspect of teaching and learning: The teacher–student relationship must be grounded in what Noddings (1984) has termed an "ethic of care." As Goldstein notes, "Caring is not something you are, but rather something you engage in, something you do" (1997, p. 14). In quality teaching and learning contexts, caring involves "stepping out of one's own personal frame of reference and into the other's" (Noddings, 1984, p. 24) during the encounters the teacher has with each student. The intensity and longevity of such encounters will vary. What must remain constant for real caring to occur is a willingness on the part of the "one caring"—the teacher—to give primacy to the "cared for"—the student.

A review of educational literature across subject areas at the elementary level indicates that the components of this framework are widely espoused and well supported. As a former classroom teacher, I fully recognize that day-to-day complexities often limit the extent to which the ideals embodied in this view of quality education can be realized. Theoretically pure examples of teachers who day in and day out authentically engage students in constructivist-oriented, "minds-on" activities through an ethic of care are rare. On the other hand, almost all teachers I have met and/or worked with strive to enact one or more of the mutually reinforcing components of this framework into their teaching every day.

METHODOLOGY

I began my research at Glendale Elementary school by conducting several site visits during the 1999–2000 school year. Later, I moved into a nearby neighborhood, so during the 2000–2001 academic year, I was on site an average of three full school days per week. During this time, I averaged 20 hours per week observing teachers at work in their classrooms. I conducted both individual interviews and focus group interviews with teachers, administrators, parents, a school board member, and community members. In addition, I analyzed on-line and archived district- and school-level documents to assess the origins of curricular and administrative efforts designed to improve student achievement.

I frequently analyzed the data, focusing on two key questions: How have district- and school-level administrators and teachers responded to the Texas accountability system (or TAS)? What impact has this response had on the overall quality of instruction received by the children at Glendale Elementary? I looked for "patterned regularities" (Wolcott, 1994) and checked the accuracy of possible patterns through follow-up interviews or follow-up document analysis. In pouring over and evaluating more than 2,000 pages of field notes, documents, and interview transcripts, I engaged in what Denzin (1989) refers to as "interpretive interactionalism." In other words, I derived tentative themes through a coding of the data and, in many instances, I challenged these tentative codes by re-coding the data (Miles & Huberman, 1994).

RESEARCH SETTING: SCHOOL AND COMMUNITY

The newly attached façade of Glendale Elementary School belies the fact that the school has served the Twin Oaks community for over 40 years. A walk through the open-air hallways reveals classrooms, computer labs, and a library. All are colorful and rich in resources. Students, wearing some combination of the school's red, white, and blue uniform dress code, greet visitors with a friendly smile and a "hello," or "*hola.*" Although Glendale's student body consists mainly of Latino children from low socioeconomic status (SES) families, nothing about the facility projects an image of a "poor" urban school.

Located 20 minutes from the downtown area of a major city in Texas, Twin Oaks ISD encompasses approximately 44 square miles and approximately 180,000 residents. The district's total student population is 31,357; almost half the students, 15,920, attend one of the 25 elementary schools (TEA, 2000a).[4] At Glendale Elementary, the total enrollment is 738; the student body is 68% Latino (compared to 44% for the district as a whole), 18% White (compared to 41%), 11% African American (compared to 7%), and 3% Asian/Pacific Islander (compared to 8%). District documents reveal that between the 1984–1985 and 1999–2000 school years, Glendale's overall student population nearly doubled, and the percentage of Latino student rose from less than 15% to 68%.[5] In interviews, teachers, administrators, and long-time community residents repeatedly described the district's demographic shift as "dramatic."

A review of Glendale's TAAS data for 1994–2000 reveals significant gains in test scores for all student groups and progress toward closing the achievement gap between student groups (see Table 5.1).

In every year since the inception of the current accountability scheme, Glendale has earned at least an "Acceptable" rating from the Texas Education Agency (TEA) based on the students' performance on the TAAS. In 1997, the school earned the more coveted "Recognized" rating.[5] This record represents a significant achievement, given the poverty, mobility, and limited English proficiency (LEP) of an increasingly large percentage of the student body. As Table 5.2 demonstrates, each year over a quarter of the students either left or newly entered Glendale; and both the overall percentage of students classified by the state as "economically disadvantaged" and the overall percentage of LEP students increased dramatically. Meanwhile, the overall percentage of students the state allows to be exempted from the TAAS because of language or special education issues decreased significantly.

TABLE 5.1
Percentage of Glendale Students Passing the TAAS, 1994–2000

	'94	'95	'96	'97*	'98	'99**	2000	%change
All Students	54	59	61.4	78	82.5	72.9	70	+16%
(N =)	(617)	(725)	(768)	(732)	(728)	(737)	(738)	
AfricanAm.	35.9	35	26.1	53.3	50	65.2	75	+39.1%
Hispanic	35.2	47	48.1	71.4	85.5	70.5	60.2	+25%
White	69.1	80.8	77.8	86.7	83.7	75.8	86.4	+17.3
Econ. Disadv.	39.4	44.4	44	70.1	75.8	69.3	60.5	+21.1

Note. *School earned a "Recognized" rating. All other years, school earned an "Acceptable" rating.
**Beginning in 1999, results include special-education test takers in third through fifth grades and Spanish TAAS test takers in grades 3 and 4.

TABLE 5.2
Demographic and Testing Data for Glendale Elementary, 1994–2000

(Percentages of Glendale students fitting each category)

	'94	'95	'96	'97	'98	'99	2000	%Change
Mobility Rate	30	30.1	30	28.4	24.8	24.4	25.9	− 4.1%
Econ. Disadv.	68.1	71.2	74.3	75.5	77.7	78.4	79	+10.9%
L.E.P.*	34.4	40.4	41.5	41.3	49.3	48.7	49.8	+15.4
Exemp. Rates**								
L.E.P.[6]	NA	23.8	20.5	16.1	15.8	15.8	9.9	−13.9%
Special Edu.	NA	17.1	10	10	6	6	7.3	−10.4%

*Limited English Proficient
**Percentage of students exempted from taking TAAS because of language or special education issues.

NEW YEAR, NEW RESPONSE

Based on several interviews with teachers and administrators and limited classroom observations during the 1999–2000 school year, I tentatively concluded that the TAS had motivated school personnel to improve overall educational quality at the school. The accountability system had revealed academic weaknesses and failures among low-income children of color. In response, Glendale's principal and teachers took such actions as funding teachers' professional development and purchasing classroom libraries of "leveled texts."[7] Together, these efforts improved the quality of literacy instruction in the classrooms. Demonstrating their understanding of instructional strategies such as "guided reading" (Fountas & Pinnell, 1996), teachers used the expanded classroom libraries to deliver higher quality, more individualized literacy instruction.

As I settled into the school at the beginning of the 2000–2001 school year, I fully expected that my ethnographic investigation of Glendale Elementary would produce a complex portrait of administrators and teachers at one urban elementary school who had been motivated by the TAS to improve educational quality. It soon became clear, however, that a dramatic shift underway at the district level would significantly affect Glendale's current and future response to the TAS. Teachers sensed that complying with the plethora of new mandates from the district would require devoting more instructional time to the TAAS. Few anticipated the magnitude of the time and effort that would be expected, however.

In early October, almost two months into the school year, Glendale staff learned the details of the district's new "High Performance Blueprint" from the local newspaper. An article titled, "District Working on 'Recognized' Status" described a new data-utilization scheme called Schools Working to Ensure Every Student Exceeds Exemplary Performance (SWEEP). The district superintendent explained that a newly purchased data software package would make possible systematic "sorting and analyzing [of] test scores." This, in turn, would allow teachers to more effectively "identify student weaknesses." "But," the superintendent warned, "only strong leadership by principals and area superintendents can ensure that the necessary interventions are taking place."[8] The article also noted that teams of curriculum writers would be producing curricula designed to address students' weaknesses, and that, according to the superintendent, teachers would be expected to "stick close to the approved curriculum."

Following the publication of this article, one outspoken but talented classroom teacher voiced some of the collective angst in the teachers' lounge when she shrilled, "*Teach* the curriculum!? *Teach* the curriculum? Oh, that makes me so mad!" She bemoaned the dwindling amount of time she had available to "teach the curriculum," given the number of her planning hours that were now needed for bookkeeping and other administrative tasks. One new mandate, for example, required teachers to create and submit to administrators detailed yearly lesson plans in each subject area. Teachers were expected to specify when and how they would address specific state curricular objectives as well as TAAS objectives. These plans were to be provided to administrators as initial "evidence" that teachers were "sticking close to the approved curriculum." In addition, this teacher lamented the substantial amount of instructional time now given over to conducting an expanded battery of reading assessments for each student.[9]

Glendale teachers repeatedly expressed their unhappiness with new district-level mandates, especially the call for schools to administer more TAAS practice tests. The new requirements increased teacher workloads, adding even more work hours onto their days, but, just as importantly, they stole instructional time away from activities teachers believed to be of more importance. Furthermore, teachers frequently remarked on the negative impact the district's demands had on the overall atmosphere of the school. In the first month of the school year, for instance, one veteran third-grade teacher noted that the school climate was "*nothing* like it has been the last three years. *Nothing*!" [emphasis in original] Teachers (and school administrators) were skeptical of the district's publicly professed explanation that the changes were needed to ensure that every student would "exceed exemplary performance." Instead, many saw SWEEP as an attempt on the part of "new and very ambitious" district-level administrators to improve their own standing in the community by forcing teachers to do something they had not previously been expected to do: systematically teach the TAAS.

Among the components of the district's blueprint, the expanded testing and assessment regimen proved to be the most detrimental. The overall quality of classroom-level education suffered on two counts: testing and assessment stole whole days, even weeks, of valuable instructional time. Moreover, being constantly bombarded with disaggregated test data and knowing that district administrators were overtly monitoring these data to see whether the school would achieve the coveted Recognized status produced such high levels of anxiety among teachers that many felt compelled to spend even more instructional time engaging in TAAS-like drilling. Thus, the curricula narrowed, telescoping around not only the content, but the format of the TAAS.

Lost Instructional Time

When I asked teachers to calculate the total amount of time required to individually administer the district's expanded battery of reading assessments to each child, I received a range of responses. One kindergarten teacher estimated "an hour or so" per child, while another reported spending two hours per child (diverting 30 hours of instructional time for the entire class). A first-grade teacher estimated 45 minutes per child.

The time given over to assessments either prevented or made it extremely difficult for teachers to engage students in higher-quality curricular activities during most of the first month and the last six weeks of the school year. Teachers explained that while they were occupied individually assessing children, they assigned relatively simple, non-challenging activities to the rest of the class. They gave priority to cut-and-paste or paper-and-pencil worksheets that children could complete quietly and independently. As one first-grade teacher recounted,

> . . . [W]e started out with [activities] they knew from kindergarten . . .
> or [an activity] they could pretty much do independently. [I] just
> found lots of easy, *easy*, worksheet activities that they should already
> have some kind of background in so that they could just do those independently while we do our *two weeks' worth of assessing*. [emphasis in original]

Another teacher described her students' activities during the individual testing periods as involving

> *Lots* of seat work, independent seatwork. . . . [I would tell them]
> "Do that by yourself. Don't come and bother me when I'm testing."
> That went on probably two to three weeks into October. And that's
> not normal. I *hated* it. [emphasis in original]

In early November, when I asked a teacher if she felt her students had been affected by the lost instructional time, she quickly responded,

> They *definitely* suffered because they could be way beyond where
> they are now. Those [students] that are strong and good, well they
> made that growth anyway, because they were going to because they
> already had that foundation. . . . [But the weaker students] needed
> that one-on-one in small little groups, with me sitting with three or

four. I couldn't do it for two or three weeks because I had to this test, and this test, and this and this and this. [emphasis in original]

In addition to the time loss occasioned by the administration of reading assessments, six full days of teaching were lost to the administration of three TAAS practice tests. In October, January, and March, students in the third through fifth grades took a full-scale practice TAAS. Many teachers acknowledged that TAAS practice tests did yield "valuable information" useful for guiding and/or reorganizing their classroom instruction. Most felt, however, that three full-scale TAAS administrations (versus the previous single annual practice test) were "too much."

The Curriculum Narrows

As the year progressed, in faculty meetings and grade-level meetings, teachers were bombarded with scores and other data generated by the TAAS practice tests. This information was accompanied by stern messages from district-level administrators warning teachers that "time is short and the stakes are high," or urging teachers to use the data to "work smarter, not harder." Anxiety levels among and between administrators and teachers rose as rumors circulated that the school might not "make it" (i.e., be awarded "Recognized" status). Their readings of the data from the practice tests at Glendale prompted district-level administrators called "Instructional Specialists" to make frequent visits to the school. Consistently, they advised teachers to link their teaching more explicitly to the format of the TAAS (e.g., directing teachers to end each lesson with an actual TAAS-formatted question).

Prompted by these official warnings and instructions, as well as by their own anxieties, Glendale teachers began to spend more and more time "teaching the test." The breadth and depth of the curriculum presented to students narrowed, telescoping around material specifically covered on the TAAS. As one third-grade teacher explained:

We just don't have the time to teach integrated units. Time is a *luxury*, now. It used to be, if you felt like you wanted to try something new, and you could justify it, it was fine to do. But *now*? Boy, if it's not a *testable* TEK (Texas Essential Knowledge) in math or reading, don't teach it. Don't go there. We don't have time for it. We have to get these scores up, and that's a narrow focus, and I don't like that. . . . [emphasis in original]

This teacher, who frequently demonstrated exemplary classroom instruction, left Glendale at year's end.

In early spring, anxiety levels concerning whether or not the school would "make it" were so high that the principal directed the third-grade teachers to write "NA"—"Not Applicable"—on students' report cards for their third-quarter science and social studies grades. According to one veteran third-grade teacher, "We were told to forget teaching science and social studies and focus on reading and math for the third quarter." When I asked her if this had ever been done before, she exclaimed, "No! It was *never* like this in the past." [emphasis in original]

The narrowing of the curriculum was not lost on students. In a group interview with fifth-grade teachers, one teacher reported that several of her students had formed the opinion that science and social studies were "not important because they are not on TAAS." Moreover, her students put far less effort into completing their science work compared to mathematics. Another fifth-grade teacher confirmed her colleague's observations and quickly added, "But what do you expect? We're teaching the TAAS *all* the time." [emphasis in original]

"Actual Teaching" versus "TAAS Teaching"

During my classroom observations, I began to notice an overt dualism in teaching as the year progressed. In many classrooms, teachers consciously divided their time between "actual teaching" and "TAAS teaching." An especially clear example of this pedagogical dualism involves a fifth-grade classroom. The teacher's ability to draw students into short novels, or "chapter books," and her encouragement of their efforts to represent what they knew and liked about each book in a variety of ways had impressed me on several occasions when I was present in the classroom as an observer. The teacher permitted multiple interpretations of story events and allowed students a range of options—including making dioramas, posters, and mobiles—to represent their understanding of each book. The students' creations were displayed prominently around the classroom.

During an interview, I asked this teacher to explain her instructional goals. She replied, "My goal is to make them read independently and discuss this book independently." To encourage independence, she pushed students to relate stories to themselves and their lives. It is this style of instruction that she refers to as her "actual teaching," and it stands in stark contrast to what she calls her "TAAS teaching." I observed the latter as well. On some occasions, she would clearly signal the change. For instance, she instructed her students to "Forget *everything* in your head. Use an eraser and get rid of it!" Later on, she reminded them, "Everything you need to know is right here," as she displayed one of many TAAS passages on the overhead screen.

In a fourth-grade classroom, I observed a teacher struggle to "TAAS teach." Her difficulty was not in how to help her students learn to summarize a story, an event, or an experience through "actual teaching," but how to "TAAS teach" the art of summarizing. She started the lesson by reminding her class that a good summary answers "who, what, where, when, why, and how" questions. The students seemed to have little difficulty providing answers to these questions for the story they had read and appeared comfortable offering story details as well. As students responded, the teacher wrote their answers on a dry-erase board.

Once the answers to the who, what, etc., questions had been recorded, however, the teacher seemed to switch into "TAAS teaching" mode. "That's *not* a correct summarization," she informed her class. "A correct summarization is only one sentence long." She then asked the students to generate a one-sentence summary that included the "most important" information about the story. Although the students had little difficulty summarizing the story based on the information already available, they struggled mightily to construct a single-sentence summary. The teacher listened to the students' responses and critiqued each summary as "wrong" because it did meet not the single-sentence criterion. She then set out to demonstrate how to use the available information to construct a "correct," single-sentence summary. As the class helped negotiate the "most important" details of the story and the teacher began constructing a "correct" summarization, she realized how very difficult it was to create a single-sentence summary of a story with so many events and characters. After many attempts, mostly without the help of the students, she finally produced the following "correct" summary of the story: "Patricia, Stewart, and Weinstein wanted to buy Ms. Eula a bonnet she always wanted, so they sold decorated eggs at Mr. Kapinski's store, but after all Mr. Kapinski gave them the bonnet for free." Although her summary fits the TAAS rule, the sentence is poorly structured, even grammatically problematic.

In a follow-up interview with this teacher, I asked her how she had come to define a "correct" summarization as one consisting of a single sentence. She reported that she had learned this from a district Instructional Specialist (who had also explained many other "TAAS teaching" rules to her). She confessed that prior to receiving these teaching tips from the Instructional Specialist, she had been "doing it wrong" with her students.

Teacher–Student Relationships Undermined

Teachers who felt compelled to engage in what they considered inferior modes of instruction for extended periods of time experienced a great deal of dissonance. Replacing the previous child-centric reform efforts at Glendale with a district-mandated emphasis on achieving Recognized status as a first priority for the school left many teachers feeling remorseful, even guilty, over having "neglected" their students.

A kindergarten bilingual education teacher described an incident that occurred in her classroom that demonstrated to her the impact on the children of the school's new focus on ratings. After reprimanding the class for leaving the activity center areas in utter disarray, she asked the class, "What do you need me to do to make sure this doesn't happen again?" After a short silence, a little girl responded, "*Necesitamos más ayuda* (We need more help)." The child's remark alerted the teacher that to meet the demands of the new assessment regimen, she had diverted her attention from the daily educational needs of her children. At the same time, this teacher fully recognized that assessment was now a crucial part of her teaching and that assessment results were supposed to guide her instruction.

In interviews, teachers acknowledged that the assessments did provide them with some useful information about their students, but these same teachers questioned the overall worth of the assessments and TAAS drilling, given the impact of this kind of instruction on student–teacher relationships. One teacher commented that the time given over to constant testing actually prevented her from "knowing" her students in more complex, personal ways. "How can you have a parent conference [in October] to report on the student when 50 percent of your instructional time has been taken up with assessments?" This teacher went on to explain that six weeks into the school year, she still felt ill prepared to speak with parents about their child's strengths and weaknesses because so much of her time had been given over to test-based assessments of individual children:

> It was horrible! . . . I was *never* so embarrassed, reporting to the parents, "I don't know a whole lot about [your child]. This is what the *testing* showed, but one-on-one, I can't tell you a whole lot because

we've not met that often in our small instructional groups. [emphasis in original]

"It was *very* embarrassing," she went on, "professionally, and just as a person sharing what I knew about their child and what I was going to do to help them. It was the most awkward year for [parent–teacher] conferences. I hated them." Given that this teacher had taught for nearly 20 years and was one of the school's strongest teachers, her comments seem especially poignant.

As the 2000–2001 school year progressed and the deleterious effects of the district-mandated response to the accountability system mounted, I sought a deeper understanding of the new approach. I reviewed past and present district documents and conducted extensive interviews with veteran teachers, administrators, community members, and a school board member. Through a comparative analysis of the district's varied responses to the TAS over time, I discerned two broad types of approaches: a reform-focused response and a ratings-focused response. Each is informed by distinct—and vastly different—underlying assumptions concerning children, teachers, and the value of curricula and pedagogy. The next section examines these two responses and compares their underlying assumptions.

Accountability and Children: "Special Needs"
verus "Impediments"

At the heart of the district's earlier reform-focused responses to the TAS were the educational needs of the rapidly changing student population in general, and the educational and social needs of the "new" student in particular. Both the district and the school initiated efforts designed to enhance teachers' understanding about the multifaceted nature of learning and the acquisition of knowledge. Moreover, these reform-focused efforts pushed teachers to recognize the new students' social and emotional needs and to create more and varied opportunities for these students to experience academic success. Notable examples of district support for this student-centered approach include funding the implementation (and the associated training) of innovative teaching strategies (e.g., see Caine & Caine, 1994; Chipman, 1986; Sylwester, 1995) such as "Tribes" (Gibbs, 1987), "multiple intelligences" (Gardner, 1983), and "brain-based" learning. In interviews, veteran teachers frequently cited these strategies as having a major influence on their teaching.

In contrast, the district's newly formulated ratings-focused response constructed low-income, LEP, Latino students as "challenges," even "risks," with the potential to sink the district's chances for winning a Recognized rating. In 1998, the school district hired a high-profile accounting agency to conduct a "School Performance Analysis."[10] According to the report's executive summary, "The purpose of this service [was] to provide the district and its constituents with an objective analysis of how effectively the district maximizes the educational return on its resources." The authors of the analysis concluded that the district "[was] yielding a good and improving educational return on its resources," and they acknowledged that "student performance" had improved, and that the district had "posted impressive gains in student test scores, both in absolute terms and relative to peers." At the same time, however, the School Performance Analysis contains findings that, if not quite constituting invidious distinctions, do seem to construct low-income, LEP, Latino students as a serious stumbling block. For example, the report describes "the large and expanding LEP and economically disadvantaged enrollment" as "a principal factor" that could "impede [the district's] return on resources."

Accountability and Teachers: "Professionals" verus "People"

In the context of the district's reform-focused response to the TAS, teachers, especially veteran teachers who had experienced the dramatic demographic changes firsthand, were positioned as professionals capable of expanding their expertise sufficiently to effectively teach the district's "new" students. One school administrator who had experienced many of the reform-focused efforts as a classroom teacher recalled the district's overt efforts to "re-tool" teachers to "empower" them to become stronger professionals. Several veteran teachers made independent reference to the district's reform-focused response efforts as part of a "fifteen-year plan" to improve overall educational quality and raise all students' achievement levels. During the 1999–2000 school year and early in the 2000–2001 school year, most veteran teachers at Glendale seemed to believe that this plan was still underway and that real progress was being made.

The district's ratings-focused reforms, by contrast, presented teachers with an expanding list of curricular and pedagogical "nonnegotiables." Rather than focusing on the professional capacities of teachers to improve student achievement levels, district administrators emphasized strict adherence to an approved agenda. As the superintendent explained (in the local newspaper's coverage of the district's "high performance blueprint"), "We're not hiring *people* to go in and teach what they feel good about. We're hiring them to teach the curriculum." [emphasis added] The superintendent later reiterated this clear preference for "strong instructional leadership" over teachers' classroom expertise, noting that "only strong leadership by principals and area superintendents can ensure that the necessary interventions are taking place." At Glendale, the "necessary interventions" meant teachers were expected to more explicitly link their teaching to the format of the TAAS.

This shift from teacher quality concerns to instructional leadership concerns was facilitated by the findings of a second study of the Twin Oaks ISD. During the 1999–2000 school year, district administrators and researchers from a major Texas university jointly investigated the interaction between the district's recent reform efforts and the achievement levels of all students. The study found significant gains in TAAS scores among all student groups between 1994 and 1999, but the researchers noted that these gains had occurred primarily at the elementary level and not at the secondary level.

The authors of the study's final report explained this uneven success by suggesting that although the district may have adequately assessed the "problem of the problem" (e.g., see Getzels, 1975; Getzels & Csikszentmihalyi, 1976)—that is, administrators had accurately identified the lingering achievement gap—they had been less effective at formulating the "problem of the solution"—that is, the district's efforts to close this gap had been less effective at the secondary level. In arriving at this conclusion, the authors relied on results of a survey that asked principals to list any and all reform efforts related to improving student achievement. Based on the responses, the authors identified 74 reform efforts underway within the district and suggested that such a high number indicated a lack of focus. However, a veteran teacher who participated in the study at both the school and the district level believes that the wording of the survey instrument led principals to over-identify reform efforts. According to this teacher, principals, who are expected to demonstrate that they have been doing everything humanly possible to increase student achievement, created "laundry lists" of teaching strategies rather than limiting themselves to reporting only ongoing, school-wide reform efforts.

This over-identification of "reform efforts" proved to be a powerful tool in the hands of district-level administrators, who were eager to promote strong instructional leadership models of educational administration. The move toward a ratings-focused response more explicitly focused on TAAS scores could be justified as a much-needed means of reestablishing control over what appeared to be a chaotic array of school-level reforms. At a public presentation of the study's findings, the district's chief academic officer (CAO) stated, "We were *shocked* to find out just how much was going on out there . . . that we had absolutely no control over."[11] [emphasis in original] In articulating the new ratings-focused response, administrators shifted the discourse away from teacher quality and child-centric curriculum and pedagogy toward the importance of strong administrative leadership. The next section traces the effects of this shift in discourse on the value assigned to classroom instruction.

Accountability and Pedagogy: "Child-Centric versus "TAAS-Focused"

The district's reform-focused efforts had constructed "academic success" broadly, incorporating both the educational and the social and emotional needs of low-income, LEP children of color. The ratings-focused efforts adopted a far more narrow definition, one that gave priority to instruction explicitly linked to TAAS content and format. This redefinition was shaped by the second study's evaluation of district- and school-level efforts designed to close the student achievement gap. Investigators attached a high value (i.e., "direct impact") to pedagogical efforts that increased TAAS scores and a low value (i.e., "unintended impact") to reform efforts that did not help increase TAAS scores. The authors of the study interestingly cite as effective certain reform-focused response efforts favored by Glendale teachers, namely "brain-based teaching" and "multiple intelligences" approaches. For instance, "brain-based teaching" is described as having had a "direct impact," helping raise TAAS scores for *all* students, and especially for those at the elementary level. The implementation of "multiple intelligences" approaches also could be useful, but it had an "unintended impact" of "reducing the focus on drill in basic skills in favor of other artistic, musical, or physical activities. As a result, students' TAAS scores may not show improvement or may even decline." It is not clear how investigators were able to so closely correlate the relationship between teaching strategies and TAAS data, nor how they could link the size of the achievement gap to specific types of reform efforts.

The final piece of the ratings-focused response puzzle, and the piece that most directly links the two studies of the Twin Oaks ISD to the SWEEP initiative, is a booklet titled "High Performance Blueprint" issued by the district's Office of Accountability. Laden with business-efficiency jargon, the booklet opens with this "strategy statement": "We are embarking on a comprehensive benchmarking strategy resulting in continuous quality, increased productivity, and cost improvement for the district." Next comes a quote from noted business author George Labovitz (1997), "Our research and our experience have convinced us that growth and profit are ultimately the result of alignment between people, customers, strategy, and processes." The booklet then describes the district's efforts to create an organizational structure with a "laser-light focus" on increasing student achievement and earning a higher state rating. To help bring about this new laser-light focus, the district's thirteen "Strategic Goals-Objectives" were "streamlined" to four. The first new Goal-Objective states, "[The district] will be identified as an 'Exemplary' district by ensuring increased and sustained academic achievement for each student."

DISCUSSION

As Skrla and colleagues (2000b, p. 18) point out, "State level policies [such as the Texas Accountability System] are blunt instruments." My experiences at Glendale Elementary School over the past two years, however, lead me to conclude that although the Texas Accountability System might indeed be a complex equation made up of multiple, interacting variables, it is the TAAS test that is the blunt instrument. For teachers and children at Glendale, accountability is TAAS and TAAS scores are, as Linda McNeil (2000b) has observed, "the *only* language of currency" (p. 730) at the school [emphasis in original]. Drawing on this currency, local administrators created curricular policies that reduced and truncated instructional time, telescoped curricula around content and processes that are "testable," facilitated a dual, almost schizophrenic view of pedagogy, and undermined the relationship between teacher and student.

Consistent with the findings of Smith (1991), who studied the impact of "external" standardized testing on the work of teachers, the newly expanded assessment and testing regimen took away "real" instructional time as well as what one teacher referred to as "build up time and recuperation time." Teachers understood that TAAS practice scores would be monitored by district-level administrators and would be used, among other things, to judge teachers' abilities. Thus, they felt compelled to leave nothing to chance. They transformed "build-up time" into practice time, helping their students prepare for the practice TAAS tests. Realizing how difficult it was for their students to sit quietly for hours on end, sometimes for consecutive days, teachers then transformed part of the "recuperation time" following the TAAS practice administrations into "free time," "game time," or other non-curricular activities that allowed students to relax. Most third- through fifth-grade teachers spent the remaining recuperation time reviewing the practice TAAS questions with their students, item by item.

As the disaggregated data from each administration of the TAAS practice poured into the school, so too did explicit and implicit messages of disappointment and concern on the part of district-level administrators. In meetings, teachers heard, "If we're going to 'make it,' we're going to have to . . ."; and "Time is short, and stakes are high." So warned, teachers returned to their classrooms and did what they were "supposed to do." Glendale's assistant principal acknowledged that the area superintendent would be surprised to see that the children were being taught the TAAS on such a consistent basis. "But," she quickly added, "what does he expect!?"

The unrelenting emphasis on the TAAS narrowed the curriculum within subject areas as well as between subjects. Not only were science and social studies officially abandoned, but language arts narrowed to TAAS reading and mathematics became TAAS "problem solving." Pedagogy did not telescope around "useless facts," as others have warned (e.g., McNeil, 2000a), however. Instead, it focused on problem-solving strategies that promoted the specific thinking processes students would need to decipher and then answer TAAS-formatted questions. For example, in the third through fifth grades, a patchwork of "strategy strips" ("If the question asks you to . . . then you . . . ," etc.) was taped to each student's desk, and posters displaying similar TAAS tips dominated the available wall space. Students were constantly reminded to "go to your strategy strips" or "look at the poster" and were repeatedly taken, lock-step, through these strategies. Instructional primacy was placed on making sure children followed the steps exactly. As a result, teachers exacted more and more compliance from students. Children were reprimanded for drawing on self-created strategies even though these strategies might have been more useful to them as individuals. The TAAS problem-solving strategies did not help students recognize and understand what Bruner (1960) referred to as the "structure of the discipline," but were instead focused solely on helping students decipher a TAAS-formatted problem (e.g., strategies for "finding the math" in a word problem). Thus, although teachers were required to teach these problem-solving techniques, they appeared to have little value outside the context of a standardized, multiple-choice test such as the TAAS.

Describing the dualistic teaching that the ratings-focused response promoted, one fifth-grade teacher openly acknowledged that she struggled to make sense of the "two opposing schools of thought" she was presented. One advocated that students bring no prior knowledge to their reading; the other advocated that students mine their prior knowledge to comprehend, or make meaning of what they read. This teacher eventually concluded that, "One is for 'real life' and the other is for the TAAS." To which another fifth-grade teacher added cynically, "But the TAAS *is* 'real life.'"

This notion of the TAAS as "real life" was a recurring theme. Teachers were frequently told that not viewing the TAAS as important, not explicitly linking their teaching to the TAAS, was a disservice to students. For example, the district administration arranged for a school visit by a secondary teacher who has had high levels of TAAS success with her students. She acknowledged that she is known as "the TAAS lady." She justified explicitly teaching the TAAS to students this way: "It is important because to do *anything* in life, kids are going to have to take tests." [emphasis in original] She pointed out that to get into the local community college, students are required to take a standardized test, and "even to work down at the corner 7-Eleven [convenience] store, people are required to pass an English-language proficiency test." This configuration of the TAAS as having "real world applications" seemed designed to motivate both the students who had to take the test and the teachers who had to prepare them for it.

Neither the district's reform-focused nor its ratings-focused responses sufficiently addressed or challenged the predominantly White teaching staff's "deficit" orientations (Valencia, 1997) toward low-income children of color. As teachers were exposed to "multiple learning styles" or "brain-based teaching," their deficit orientations emerged in subtle ways. For example, that African American children are body-kinesthetic learners and that Latino students are more social, and thus learn better by working in group situations, were commonly held myths at Glendale. These "child-centric" modes of instruction did, however, push teachers to create more opportunities for children of color to experience academic success. The forms of "deficit thinking" (Valencia, 1997) generated as a result of the district's ratings-focused response not only had no equivalent positive effect, they seemed to nurture old stereotypes. For example, teachers trying to account for continuing low TAAS scores among Glendale's third-grade bilingual education students hypothesized that Hispanic students had a difficult time with the problem-solving and measurement TAAS objectives because they lacked proper role modeling at home. Glendale's assistant principal, in summarizing the substance of the teachers' meeting for me, explained that Hispanic children were not good problem solvers because of an emphasis on *machismo* in Hispanic culture. When a Hispanic family is faced with a problem, she continued, women and children are told to leave so the men in the family can resolve the problem. Hispanic children are not good measurers because there are no measuring instruments in Hispanic households. Because Mexican recipes call for a "pinch" of this or a "dash" of that, she reasoned, mothers don't use measuring spoons or cups when they cook. Consequently, according this assistant principal, their children never see measurement being modeled.

No doubt, these deficit orientations were present prior to the initiation of the ratings-focused response, but the TAAS-related pressures during the 2000–2001 school year created conditions that allowed such orientations to surface in far more ugly and potentially damaging ways. Low-income LEP students were constructed as "impediments" to district success. Teachers were explicitly told that past modes of instruction that incorporated "multiple learning styles" were not only not effective but had the "unintended consequence" of actually lowering TAAS scores. What teachers had come to understand as "quality instruction," largely through exposure to the district's reform-focused initiatives, was undermined. As one teacher put it, "We've gone from trying to address the needs of the children to trying to address the needs of the test."

CONCLUSION

As the "reform by comparison" (Corbett & Wilson, 1991) movement in Texas has grown, so too have the pressures brought to bear on school districts to improve education. Long-time residents of Twin Oaks who have been active in educational politics in the district suggested in interviews that local political and economic issues played a significant role in the district's newly formulated ratings-focused response to the TAS. Local politicians broadcast school ratings as a way to attract business and real estate companies, which in turn attract middle- and upper-middle-class home buyers—and voters. It is nearly impossible to drive through any major Texas community without seeing a new housing development with a nearby billboard assuring parents that buying a home here will make it possible to "Send your children to a 'Recognized' school." Along with commanding higher real estate prices, a district with high ratings can boost local tax revenues and, potentially, protect political incumbents. With the Twin Oaks area struggling to meet the costs of increased social services coupled with a deteriorating tax base due to "White flight" and lowered property values, local politicians and business groups pressured the district to improve its rating.

Glendale Elementary School's students improved their scores on the 2001 TAAS. Nevertheless, I could not find a single Glendale teacher who believed that the overall quality of education the children received had increased. I have not yet completed analyzing the data I gathered over the last two years—and continue to gather. Still, one conclusion seems clear: As educators shift their focus from concerns related to student achievement to concerns related to earning a higher state rating, overall educational quality suffers.

NOTES

1. The school and district names are pseudonyms.
2. Over the past three years, Glendale has received funds to develop the three Annenberg imperatives: Increase teacher learning, personalize the learning environment, and reduce school size. By "reducing school size," this imperative targeted school reorganization following a school-within-a-school model.
3. This quote and the ones provided in later paragraphs are taken from information posted on the district's website. Protecting the school and district's anonymity precludes providing the URL for the site.
4. This data covers the 1999–2000 school year.
5. These data are taken from information posted on the district's website. Protecting the school and district's anonymity precludes providing the URL for the site.
6. The initiation of the Spanish TAAS in 1999 may have contributed to a slight decrease in the number of LEP exemptions, but only for students in third grade. According to Texas policy, only children enrolled in a bilingual education (BE) classroom—or those children receiving instruction in Spanish—can take the Spanish TAAS. Because Glendale has an early exit model BE program, all English Language Learners (ELLs) are transitioned to "regular" classrooms in fourth grade. Thus, LEP exemptions are used exclusively for fourth and fifth graders. And the number of those exempted in the fourth and fifth grades has been reduced.
7. In a leveled text, the reading difficulty level is held constant throughout the book.
8. Just prior to the 1999–2000 school year, the Twin Oaks ISD reorganized into "learning communities." Headed by an area superintendent, these

units contain schools in an elementary, middle school, junior high school, and high school "feeder" pattern.

9. The Texas Education Code, §28.006(c), states that each school district shall administer a reading instrument twice per year for each child at kindergarten, grade 1, and grade 2.

10. The performance analysis was conducted by Standard and Poor's, which is a branch of the publishing–testing company, McGraw-Hill. Kohn (2002) has warned that publishing companies such as McGraw-Hill use "front" organizations like Standards and Poor's to shape state- and local-level curriculum policy that benefits them financially. This connection between the Twin Oaks ISD, curriculum and assessment policy, and Standard and Poor's/McGraw-Hill is still being explored.

11. At this same meeting, the CAO was challenged concerning the difference between a "reform" and a "teaching strategy." He acknowledged that there may indeed have been an over-identification of actual "reforms."

REFERENCES

Bruer, J. T. (1999). In search of brain-based education. *Phi Delta Kappan, 80*(9) 649–657.

Bruner, J. S. (1960). *The process of education.* Cambridge, MA: Harvard University Press.

Caine, R. N., & Caine, G. (1994). *Making connections: Teaching and the human brain.* New York: Addison-Wesley.

Cary, D. A., Fennema, E., Carpenter, T. P., & Franke, M. L. (1995). Equity and mathematics education. In W. G. Secada, E. Fennema, & L. B. Adajian (Eds.), *New directions for equity in mathematics education* (pp. 93–125). Cambridge: University Press.

Chipman, S. F. (1986). Integrating three perspectives on learning. In S. L. Friedman, K. A. Klivington, & R. W. Peterson (Eds.), *The brain, cognition, and education* (pp. 203–32). Orlando, FL: Academic Press.

Corbett, D., & Wilson, B. (1991). *Testing, reform, and rebellion.* Norwood, NJ: Ablex.

Denzin, N. K. (1989). *Interpretive interactionalism.* Newbury Park, CA: Sage.

Fountas, I. C., & Pinnell, G. S. (1996). *Guided reading: Good first teaching for all children.* Portsmouth, NH: Heinemann.

Gardner, H. (1983). *Frames of mind: The theory of multiple intelligences.* New York: Basic Books, Inc.

Getzels, J. W. (1975). Problem-finding and the inventiveness of solutions. *Journal of Creative Behavior, 9*(1), 12–18.

Getzels, J. W., & Csikszentmihalyi, M. (1976). *The creative vision: A longitudinal study of problem finding in art.* New York: Wiley.

Gibbs, J. (1987). *TRIBES: A new way of learning and being together.* Santa Rosa, CA: Center Source Publications.

Goldstein, L. S. (1997). *Teaching with love: A feminist approach to early child-hood education.* New York: Peter Lang.

Guerrero, M., & Sloan, K. (2001). A descriptive analysis of four exemplary K–3 Spanish reading programs in Texas: Are they really exemplary? *Bilingual Research Journal, 25*(1, 2), 253–280.

Hoffman, J. V., Pennington, J., Assaf, L., & Paris, S. G. (2000). *High stakes test-ing in reading: Today in Texas, tomorrow?* Paper presented at the annual meeting of the American Educational Research Association, New Orleans, LA, April, 2000.

Kohn, A. (2002). The 500-pound gorilla. *Phi Delta Kappan, 84*(2), 112–19.

Labovitz, G. (1997). *The power of alignment.* New York: John Wiley & Sons, Inc.

McNeil, L. (2000a). *Contradictions of school reform: Educational costs of stan-dardized testing.* New York: Routledge.

McNeil, L. (2000b). Creating new inequalities: Contradictions of reform. *Phi Delta Kappan, 81*(10), 728–734.

McNeil, L., & Valenzuela, A. (2000). Harmful effects of the TAAS system of test-ing in Texas: Beneath the accountability rhetoric. In M. Kornhaber, G. Or-field, & M. Kurlandar (Eds.) *Raising standards or raising barriers? Inequity and high-stakes testing in public education* (pp. 127–150). New York: Century Foundation.

Miles, M. B., & Huberman, A. M. (1994). *Qualitative data analysis: An ex-panded sourcebook.* (2nd ed.) Thousand Oaks, CA: Sage.

National Council of Teachers of Mathematics. (1989). *Curriculum and evalua-tion standards for school mathematics.* Reston, VA: Author.

National Council of Teachers of Mathematics. (1991). *Professional standards for teaching mathematics.* Reston, VA: Author.

National Research Council. (1996). *National science education standards: Ob-serve, interact, change, learn.* Washington, D.C.: National Academy Press.

Noddings, N. (1984). *Caring.* Berkeley: University of California Press.

Scheurich, J. J., Skrla, L., & Johnson, J. F. (2000). Thinking carefully about equity and accountability. *Phi Delta Kappan, 84*(4), 293–299.

Schwab, J. J. (1964). Structure of disciplines: Meaning and significances. In G. W. Ford & L. Pugno (Eds.), *The structure of knowledge and the curriculum* (pp. 6–30). Chicago: Rand McNally.

Skrla, L., Scheurich, J. J., & Johnson, J. F. (2000a). *Accountability for equity: Can state policy leverage social justice?* Paper presented at the annual meeting of the American Educational Research Association, New Orleans, LA, April, 2000.

Skrla, L., Scheurich, J. J., & Johnson, J. F. (2000b). *Equity-driven achievement-focused school districts: A report on systemic school success in four Texas school districts serving diverse student populations.* Austin, TX: Charles A. Dana Center.

Smith, M. L. (1991). Put to the test: The effects of external testing on teachers. *Educational Researcher, 20*(5), pp. 8–11.

Sylwester, R. (1995). *A celebration of neurons.* Alexandria, VA: Association for Supervision and Curriculum Development.

Texas Education Agency (TEA). (2000a). *An overview of the Academic Excellence Indicator System for the state of Texas.* Retrieved June 12, 2001. Available at: http://www.tea.state.tx.us/perfreport/aeis/about/.aeis.html

Texas Education Agency (TEA). (2000b). *Selected AEIS data six year history.* Retrieved June 2, 2001. Available at: http://www.tea.state.tx.us/perfreport/aeis/hist/state.html

Valencia, R. R. (1997). *The evolution of deficit thinking: Educational thought and practice.* London: Falmer.

Valenzuela, A. (1999). *Subtractive schooling: U.S.-Mexican youth and the politics of caring.* New York: State University of New York Press.

Wolcott, H. F. (1994). The elementary school principal: Notes from a field study. In H. F. Wolcott (Ed.), *Transforming qualitative data: Description, analysis, and interpretation* (pp. 103–148). Thousand Oaks, CA: Sage.

6

Standardized or Sterilized?
Differing Perspectives on the Effects of
High-Stakes Testing in West Texas

ELAINE HAMPTON

When I drive along the Rio Grande in West Texas, I see miles and miles of *Tamarix*, an invasive plant commonly called saltcedar. Much of the habitat along riparian areas is infested with dense stands of this shrub, which was introduced to our continent in the late 1800s. It deposits salt in the soil, creating high saline conditions favorable to its own growth but toxic to most other species. The *Tamarix*'s very extensive root system crowds out other plants, and it uses more water than native species. In some cases, entire riparian areas have dried up as the result of a *Tamarix* invasion. Finally, by eliminating nearly all other grasses, forbs, and small trees and shrubs, *Tamarix* standardizes the riparian community and sterilizes the rich plant diversity (Muzika, 1997).

Assessment can be the stimulus for a rich learning environment that is full of diversity and that provides a fertile bed where thoughts and ideas can sprout and grow.[1] An example of this kind of fertile setting is the annual coming together of high school students who live along the Rio Grande in the United States and Mexico. The students gather to present the results of their river water quality monitoring and to report on the progress of their community environmental improvement projects. They have to defend the quality of their ten water-monitoring tests to students from other teams and to community judges. In addition, they must convince the judges that their projects reflect research into the community's needs and an understanding of several points of view in dealing with environmental issues (Hampton & Licona, 1998).

In too many educational settings today, however, this authentic approach to disciplinary knowledge (see Sloan, this volume) is the exception rather than the rule. More commonly, education occurs in a

"*Tamarix*-infested" environment fraught with rigid standards and high-stakes tests, where the landscape is altered into one of sameness that chokes children's and teachers' creative potential and crowds out the rich variety of curricula necessary to prepare students for a complex future. My goal in this chapter is to provide evidence of the *Tamarix*-like impact of Texas' system of accountability and the sterilizing, if not suffocating, uniformity it engenders.

I report selected findings from a larger study conducted in 1997 that compared a school district in New Mexico where high-stakes testing was not in place with the nearby Ysleta Independent School District[2] in El Paso, Texas, which was participating in the Texas Assessment of Academic Skills (TAAS) high-stakes testing program (Hampton, 1997). In that study, I drew primarily on data gathered from 24 schools (where I had administered surveys and conducted focus groups with teachers and administrators) to examine whether the TAAS supports quality student learning.

In both states, teachers felt the negative effects of testing. Teachers in the Ysleta district, however, reported much more pressure to improve their students' test scores. They narrowed their curriculum to TAAS format and content, and they focused more on students whom they thought were close to the passing range, at the expense of the children who were well above or below this range. For purposes of providing an in-depth examination of how school personnel experience high-stakes testing, I focus herein on the Ysleta Independent School District.

At the time of this study, the Ysleta Independent School District was nationally acclaimed for rapid and impressive increases in test scores. Superintendent Anthony Trujillo took over the Ysleta District in 1992. He implemented a hard-nosed approach to management, focusing on accountability via increased scores on the state test. By 1997, scores on these state tests had risen, especially for Hispanics, and Trujillo and the Ysleta district were credited in national news reports for these increases. Ysleta was nationally recognized by Texas Comptroller John Sharp and U.S. House Speaker Newt Gingrich in 1998–1999 for high test scores and a dropout rate that was impressively low in comparison to other Texas districts (Lueng, 1999).

Trujillo's hard-nosed approach was passed along to building-level administrators and often interpreted in the narrow and detrimental manner described in this chapter. In the next few years, Ysleta's district administration collapsed. Trujillo was fired amid allegations of the misuse of power, and the district was eventually taken over by the state education agency amid various controversies and questionable practices

(Stover, 2001). The same year, the Ysleta District was one of three in the state that was cited and received an unacceptable rating for dropout data too inaccurate to be trusted (Texas House of Representatives, 1999).

The data in this research from 1997 describe detrimental effects of the high-stakes testing environment, which are ongoing. As a faculty instructor in the university field program, I teach interns in four of the Ysleta schools[3] and visit regularly in the classrooms. The Ysleta district today hosts some schools whose high test scores are based on a more inclusive curriculum and thinking-centered learner strategies. For example, Alicia R. Chacon International Magnet School is a kindergarten through eighth grade (K–8) year-round school in the Ysleta district often recognized as a leader in bilingual, dual language education. Rather than seeing students working individually on drill sheets, I often see students working together to explore complex mathematics and science problems and developing their literacy skills through a variety of writing and reading activities.

With this caveat in mind, the majority of the following analysis centers on a less sanguine portrayal of high-stakes accountability based on survey, focus group, and interview data from teachers and administrators in the Ysleta district. The teachers consistently perceive the TAAS program as detrimental to their students and as responsible for a narrowing of their curriculum to a point at which it is unhealthy and dissatisfying. Although the administrators show greater respect for the TAAS program's ability to accurately measure student learning, their comments reveal an artificially constricted, sterilized educational program.

BACKGROUND

The origins of the *Tamarix*-like education that today finds expression in high-stakes testing systems (McNeil & Valenzuela, 2000) may be traced to a paradigm introduced in the early twentieth century when ideas from behaviorist psychology and strategies for assembly-line efficiency began being applied to educational practices (Callahan, 1962; Gould, 1981). Advocates of the new approach presumed that knowledge could be broken down into small pieces, taken out of context, and learned in order (Eisner, 1994; Medina & Neill, 1990; Vygotsky, 1978). Summed, these small pieces result in something we may call "knowledge," and once consumed, these bits of information constitute a child's "education." Freire (1996) calls this perspective the "banking concept of education." The learner's role is to passively accept and store deposits of knowledge and then to catalogue what has been stored. But, as Freire (1996) points out,

. . . in the last analysis, it is the people themselves who are filed away through the lack of creativity, transformation, and knowledge in this (at best) misguided system. For apart from inquiry, apart from the praxis, individuals cannot be truly human. Knowledge emerges only through invention and reinvention, through the restless, impatient continuing, hopeful inquiry human beings pursue in the world, with the world, and with each other. (p. 53)

To be sure, high standardized test scores *can* come about with curricula that are relevant and interesting to students (Resnick, Bill, Lesgold, & Leer, 1991). For example, elementary school students in Austin who participated in a problem-centered, non-TAAS mathematics curriculum showed impressive gains in their TAAS mathematics scores. African American and Hispanic students, in particular, significantly improved. This experience led the district to conclude, "Active student involvement, development of conceptual understanding, problem-solving set in a real world context, variety of instructional strategies, and assessment embedded in classroom instruction are among the best practices listed as positively influencing student achievement" (Austin Independent School District, 1998, p. 3). One could therefore argue that if teachers just teach well, the TAAS will take care of itself. Indeed, innovative teachers who modify their curriculum very little often still have classrooms in which the students earn impressive TAAS scores. As will be demonstrated here and in other studies (Herman & Golan, 1993; Sloan, this volume), however, that is not the reality in most classrooms in high-stakes environments.

The "high saline soil" within the current system prevents both teachers and children from developing their full potential. The growth of new "species" of curricular options is thwarted by the toxins emitted by the real and perceived pressure to focus on the TAAS. The teacher and administrator data presented in this chapter indicate that the imposed testing system has diminished curriculum and constrained what qualifies as relevant content, has limited professional development, and has restricted class and scheduling options.

THE STUDY

The Ysleta Independent School District is the second-largest district in the El Paso area. At the time of the study, there were 32 elementary schools, 10 middle schools, 7 high schools, and several alternative school programs. From these, nine elementary schools and three middle schools were selected for the study. Neither quality of education nor test score ranking was considered in the selection. The schools were chosen on the basis of their similarity to those in the New Mexico sample in terms of student body size and ethnicity. The overwhelming majority of the students were Latino, and 63% had been identified by the Texas Education Agency (1995) as economically disadvantaged. All but two schools reported over 90% of the student body as Latino. Of the two with lower percentages, one reported 72% and the other 78%. Spanish was the home language for many of these students.

Thirteen administrators, principals from nine elementary schools and principals and assistant principals from three middle schools, were interviewed about their role in administering the TAAS, how they prepared for the test, how the results were used, and how the test affected their school's curriculum. A total of 60 teachers from these same schools provided information about the impact of the TAAS on their practice by responding to a survey (N=42) or by participating in a focus group interview (N=18).[3] The survey instrument, the modified Teacher Questionnaire (Herman & Golan, 1993), contains 80 Likert-type items probing teachers' perceptions of the effects of testing on the teaching and learning process in the schools. The items were charted in subscales to capture the broader attitudes. The survey results were computed into averages and percentages.

Teachers who participated in the two focus groups were drawn from several disciplines to ensure a curriculum content balance. The focus group participants also reflected the schools' ethnic demographics: majority Hispanic. The teachers were asked to respond to the open question, "In your experience with the state-mandated, standardized testing, what effects have you observed on the curriculum, on the students, and on your school climate?" The analysis presented here is further supplemented with information provided by 56 university students who were interning in 15 schools in the district when the research data were being collected. The interns, who were teaching and observing four days per week, responded to an informal survey about the amount of time they observed teachers devoting to test preparation.

RESULTS

Constricting the Middle School Curriculum

Principals from three middle schools were interviewed, and teachers from these schools participated in the survey research. A focus group interview with 10 teachers was held at Middle School 2. When the most recent TAAS results were published, this school's math scores had increased by a very impressive 28 percentile points. This achievement resulted in the district presenting the school with a formal recognition. The principal attributed the improvement in test scores to extensive changes that had been made at the school: classes and time schedules had been drastically restructured, a student tracking system had been imposed, and the curriculum had been revised to match the contents of the test. At the other two middle schools, principals undertook similar restructuring and reported some improvement in test scores, but no change as dramatic as that experienced at Middle School 2.

The school's new schedule allotted significantly more time to instruction that mirrored the test format, and it allowed for greater amounts of remediation. The principal and teachers described a complex series of programs targeting students who did not do well on the TAAS. One remedial class—known as "TAAS-Up Class"—was for students who had scored below the 70th percentile. The principal explained that students in this class received direct TAAS instruction in writing during the fall semester and in math during the spring semester. Another remedial class was designed specifically for students who had scored between the 70th and 85th percentiles. Children in this group were known as "bubble students" because, with extra help, they could increase the school's average passing score on the TAAS. The "bubble students," who represented about 40% of the student body, also attended a computer-assisted instruction class that focused directly on the TAAS.[4] The principal and teachers reported that students were not ability grouped; yet the principal described the remedial classes this way:

> When we created this remediation, it minimized the number of electives, but not entirely. The kids have three electives to choose from. If you don't pass TAAS Reading, you have to go to Reading Improvement, another block class. So, you could go to TAAS-Up and Reading Improvement. We took all the seventieth percentile to eighty-fifth percentile students into an on-level reading class. This is a special class, also. So, we got you any way you go!

In addition to this restructured schedule, the principal described a process of improving math scores by teaching math in all the other curriculum areas. Teachers in every class, from language arts to physical education, taught math during their own class time:

> This process provides a great increase in the quantity of math instruction the students receive. The math teachers created worksheets

and activities that they give to all the other teachers to use during the 35-minute advisory class each day, so the children get extra math during advisory. The math teachers grade these, and it goes on the math scores.

In addition, a warm-up activity, described as a reading, math, or writing question in the TAAS format, was implemented in every class for 15 to 20 minutes each day. The "curriculum inspector" (as the teachers dubbed her), a middle-level administrator, checked all the teachers' plans to make sure they were teaching this TAAS warm-up.

For many students, these changes resulted in an overwhelming increase in math-related activities. For instance, during their two-day block schedule cycle, these students had one math class based on TAAS objectives; possibly a second math class or "TAAS-Up Class"; a computer TAAS class; a 35-minute TAAS math "advisory" class (every day); and in all the remaining classes, a TAAS focus that resulted in the first one-third of class time being devoted to a TAAS math or writing problem.

Just as the students' day was redesigned to hone in on TAAS instruction, the curriculum was redesigned to hone in on TAAS content. Most of the administrators interviewed described this as "curriculum alignment," meaning that classroom instruction deliberately focuses on the 29 objectives covered by the TAAS tests. For the principal at Middle School 1, this overlap between the TAAS and classroom curriculum "helps clarify what is expected and what they [students] should be able to do by a certain point." He elaborated:

> This test is aligned with the curriculum. There are thirteen math objectives, seven writing objectives, and nine reading objectives tested on TAAS; so we aligned our curriculum to these objectives. To say we have to "teach the test" is not really accurate because the objectives are written into the curriculum frameworks. Some of the objectives are easy ones and some are real hard ones. We place most emphasis on the ones that the kids can pass and need help on. We want to get those that are within our grasp.

To help teachers design TAAS-like tests for use in their own classrooms, this administrator further provided the school's teaching teams with regular opportunities for professional development in writing test questions. His statement that teachers in his school do not teach to the test revealed his faulty and problematic premise that the state's curricular framework is reducible to the test items around which they coached students. Indeed, teachers at his school focused their instruction primarily on those items that they believed would be tested. Accordingly, they commonly created their drill exercises by copying pages from previous years' TAAS test booklets.

When teachers teach to standardized tests by providing daily skill instruction in the format of the test, their instructional practices are not merely ineffective; they are also detrimental. Learning isolated facts and skills is more difficult for students because there is insufficient context to mentally organize the information in ways that make it relevant and, thus, easier to remember and meaningfully apply to one's life. Moreover, in the real world, problems do not come in neat, step-by-step pieces; thus, learning skills apart from their context reduces students' ability to solve real problems (Corbett & Wilson, 1993; Herman & Golan, 1993; Shepard, 1992). Nevertheless, hoping to improve their students' scores, teachers in the Yselta district had resorted to using study tools such as TAAS MASTER (published by ECS Learning Systems) and drill sheets that present study items in the exact format used on the TAAS, complete with bubbles.

The National Council for Teachers of Mathematics (1989) advocates a problem-based approach to learning mathematics in which students focus on thinking through complex problems and examine approaches to solving the problem. The drill sheets, in contrast, present many isolated concepts. On a single drill sheet, for example, students were asked to answer one multiplication word problem; put four cities' temperatures in order from coldest to warmest; write a check to the teacher on a sample check form; measure a rectangle in centimeters; and divide the rectangle in eighths. Teachers in the schools involved in this study reported using drill sheets like this one up to two hours per day, and assigning them for homework as well. A strong emphasis on isolated mathematical facts drew approval from the principal at Middle School 3, who praised the TAAS for forcing educators to take a linear approach to mathematics:

> Math is structured where you have to know one concept before you
> can go on to the next. This self-paced curriculum will help with that
> structure. The classes will be heterogeneous to begin with, then sep-
> arated sort of like a race. [The plan was to group students according
> to their scores on each isolated concept.] We don't want the kids to
> see it as tracking, but a different way to learn. Since math builds on
> itself, if you skip a concept, you have to make sure they learn it well
> before going on. At the three- or six-week break, those who have

learned the concept well go on, and those who have not have a different approach in their class.

Drill sheets were only one of many methods used to tailor classroom instruction and delivery to the TAAS format. In Middle School 2, every essay every student wrote had to use the TAAS two-page format. An administrator at Middle School 3 encouraged his language arts teachers to have their students use the TAAS-style eight-step paragraph structure (topic sentence, subject 1 and detail, subject 2 and detail, subject 3 and detail, and concluding sentence) in every paragraph they wrote. In addition to the strategies school staff developed on their own, the district and individual sites hired professional development consultants, selecting them on their ability to present ideas and lessons in the TAAS format.

In the following excerpts, teachers from Middle School 2 describe their contextless, TAAS-focused teaching, the stress it causes them, and the monotony their students experience.

> TEACHER 7: We had a workshop with [a particular consultant]. She gives seminars on taking TAAS. She helped us focus on TAAS objectives, and we decided to structure all our six-week tests like TAAS. So they [the students] all do multiple choice and the two-page essay as on the TAAS writing test. We all have to incorporate all the objectives that are on our school's timeline on that six-week test. So, in reading, I structure the reading passages and the questions as they are on TAAS, and then I have to ask questions on math and capitalizing and spelling, just like they see it on TAAS. These six-week tests are twenty-five percent essay, so everybody focuses on one type of essay, say persuasion. Everyone has to have their six-week test with that type of essay question . . . all eight classes. We all use the same type of outlining or mapping for the essay, so they [the students] know exactly what to do. They do get tired of taking eight tests on the same format. I think this does test the kids' writing ability well, but everything is in this certain format of a two-page essay, like TAAS. Sometimes I tell them they can write a "regular essay" that they might do after they get out of school. They are finally starting to see this basic format and the organization. To me it has been very beneficial because I have become more focused on what I am doing.
> TEACHER 8: I think the kids get stressed-out sometimes.
> TEACHER 9: I do too.

TEACHER 8: It is every teacher, every day. It has gotten to where the kids are geared towards the objectives: "Which objectives are we on today?"

TEACHER 10: Especially writing the essays. On our six-week tests, each teacher requires a TAAS-formatted essay. Within one week, they will have written eight TAAS-formatted essays. They do get tired. You see that. It is straining. One test you will get a really good essay, and the next time you can tell you are the last class [of the day], because it is not good.

TEACHER 11: We do a lot of phrasing practice and circling and underlining, because you don't want the vernacular to beat them—and that is what beats them on the TAAS. Rarely is it that they don't know what they were doing.

TEACHER 6: As long as it is not TAAS tested, we can't teach it. They have to learn that the world does exist besides TAAS. It seems like there is not much room for pleasure, or what you do in the outside world, or life skills—nothing but the TAAS and preparing for the high school TAAS. The way I see it, I am preparing them so they are going to succeed in high school, not so much after that.

TEACHER 5: We've revamped all the curriculum, so to speak, to make sure the TAAS objectives are included in our regular curriculum. We've taken each of the TAAS objectives and divided them up in a timeline, so that in each six weeks we have covered all the objectives. We are focusing on those objectives and trying to get our content area in at the same time. It is very stressful. Very stressful. It is a lot of work, because even though there are a lot of materials out there for TAAS, they are not geared for the specific curriculums.

TEACHER 6: We are really limited in that we cannot do stuff that is not TAAS. Seems like it's all TAAS preparation, TAAS work. They're the same, I guess. Even though we are not teaching the TAAS, it is a lot of TAAS preparation. It's hard covering all the math objectives in the TAAS-Up Class in six weeks—even less than six weeks. So in less than six weeks we have to cover thirteen objectives, plus the reading. It is real hard to get writing and reading in math.

Standardizing the Elementary School Curriculum

Administrators at the elementary schools in the research sample believed that TAAS alignment was helping them by giving them a focus and providing valid insights into which programs should be modified and which students were not learning. With one exception, none of these principals objected to the narrowing of the curriculum caused by the TAAS, and none questioned the wisdom of using this one tool as the only indicator of the quality of their educational programs. Most interpreted educational improvement as improved TAAS scores. One principal, in describing her concept of curriculum alignment, began by defending it, but ended on a note of doubt:

> We now have objectives and learning targets defined on TAAS. Those objectives now become our lesson objectives. We used to be textbook driven; now we are objective driven. It is good to align the curriculum. If something is not TAAS-related and does not meet one of those objectives, there is no need for us to be doing it. We have to justify. It helps the kids have common information. It sometimes stifles the creativity of teachers. As it gets close to TAAS, we become obsessed.

Another principal confirmed that at her school, they prepare for TAAS ". . . a lot from day one. We teach what we test and test what we teach." Several principals stated that the alignment included kindergarten, first-, and second-grade teachers helping the third-grade students prepare for the TAAS, the first grade level where it is administered. They did so by aligning their own curriculum with what was tested on the third-grade test.

Another principal described alignment as "determining the deficiencies in the curriculum from the test results and targeting these areas." At her school, teachers used TAAS practice books for 45 minutes every day, in every class. She referred to this as "daily enrichment." The principal at a different elementary school reported that they used the item analysis of the TAAS test results to group students according to the objectives they were weak in and then provided remediation. Many schools in the district hired the services of a particular Texas teacher who provided TAAS-focused professional development. According to administrators, this teacher/consultant had "taken the TAAS objectives and made a curriculum on it. She gives strategies to use, codes, and tools. She uses manipulatives and breaks down math."

TAAS-dominated curriculum was widespread and appeared to persist throughout the school year. In an informal survey of 56 university students (Hampton, 2000) working as interns in different classrooms in 15 elementary schools in the district, 14 reported that the teacher focused on TAAS practice most of the day, 30 reported that TAAS practice was a regular part of the curriculum, and 12 reported TAAS practice occurring rarely. Over half reported that the math curriculum was the prescriptive, standardized content and format described in this chapter and that all teachers in the school were instructed to follow this curriculum daily. Every math question was presented to the students in the TAAS bubble format.

The principal of a school that scored well on the test described her school's testing environment as a "worship" of TAAS.

> Since it is with us, we build on it and show that it can be done. I have seen growth and pride because we are a recognized school. I see quality in our classrooms. The kids know it is very important, so we celebrate. Last year everyone got to go to a skating party before the test and a barbecue after the test. The children in kindergarten, first, and second grades adopt a TAAS-tested grade and bake them cookies, and make banners for them, and give them rewards during the test. It seems to be less an assessment tool and more a "worship practice."

In sharp contrast to the generally positive opinions of the TAAS offered by elementary school administrators, teachers at the elementary level expressed serious reservations. Eight teachers participated in the focus group interview at Elementary School 1, a model school recognized by several agencies for quality teaching. The school had received the state's coveted "exemplary" rating (one level above the "recognized" rating that Middle School 2 had been awarded), indicating that their students' scores were in the top category. The teachers reported that they were still able to implement sound instructional practices that involve critical thinking. However, they expressed great concern about the controlling effect of the TAAS test and its power to restrict their autonomy in teaching. As one teacher put it, "It demeans my intelligence that they can just look at the scores in my class and not have any idea what kind of teacher I am, what kind of students that I have. It is terribly demoralizing as a professional. You know, you work so hard—and your whole worth comes down to how well you did on that TAAS."

"Teacher 1" in the focus group described the effects of the TAAS this way:

[A few weeks ago], I mentioned that I felt so guilty because I am doing projects only. I visited New Zealand a few years ago, and that is what they do. That is how the children develop their literacy. No one feels guilty about it. That is exactly what you do. But here, it is, "Oh my gosh! I need to go back to the dittos." I always end up going back to the dittos. And I call it transfer, but I know it is just my safety net. I want to be able to give the kids what I know they need. But I also want to make sure that they show up on paper. If they don't, everything else becomes invalid, and that is sad.

The focus group was held in the bilingual classroom of this award-winning teacher. The room was filled with complex student work in Spanish and English. She and her colleagues (all in the focus group) taught together as a team, shared projects and information, provided moral and emotional support, and spoke with a united voice:

TEACHER 2: In the race to be the top district and the top school, I think we are really narrowing it down to just one form of what you know. Even colleges look at how you are involved in sports, community work, your grades, you as a social being. And here we are just using one indicator. We all work extremely hard to make sure the kids have success. And success is not what is measured on the TAAS. Success is feeling good about themselves, feeling good about what they are doing, feeling like they are improving. We are trying to help the kids become whole individuals . . . whole. We are working on all aspects of it. Just targeting test-taking and TAAS is not right. It [our complaint] is not sour grapes. Last year we scored highest in math and language arts. We were very high the year before. It is not that we can't do this. But there is so much more to education.

TEACHER 3: Unfortunately, this test correlates highly with educational success in a lot of people's eyes. Unfortunately, people in power see it that way. But it doesn't represent success at all. If you are producing mechanical idiots that can't think their way out of a paper bag . . . that is what we are doing. So-called experts say that TAAS is supposed to measure children's critical thinking skills as well as basics. Yet, when children are taught to test and not how to be critical thinkers, the whole point of the test is meaningless. This [pointing to students' projects displayed around the room] is what our team does.

And you feel guilty because you are doing this kind of stuff and you are not doing the ditto stuff. If the results on the TAAS are not great, it makes it look like this was worthless. Like I have been playing.

TEACHER 4: It is degrading for the child as well as the teacher. Now, some form of testing is important. But we have gone overboard. It is like you ask for a drink of water and they drown you. We have blown it out of proportion. Too much emphasis on it.

TEACHER 1: Yes, exactly.

Important concepts and life skills were put on an artificial timeline or eliminated because of the TAAS pressure. The teachers felt that they faced a curriculum so predetermined and rigid, with so much pressure to cover this material, they could not teach important subjects such as science and social studies or cover significant topics that were interesting and relevant to the children.

TEACHER 3: When I come back the first of April, I have got to get to that ditto machine, and I have got to run off thirty-nine million copies of the math test, because we will have three weeks until TAAS. We do reading all afternoon. Forget science and social studies. We'll do those in May. And then when TAAS is over—do whatever you want to do. Then you can really teach. Most teaching gets done in May . . . all my projects. I am not doing protractors until May. It is not on the test. I am teaching circumference, diameter, and radius because that is on TAAS. We do the fun unit in geometry in May. Get those dittos out, darlings!

TEACHER 2: Yesterday, the kids had their presentation on "growing up." They were very interested and needed to talk. We talked about it. You have to, or they won't focus on anything. It was a good discussion, and you bond with the kids. We spent about forty-five minutes talking, and I was sitting there thinking, "Oh, we have to hurry up and study math!"

The Tyranny of the 70th Percentile

Shepard's (1992) research indicates that with increased emphasis on test scores, hard-to-teach children are denied access to quality education.

They are targeted for grade retention, referred to special education, or placed in low-level, remedial classes with an even greater focus on drilling isolated facts. Teachers and administrators in this study described how instruction was narrowed to focus on those students who were performing just below or just above the 70th percentile to ensure greater numbers of students passing. They worried that students not in this range were being overlooked. "We are mostly concerned for those kids that are barely passing," one teacher said. "There really is not much encouragement for kids who are advanced. It is very time-consuming to try to do extra projects for these kids. You don't have time to do something that is not on the objective list." Another teacher described the district as guilty of "reverse discrimination":

> TEACHER 12: Anyone who does not pass TAAS has to go to summer school. That will be expensive. But there are no funds available to hold open our computer lab, which is where they really need to be writing. There will be no funds available for the bright child . . . an enrichment program to extend their learning. As a parent of a pretty smart kid, I resent that because I am paying taxes. And now I am paying to send my son to a private school to get what he is not getting with my tax money. And I highly resent it. I am not saying these kids don't need to go to summer school. But I am saying, if we are going to work with that group of people, why don't we have something rewarding for the children who have mastery? It is reverse discrimination. This district is the worst I have seen for that.

TAAS pressures led one teacher to automatically (but unconsciously) rate her fifth graders as they entered the room. She would tell herself, "I don't need to work with that one, because he is way below [or way above] seventy." With others, she would note that she should spend extra time with him/her because that student was close to the 70th-percentile range. She said she felt terrible when she realized she had been doing this. She had always believed that all her students were equally deserving of her attention.

Similarly, McNeil and Valenzuela (2000) and Haney (2000) provide evidence of specific negative effects on students who have the greatest educational need. Valuable educational expenditures are diverted from high-quality curricular resources in favor of test-preparation materials and activities. Because the TAAS is a minimum-skills test, teachers aim at the lowest level of skills and information. Classroom activities often are selected solely because they will help raise test scores. Moreover, the

TAAS does not consider the children's culture or experiences, nor is it aligned with what is known about how children learn. McNeil and Valenzuela argue that the strong emphasis placed on the TAAS has caused a decline in overall educational quality in the state. They have identified classroom practices in many Texas schools as narrowing to little more than test preparation. They also note that these practices are more evident in districts that reward the administrators financially for high scores.

The Impact of the TAAS:
Highlights From the Teacher Survey Data

Data analyses show that the Texas teachers strongly emphasized basic skills lessons at the cost of lessons that required higher-order thinking (see Hampton, 1997). The TAAS program significantly influenced the decision to narrow instruction to mainly TAAS format and content, and it detracted from the school's ability to focus on good instruction. The teachers reported spending great amounts of time on direct TAAS instruction. Some of the experiences reported by the Ysleta teachers were echoed by their counterparts in New Mexico, where standardized, but not high-stakes, testing was in place. The Texas teachers, however, felt significantly more pressure to improve test scores. They devoted significantly more time to testing and they reported significantly more attention paid to test scores than did the New Mexico teachers. Testing also had more impact on curriculum and instruction in Texas than it did in New Mexico, but the difference was not statistically significant. Overriding the comparison, however, were consistent data from all teachers indicating that the testing program negatively affected their practice. Teachers in both districts agreed that the state-level testing did not give accurate readings of student attainment.

　　The survey instrument included nine subscales probing the testing program's impact on teacher practice. In four of the subscales, there were no significant differences.[5] One of the subscales was entitled, "School Attention to Good Instruction." It included a rating of "weak," "moderate," or "strong" on areas such as implementing innovative instruction and a school focus on improving student learning. Over 75% of the teachers surveyed rated these areas between "weak" and "moderate." When asked how much attention they were able to give to higher-order thinking and problem solving, 93% responded between "a little" and "moderate" (on a three-point scale: "a little," "moderate," "a lot"). When asked how much attention they were able to give to drilling students in basic facts, 50% marked "moderate," and 43% marked "a lot." Only 2% of the teachers rated attention to test preparation as "little."

On the subscale "Time in Test Preparation," teachers were asked to rate the amount of time they spent on the items listed. The scale rating was "none," "one day," "a few days," "a week," "4 weeks," or "throughout the year." Specifically, three of the items on this subscale asked teachers to rate giving students test review worksheets, giving students practice in items formatted like the test, and instructing students in test-taking strategies. On these three, the teachers marked "throughout the year" over 80% of the time. When asked questions about giving students commercially-produced practice tests and old forms of the test for practice, over half of the teachers reported doing this for "four weeks" or "throughout the year." University interns working in the area classrooms described this practice-test-style curriculum as going on throughout the year. They reported that in math classes every day the children were working drill sheets that were formatted like the test, covering content that was to be tested. The middle school language arts teachers in this research described their ongoing practice of teaching children to write in the same paragraph structure as required on the test.

The survey data indicate that the teachers felt that the testing program forced them to implement and spend the great majority of their instructional time on a curriculum that was drill based and that left little room for thinking-centered instruction. These data consistently support the qualitative findings derived from the focus group interviews.

CONCLUSION

As stated in the beginning, Ysleta bears a distinct privilege in the state of Texas for its high scores and school ratings. However, in the high-stakes testing environment in the district, administrators and teachers provided disheartening information about the impact of testing. The administrators described curriculum changes that labeled children, grouped them for intense test drill programs, and focused the school's instructional program on a narrow, sterile curriculum in which direct test instruction occurred daily in the majority of the schools. Most administrators did not express concern over this shift in educational priorities. The teachers' survey responses and comments also confirmed the implementation of a narrow, test-driven curriculum. Unlike most of the administrators, however, the teachers expressed dissatisfaction and concern over the fact that the TAAS focus crowded out coverage of many other important subjects. The teachers worried about the practice of focusing most of their classroom instruction on those students who were scoring near the 70th percentile, leaving the needs of the other children unmet. The level of the teachers' frustration was evident as I conducted my research. Because I was very conscious of their valuable and limited time, I tried to keep the interviews on schedule and prompt. The teachers deliberately slowed the pace. They told me that it was very therapeutic to be able to voice their intense feelings about the detrimental effects of this test.

The TAAS test, on its own, is neither good nor bad. It is simply a tool, like a hammer or a computer. But when misused, assessment can be a weapon. Testing is misused when it is the only instrument for evaluating the condition of education. It is misused when administrators and policy makers far removed from the classroom make the test results the basis for rewarding or punishing teachers, students, and schools. It is misused when it is allowed to gain so much power that it forces a narrow, standardized curriculum on a huge state rich with cultural diversity.

When the testing system was legally challenged in 1999, the judge upheld the system because it provided the same curriculum for all students (McNeil, 2000). The court interpreted this sameness as equity. McNeil describes this confusion, "In the lawsuit, access to a test score came to displace access to an equitable education" (p. 510). The research described in this chapter further defines that sameness as a detrimental narrowing of opportunities and resources for students in a majority Latino/a community. The children get the same access to the TAAS test and the prescriptive curriculum it has spawned. They get the same curriculum every day, in every class, and in the same format, with the same bubble sheets and the same ditto sheets.

The TAAS test has been misused to the extent that the curriculum across schools is so standardized that it has become sterilized. Diversity is limited; monotony prevails. The saline environment has poisoned the growth of interactive, relevant, student-centered learning experiences. The schools have become stark, dry, and uninviting. They have become standardized and sterilized.

NOTES

1. The U.S. Department of Education and the National Science Foundation's 1994 document, *Joint Statement of Principles on Assessment in Mathematics and Science Education,* defines a quality assessment program for students as one that will "be coherent and comprehensive; be equitable and engage all stu-

dents; be integrated with instructional strategies and curriculum materials to promote effective student learning; and provide information that will help yield valid inferences about students' learning." (p. 4) The *Statement of Principles* also explains that many different methods of assessment should be used, and that assessment should be an integral part of the learning process, not the end result. Particularly in border communities with blends of languages and cultures, evaluations of students' growth should involve varied assessments tied to vibrant curricula (Sosa, 1993).

2. The Ysleta Independent School District authorizes the use of its name but proffers no opinion regarding the conclusions made by the researcher.

3. Twenty-seven fifth-grade teachers from nine elementary schools and fifteen middle-school teachers from three middle schools responded to the survey. Eight teachers from one elementary school participated in one focus group, and ten teachers from one middle school participated in the other focus group.

4. The principal noted that because the school's integrated learning system computer lab was aligned with the TAAS, "Low-scoring students can be plugged into that system."

5. The survey instrument has been determined to be internally consistent. Factor analysis on the eight subscales confirmed a good fit between identified indicators and the measurement model. Eight paired t-tests, one for each subscale, were run to compare the results of the responses from the two districts. For more information, see UMI Dissertation Services at www.umi.com/

REFERENCES

Austin Independent School District. (1998). *Austin collaborative for mathematics education year I progress report.* Austin, TX: Author.

Callahan, R. E. (1962). *Education and the cult of efficiency.* Chicago: University of Chicago Press.

Corbett, H. D., & Wilson, B. L. (1993). *Testing reform and rebellion.* Norwood, NJ: Ablex Publishing Corporation.

Cummins, J., & Skutnabb-Kangas, T. (Eds.). (1998). *Minority education: From shame to struggle.* Clevedon, UK: Multilingual Matters.

Eisner, E. (1994*). The educational imagination on the design and evaluation of school programs.* New York: Macmillan College Publishing Company.

Freire, P. (1996). *Pedagogy of the oppressed (revised).* New York: Continuum Publishing Company.

Gould, S. J. (1981). *The mismeasure of man.* New York: W. W. Norton and Co.

Hampton, E. (1997). *Educators' perceptions of the effects of state-mandated testing in a Texas school district and a New Mexico school district along the Mexican border.* Unpublished doctoral dissertation, New Mexico State University at Las Cruces.

Hampton, E. (2000). *Student survey on TAAS implementation*. Unpublished document. El Paso, TX: University of Texas at El Paso.

Hampton, E., & Licona, M. (1998). *Project del Rio community action research evaluation report*. Unpublished evaluation report. Project del Rio, Las Cruces, New Mexico.

Haney, W. (2000). The Texas miracle in education. *Education Policy Analysis Archives, 8*(41), part 1–7. Available at: http://epaa.asu.edu/epaa/v8n41/part1.htm

Herman, J., & Golan, S. (1993). *Effects of standardized testing on teachers and learning—another look* (CSE Technical Report 334). Los Angeles: Center for Research on Evaluation, Standards, and Student Testing (CRESST).

Leung, R. (1999). *A look at bilingual education*. Retrieved May 2, 2003, from http://more.abcnews.go.com/sections/us/dailynews/bilingualed_history980529.html

Lindholm-Leary, K. J. 2001. *Dual language education*. Clevedon, UK: Multilingual Matters.

McNeil, L. (2000). Sameness, bureaucracy, and the myth of educational equity: The TAAS system of testing in Texas public schools. *Hispanic Journal of Behavioral Sciences, 22*(4), 508–523.

McNeil, L., & Valenzuela, A. (2000). The harmful impact of the TAAS system of testing in Texas: Beneath the accountability rhetoric. In M. Kornhaber & G. Orfield (Eds.), *Raising standards or raising barriers? Inequality and high stakes testing in public education* (pp. 127–150). New York: Century Foundation.

Medina, N., & Neill, M. (1990). *Fallout from the testing explosion: How 100 million standardized exams undermine equity and excellence in American public schools*. Cambridge, MA: Fair Test.

Muzika, R. M. (1997). Saltcedar. In *Links to invasive species*. Retrieved May 15, 2003, from http://www.nps.gov/plants/alien/fact/tama1.htm

National Council of Teachers of Mathematics. (1989). *Curriculum and evaluation standards for school mathematics*. Reston, VA: Author.

Resnick, L. B., Bill, V. L., Lesgold, S. B., & Leer, M. N. (1991). Thinking in arithmetic class. In B. Means, C. Chelemer, & M. Knapp (Eds.), *Teaching advanced skills to at-risk students* (pp. 27–53). San Francisco: Jossey-Bass.

Shepard, L. A. (1992). *Will national tests improve student learning?* (CSE Technical Report 342). Los Angeles: UCLA Graduate School of Education CRESST.

Sosa, A. (1993). *Thorough and fair: Creating routes to success for Mexican-American students*. Charleston, WV: Eric Cress.

Stover, D. (2001, April 10). A Texas district makes student achievement a top priority—and succeeds. *School Board News*.

Texas Education Agency, National Computer Systems, Harcourt Brace Educational Measurement (Eds.). (1995). *Texas student assessment program technical digest for the academic year 1995–1996.* (Available from Texas Education Agency, 512–463–9536).

Texas House of Representatives. (1999). *The dropout data debate.* Focus Report. November 2, 1999. Retrieved November 12, 2002, from http://www.capitol.state.tx.us/hrofr/focus/dropouts.pdf

Thomas, W., & Collier, V. (1996). *Language minority achievement and program effectiveness.* Fairfax, VA: Center for Bilingual/Multicultural/ESL Education, George Mason University.

Thomas, W., & Collier, V. (2001). *A national study of school effectiveness for language minority students' long-term academic achievement final report: Project 1.1.* Retrieved December 3, 2002, from http://www.crede.ucsc.edu/research/llaa/1.1_final.html

U.S. Department of Education Office of Educational Research and Improvement Programs for the Improvement of Practice & National Science Foundation. (1994). (#PIP 94-1501). *Statement of principles on assessment in mathematics and science education.* Washington, D.C.: Author.

Vygotsky, L. S. (1978). *Mind in society: The development of higher psychological processes.* Cambridge, MA: Harvard University Press.

7

California's English-Only Policies:
An Analysis of Initial Effects

LAURA ALAMILLO, DEBORAH PALMER,
CELIA VIRAMONTES, AND EUGENE E. GARCÍA

Over the past two decades, the linguistic and cultural diversity of California's school children has increased dramatically. The number of Latino students in particular has grown rapidly (owing in part to a significant increase in immigrant populations from Latin America) and is expected to continue to do so over the next several decades (Stiles, Cohen, Elkins & Gey, 1998). At the same time, California's adult population has been growing steadily more concerned about the quality of public education. Over 70% of adults surveyed in 1992, 1994, and 1998 by Policy Analysis for California Education (PACE) polls characterized the schools as not "doing a good job" (PACE, 1998).

This public perspective and continued evidence of many Latino students' academic underachievement and underrepresentation at the college level have prompted widespread calls for change. Proposals include new teaching methods, new curricula, enhanced standards and accountability, bridges between school and work, and more strategic funding. Although such actions may be needed, they will not be meaningful unless we begin to think differently about the educational needs of all our students and the ways in which the systems we have implemented meet—or fail to meet—those needs. A change in thinking about Latino students, and particularly about those identified as limited English proficient (LEP), could foster a much-needed recognition of the value and importance of these students' language and culture.

Combined with the contemporary educational zeitgeist that embraces excellence and equity for all students, best reflected in the 1983 *A Nation at Risk,* the articulation of national goals, *Goals 2000,* and the more recent initiatives by President Bush designed to "Leave No Child

Behind," attention to Latino students and families has been significant. Most policies, programs, and publications have centered on identifying why Latinos (and others) are not thriving academically and how schools and other institutions can be "reformed" or "restructured" to meet this challenge.[1] The most recent and direct contributions to this discourse are the White House Initiatives on Educational Excellence for Hispanic Americans (2000). Overall, formal institutional and organizational efforts have attended to the "vulnerabilities" of Latinos and have noted the need for awareness of and responsiveness to issues surrounding differences in language and culture. In California, however, educational reform aimed at Latino students historically has diverged from these recommendations.

This chapter examines three such divergent efforts: Proposition 227, a statewide initiative passed in 1998 that requires all public school instruction to be conducted in English (García & Curry, 2000); the 1999 adoption of an "English-Only" statewide school accountability program (García, 2001); and the increasingly widespread use of highly scripted English-only reading programs in the schools (Stritikus, 2000). Each is a substantive educational reform initiative, and each significantly affects California's Latino students by pushing schools toward English-only educational environments. As our data—drawn from interviews we conducted with teachers and school administrators—show, together, these three policy initiatives are determining the form and outcomes of Latino student education in California. Specifically, these policies and the practices they have spawned now have, and will continue to have, negative effects. They are subtractive in nature, ignoring the linguistic resources Latino students bring to the classroom; and they are out of alignment with the attributes of responsive learning programs that have been shown to work well for these students (García, 2001).

CALIFORNIA'S "ENGLISH-ONLY" POLICY

California's Proposition 227 (California State Department of Education 1998b) is the state's most recent effort to restrict the use of a language other than English in the delivery of educational services. The initiative, known as the "English for the Children" ballot measure, and its related state education code, mandate that

- All students be placed in English-language classrooms, and that English-language learners be educated through a prescribed methodology identified as "Structured English Immersion."

- A temporary transition period not normally to exceed one year be allowed for the transition to English-only instruction.
- Instruction in a student's native language occur only in situations in which a waiver has been granted, in writing, and that such waiver be obtained yearly by parents, who must visit the school to request the waiver.
- Native language instruction be prohibited unless the student already has mastered English, is over 10 years of age, and such instruction has been approved by the principal and teacher (García & Curry, 2000).

In sum, for the 1.49 million students the state has identified as limited in their English-language proficiency, California's "English-Only" policy allows native-language instruction only through an exclusionary and complicated process.[2] There is little doubt that Proposition 227 has changed the instructional landscape for limited-English-proficient Latino students. An estimated one-third of primary language or bilingual education programs have reported moving to English-only instruction, and a majority of the remaining bilingual programs report an increased emphasis on English-language instruction (Alamillo & Viramontes, 2000; García & Curry, 2000; Gandara, 2000; García & Palmer, 2000).

At the same time, another "English-only" policy, one embedded in the state's public schools accountability system, has been substantially reshaping elementary- through secondary-level programs. As the next section explains, the single most important factor in judging the performance of public schools relies on students' scores on an English-language academic test called the Stanford 9 (SAT 9). The overriding importance of students' scores on this test has made the language-of-instruction choices of district personnel, local school principals, and classroom teachers serving LEP students extremely difficult (Alamillo & Viramontes, 2000; García & Curry, 2000).

FRAMEWORK OF THE CALIFORNIA PUBLIC SCHOOL ACCOUNTABILITY SYSTEM

The Public Schools Accountability Act (PSAA), signed into law in 1999, provides the basis for the educational accountability system in California. Embedded in this accountability program is a statewide school ranking system intended to help schools improve the academic achievement of all students (California State Department of Education, 1999).

The Academic Performance Index (API)

The Academic Performance Index (API) is the cornerstone of accountability in California. It provides a standardized numeric index scale (ranging from 200 to 1,000) for measuring the academic performance and
growth of all public elementary through secondary schools. The PSAA
stipulates that the State Board of Education adopt a statewide API performance target once state performance standards have been approved.
Because no such standards have yet been adopted, the State Board of Education set an interim statewide API performance target of 800 for the
1999 and 2000 school years. The Board (following Education Code Section 52052(c) of the Public Schools Accountability Act) also established a
minimum API growth target: Schools that met or exceeded 5% of the distance between their previous year's API score and the interim target of
800 would be considered to have achieved academic "growth" (California Department of Education, 1999).

Stanford Achievement Test, Ninth Edition

Much as the API is the cornerstone of California's accountability system,
students' Stanford Achievement Test, Ninth Edition (SAT 9) test scores
are the centerpiece of the API. First administered to all California students in spring 1998, the SAT 9 is an English-only, national, norm-referenced test. Students in grades 2–11 are tested in reading, language
(written expression), and mathematics. Students in grades 2–8 are additionally tested in spelling, and students in grades 9–11 are additionally
tested in science and social science. The scores that students achieve on
the SAT 9 tests determine their school's API ratings. The formula for calculating the API involves first determining the percentage of students
scoring within each of five predetermined "performance bands" in each
SAT 9 subject area. The bands are keyed to national percentile rankings
(e.g., performance band 1 covers students scoring within the first and the
nineteenth national percentiles; band 5 covers those scoring within the
eightieth and ninety-ninth percentiles). The band percentages are
weighted and combined to produce a summary result for each content
area. These results are then weighted and combined to produce the
school's API, a single number between 200 and 1000 (California State
Department of Education, 1999). Schools with an API below the fiftieth
percentile are deemed to be "under performing."

Linking the SAT 9 to the API has high stakes even beyond its role as a measure of students' academic performance and progress. As the sole determining factor for the API, SAT 9 scores also provide the basis for schools' eligibility for a range of rewards or sanctions. Schools that meet specific criteria become eligible for monetary awards such as the Governor's Performance Award, School Site Employee Performance Bonus, or cash allotments linked to Certificated Staff Performance Incentive programs. Eligibility, conditions, and reward amounts for these programs are outlined in Table 7.1.

The validity of high-stakes testing as a measure of accountability has been scrutinized by various professional associations, including the American Educational Research Association (AERA). In July 2000, the

TABLE 7.1
State Award Conditions/Eligibility, Amounts and Distribution

Award	Eligibility/Conditions	Amount	Award Recipient(s)	Distribution
Governor's Performance Award	Open to all schools with API scores. API scores for 2000 must show 5% growth target. All subgroups must make 80% of school target. K–8 schools must have 95% SAT 9 participation rate. 9–12 schools must have 90% SAT 9 participation rate.* Schools with API of 800+ must make at least 1 point gain.	$227 million	For school-wide use	Up to $150 per pupil at all schools meeting proposed conditions
School Site Employee Performance Bonus	Open to all schools with APIs, eligibility for Governor's Performance Award will determine eligibility for performance bonus	$350 million	All staff at school site for school-wide use	• All full-time school site staff receive bonus • Equal amount of money given to school for school wide-use

(continued)

TABLE 7.1 (*Continued*)
State Award Conditions/Eligibility, Amounts and Distribution.

Award	Eligibility/Conditions	Amount	Award Recipient(s)	Distribution
AB 1114 Certificated Staff Performance Incentive Act	Open to schools with APIs in deciles 1–5 in 1999. 1989–99 SAT 9 growth must be demonstrated. 2000 API must show at least 2 times annual growth target (minimum of 10% of annual growth target). All subgroups must make 80% of school target. K–8 schools must have 95% SAT 9 participation rate: 9–12 schools must have 90% SAT 9 participation rate	$100 million	School certicated staff	• Biggest gains received the most money, based on growth (number of API points increased over 2 times the school's target) • 1,000 certified staff in schools with largest growth get $25,000 each • 3,750 certified staff get $10,000 each • 7,500 certified staff get $5,000 each

Note.*Participation rate is calculated as follows: Percent tested = Total students tested divided by total enrollment on first day of testing (all grade levels), minus students with parent/guardian written waiver requests minus students with Individualized Education Program Exemptions. As outlined in California Education Code Section 60615, a parent or guardian may submit to the school a written request to excuse his or her child from any or all parts of any test provided pursuant to Education Code section 60640. The parent or guardian must initiate the request and the school district and its employees shall not solicit or encourage any written request on behalf of any child.
California State Department of Education, Public School Accountability Act (Sacramento, CA: Author). Retrieved February 25, 2001 from http://www.cde.ca.gov/psaa/awards/

AERA adopted a position statement calling for all high-stakes achievement testing programs to meet several conditions, including protection against high-stakes decisions based on a single test; alignment between the test and curriculum; and perhaps most important for our discussion, appropriate attention to language differences among examinees. "If a student lacks mastery of the language in which a test is given," the AERA notes, "then that test becomes, in part, a test of language proficiency.

Unless a primary purpose of a test is to evaluate language proficiency, it should not be used with students who cannot understand the instruction or the language of the test itself" (AERA Position Statement, 2000).[3]

The Public School Accountability Advisory Committee

The Public School Accountability Advisory Committee was formed by legislative action to advise the State Board of Education on matters related to establishing a comprehensive plan for school-level accountability statewide. The Committee was charged with carrying out the legislature's and governor's intent to have a reliable, valid, and fair set of assessments and a system that would nurture and promote public schools but also hold them accountable for the academic achievement of all California's public school students. As its first act, the Committee adopted a set of guidelines that included a formal commitment to recommend only assessments or processes that were valid and fair.

In its deliberations, the Committee considered two key issues: the question of whether to include the SAT 9 scores of LEP students in the Academic Performance Index or exclude them from testing for a prescribed period of years. This would allow students a period of time for English-language development. The committee also discussed whether to exclude them altogether because the SAT 9 is psychometrically inappropriate (it fails to meet either the prescribed reliability or validity standards for this population). A decision on this issue was especially important because some 25% of California's students (1.49 million) fall into this language category. A majority of these students are Latino. A final option was to include test scores for these students so as to not leave this population outside the realm of the accountability system. In reaching its decision, the Committee relied on an analysis of 1998 SAT 9 scores that showed LEP students scoring at the chance level, i.e., the equivalent score to a random response test, five to six times more than students who were not limited in their English-proficiency. This evidence that limited English language proficiency placed these students at a substantial disadvantage compared to their English proficient peers, along with the psychometric limitations of the SAT 9, led the Committee to recommend that the state exclude these students' scores from the Academic Performance Index until a reliable, valid, and fair assessment could be put in place.

The State Board of Education ignored the Committee's recommendation. Specifically, the Board adopted a plan for mandatory assessment of all students, only in English, although the Committee had concluded that doing so would be inappropriate. The result is a fatally flawed system that is likely to negatively affect large numbers of Latino students. Low SAT 9 scores may cause schools with high LEP populations to suffer the sanctions embedded in the Immediate Intervention/Under-Performing Schools Program (described later). Equally troubling is the fact that SAT 9 scores are the basis for retention/promotion decisions at every grade level at which they are administered (2–11). Further, as part of its larger assessment and accountability plan, the state has implemented a high school exit exam, also in English only. Effective in 2004, all high school seniors must take and pass this exam to graduate. Thus, sanctions apply not only to schools, but also to individual students who fall below the mandated minimum requirements. Given the inappropriate nature of these tests for those with limited English proficiency, a greater percentage of these students is likely to be adversely affected by such high-stakes exams.

Immediate Intervention/Under-Performing Schools Program

Schools that fail to meet or exceed their growth target may be identified for participation in the Immediate Intervention/Under-Performing Schools Program (II/USP), which targets schools with an API below the fiftieth percentile. This is an aggregate rank referring to all students in all grades. Additionally, schools that do not meet or exceed their 5% growth target may be identified for participation in II/USP. A school may meet its target either by meeting or exceeding 5% of the distance between its 1999 API and the interim statewide performance of 800, or by achieving an API at or above 800 in 2000. Of critical importance in this formulation is the fact that a school may not set its own growth target. Rather, the State Board of Education "may set differential growth targets based on grade level of instruction and may set higher growth targets for the lowest performing schools because they have the greatest room for improvement" (California Department of Education, 1999).

"Under-performing" schools are invited to participate in the II/USP, making them eligible to apply for $50,000 planning grants to assist them in improving their API ranking. As part of the grant, schools selected to participate are required to contract with an external evaluator and to create a broad school-site team to address ways to improve students' academic performance. Central to the stated goals of the II/USP is that participating schools demonstrate progress toward meeting their annual short-term growth targets within 12 months following the receipt of funding. Failure to meet this growth target may lead to immediate intervention. Schools meeting their growth target within 24 months after receiving funding may be eligible for monetary or nonmonetary awards under the Governor's Performance Award Program. The II/USP further stipulates the following conditions: participating schools that fail to meet their goals but demonstrate significant growth may continue to participate in the program for an additional year without loss of funding; schools that fail to meet their growth targets and fail to demonstrate significant growth within 24 months of receipt of funding are subject to a wide range of sanctions. These include the following:

- Reassignment of the principal
- Revision of attendance options to allow students to attend any public school where space is available and/or allow parents to establish a charter school
- Reassignment of other school employees and reorganization of the school
- School closure

Implications of the Accountability System

The wide range of rewards and sanctions embedded in California's educational accountability system reveal its high-stakes nature. The API system, especially, by positing the SAT 9 as the only indicator of student academic achievement, creates an inequitable framework for language-minority students, children who are already at an educational disadvantage. A system that rewards and punishes schools on the basis of student performance on a single, English-only test fails to address some of the most critical issues facing under-performing schools.

Results from a recent study conducted by an independent research firm indicate that students attending schools with APIs in the bottom 10% were socioeconomically disadvantaged (Wells, 2001). Other factors, such as high student mobility, percent of English-language learners, and school calendar (year-round or traditional) were also considered. The results suggest that multiple factors contribute to the overall education of California's public school students, especially its language-minority students. An educational accountability system that centers on a single English-only test necessarily fails to account for this causal complexity. The irony of the state's system of sanctions and rewards is that, except for II/USP coverage, those schools most in need are the least likely to receive it.

DISTRICT-MANDATED READING PROGRAMS

The scripted reading programs that have filtered into California's class-rooms include Success for All; Results; and Open Court. Here, we focus on Open Court because it was the program our respondents referred to most frequently. The other programs share many of Open Court's main characteristics, however, particularly in their scripted format and emphasis on phonics.

By January 2000, Open Court had grown from being used in one in every hundred to one in every eight elementary schools in California (Moustafa & Land, 2001). Los Angeles Unified School District implemented Open Court in summer 2000. Now the program is in use with over 300,000 K–5 students. Open Court's widespread adoption followed the publication of findings from a research project that investigated the program's use with at-risk students in Texas (Foorman, Francis, Fletcher, Schatschneider, & Mehta, 1998). Children in Open Court classrooms reportedly made greater gains in reading than children who were not in Open Court classrooms. Serious critiques of this research are emerging, however. Moustafa and Land (2001), for example, who closely examined the research supporting Open Court effectiveness (Foorman et al., 1998), provide an alternative viewpoint regarding mandated reading programs and high-stakes policies in schools. They report the following. First, the study supporting Open Court was funded by the Open Court publishers; introducing a significant potential source of bias. Second, approximately 45% of the students in the study received two Open Court sessions per day instead of the required one lesson per day. The researchers also note that the study's aggregate data combined two different sets of results from two different instructional settings. Data on children who had been in the district's classroom with contemporary reading instruction in the first grade, but who were placed in Open Court classrooms in the second grade were averaged with the data on children who were in Open Court classrooms both years. This method of aggregating data thus makes it impossible to distinguish the effect of each program.

Open Court's classroom effectiveness has not been thoroughly evaluated, and yet it has almost completely replaced other language arts materials in schools where it has been adopted. The program requires at least two hours of instruction every day; the content varies according to grade level. For example, in kindergarten and other lower grades, Open Court instruction involves emphasizing phonemic awareness and decoding. Lessons are scripted minute by minute for the teacher. For grades 4 and 5, by contrast, the Open Court program shifts to "intervention." It still requires two and one-half hours per day, and it is still scripted, but there is much more time for independent work and for drill on comprehension and written grammar. At all grade levels, however, students spend the majority of their time on phonemic awareness strategies, blending, dictation, decodables, and independent work. The program is entirely in English, and there is no variation according to a student's level of English proficiency.

THE STUDY

Given California's "English-Only" policy context, schools are facing a new set of reform challenges that move them away from primary language and/or bilingual instruction. Latino students are in classrooms where these new policies are likely to have their greatest effects. Our study was designed to empirically evaluate the combined influence of these new policies on those students. We developed new interview protocols and revisited classroom teachers we had sampled in our study of Proposition 227 (García & Curry, 2000). In the remainder of this chapter, we report these teachers' views regarding the intersection of English-only policies in California schools.

Methodology and Research Questions

Our original study focused on Proposition 227 as a policy instrument and examined its effects on the local educational policy-to-practice cycle. We asked the following questions:

- How did each school and district respond to the mandated components of Proposition 227?
- What were the specific instructional and curricular effects of this policy initiative at the district, school, and classroom levels?
- When and how did related Proposition 227 policy changes influence administrator, teacher, parent, and student relationships at the district and school level?
- What organizational roles and expectations were affected in policy articulations as a result of Proposition 227?
- Who and what were identified as critical policy agents? Why?

We began the Proposition 227 study in 1999 with 8 school districts and 16 elementary schools, each with a 30–50% LEP student population.

We selected these districts based on geographical representation in the state to include urban and rural school districts. In 2000, we expanded the study statewide, sampling 40 school district personnel, 80 principals (two per district) and 160 teachers (four per district, two per school). The 40 districts in the second sample were randomly selected from the pool of districts statewide with greater than 25% LEP students. We chose the districts to be representative in terms of size, region, and presence of Spanish and other native languages (García & Curry, 2000).

During our analysis of the data from this original study, the issue of statewide, high-stakes, English-only standardized testing arose repeatedly. We decided to pursue the issue of assessment more directly through follow-up interviews. During December 2000, we conducted 18 brief (generally under ten minutes) follow-up interviews, 8 with principals and 10 with teachers. We targeted subjects who had shown concern for the testing/evaluation issues during their first interviews. We also attempted to reach subjects from two types of schools—those that eliminated and those that maintained their bilingual education programs.[4] Our sample broke down as follows: in schools that eliminated bilingual education, we interviewed seven teachers and three principals; in schools that maintained bilingual education, we interviewed three teachers and five principals. We began the open-ended interviews with a question from our original teacher interview protocol, "How has Proposition 227 affected practices for formal assessment at your school?" We found that teachers and principals from both types of programs had a great deal to say about standardized testing, about the SAT 9 and API systems in California, and about the connections they saw between the various levels of recent school reforms in the state. We begin by reporting the teachers' views.

FINDINGS

Teachers

In both instructional settings, those that maintained and those that eliminated their primary-language programs, teachers noted several key effects of recent policy changes:

- Increased frequency of assessments in English along with a push for more English curriculum and instruction in the classroom;
- Greater pressure and accountability to transition students into mainstream English to raise test scores;

- Negative impact of English standardized assessments on the quality of learning for students;
- Negative effects of multiple state policies (Proposition 227, high-stakes testing) on teacher autonomy and pedagogical control in the classroom;
- Teachers also questioned the fundamental fairness of English-only standardized tests as a measure of the growth and achievements of their English-language-learner students.

Increased Frequency of English Assessments

As these teachers' emphasis on instructing children in their primary language diminished following the implementation of Proposition 227, they noted a simultaneous shift toward increased English assessments. This shift occurred even in schools that were able to maintain their primary-language programs. As the following teacher notes, in the classroom, Proposition 227 is not experienced as a single policy, but rather as the catalyst for a variety of interconnected changes, including the increase in English-only testing:

> This year, first graders are being tested on the language arts section of the SAT nine. The rationale is now that students are being immersed in English, we can go ahead and test them in English. So, Prop. two twenty-seven in a way has legitimized the English-only testing of English-language learners.

Greater Pressure to Transition Students into English

Not surprisingly, paralleling this emphasis on English-only assessments is a greater sense among teachers that they are being held accountable for rapidly transitioning their students into English. Educators in both instructional settings overwhelmingly expressed this concern. The pressure teachers experienced is strongly linked to school and district administrators' expectations of higher student test scores and increased API levels, to which monetary rewards are tied. In this context, teachers, feeling the pressure to push students into English whether or not they are ready, express concern that students' individual learning needs are taking a backseat to district- and state-level policy decisions. Moreover, the pressure to rapidly transition students is layered over Proposition 227, a mandate that was itself onerous, from the teachers' perspective (Alamillo & Viramontes, 2000).

Increased English Curriculum and Negative Impact on Quality of Learning

Educators in our sample asserted that increased standardized testing and the push to transition students into English instruction sooner seemed to be driving the curriculum. Both in schools that maintained their bilingual programs after Proposition 227 and in schools that dismantled their programs, teachers voiced concerns that the increased emphasis on testing was resulting in a decreased emphasis on learning. They noted that the post-Proposition 227 focus on English-language instruction parallels the emphasis on student performance on the SAT 9. This has affected classrooms in two ways. First, teachers perceive a supplemental curriculum filtering into their classrooms. "There is an increase in programs that aim at increasing test scores," one teacher explained. "We have adopted Target Teach, which is a supplement on raising test scores and lining them up with state standards. We've also adopted Accelerated Reader." Teaching to the test is usurping their teaching practices and instructional time. Moreover, the teachers note, students who fail the SAT 9 test begin to see themselves as unsuccessful, which has a downward spiraling effect on their academic achievement: "Third and fourth graders are really struggling. There are a lot of problems that come with these students being disillusioned. Many feel they can't function," one teacher remarked. Students' perceived inability to "function" suggests the deep level at which standardized testing is affecting students. The high-stakes nature of the SAT 9 only exacerbates the problem. Students' self-esteem, according to the teacher quoted in the following excerpt, is seriously impacted by the possibility of retention:

> Our principal has mandated that teachers do practice testing a month before the test. [But] the nuances in the language of the test—the idioms—are beyond students' comprehension. We've done practice testing to try to get students' fear down. There's too much pressure on students to produce. I have a real problem with that . . . third, fourth, and fifth graders are being told that they may be retained if they don't do well on the test . . . especially for second-language learners, that's a lot of pressure and stress.

The pressure is on in California's public schools, according to the teachers we spoke with, to increase standardized test scores, regardless of other concerns. These comments, from three different teachers, express the pressures they are feeling:

- "Teachers are more accountable. Also, teachers have changed teaching practices because of the increase in tests."
- "It [SAT 9] places more pressure on teachers to raise scores. I teach in a bilingual [setting] but have changed my teaching practices to align them with standards and mandated tests."
- "Teachers are on their feet more, and a lot more time is spent on strategies for reaching our goal: to be at the national norm [on the SAT 9]."

The second way in which the increased emphasis on SAT 9 test performance has affected classrooms and curriculum for language-minority students is with the introduction of English-only scripted reading programs such as the Open Court program described earlier. Teachers see the adoption of this program (or others such as Success For All or Results) as intimately connected with the focus on improving student test scores rather than as a top-down effort to ensure a meaningful learning experience for children. One teacher put it this way:

We have an accelerated English program aimed at getting students into mainstream classes much sooner. There is a push to get students into mainstream English so that they will be prepared for the standardized tests that come up.

The shift to these new programs concerns teachers because they perceive the new curriculum as lacking creativity and a commitment to deeper concept learning. One teacher explained, "There is absolutely nothing creative about the reading program. In fact, for children who are having trouble, it's completely scripted." Particularly in schools attempting to maintain their bilingual programs, district-level, forced implementation of such English-only curricula has been devastating. In describing the impact of these educational policies on their students, educators frequently alluded to the tremendous pressure placed on students to produce high test scores, as well as feelings of disillusionment among their students and among themselves.

Philosophical Disagreement with English-Only
High-Stakes Testing

All of the teachers interviewed had philosophical reservations about the educational changes brought on by increased high-stakes testing in the classroom. Teachers fundamentally disagreed with having to administer a single, English-only, norm-referenced test as the sole determinant of their students' academic achievement. As one teacher said, "SAT nine does not offer a true measure of [my] students' growth. It's not fair to students." Additionally, teachers were critical of the state's disregard for student performance on the Spanish language test, the Spanish Assessment of Bilingual Education (SABE). One teacher aptly noted:

> The state talks of multiple measures, but all they acknowledge is the SAT nine. Testing is the state's quick fix to everything. Even though students have scored high on SABE, the state only acknowledges SAT nine. The English push is so great that when kids come to kindergarten, there's a gap in oral language development in primary language.

Because of the enormous pressure on teachers and students to produce results quickly, teachers have less flexibility in the choice of assessment tools they use to measure their students' progress. Thus, teachers and students, especially English-language learners, have been denied the opportunity to demonstrate academic achievement and growth.

Reduced Teacher Autonomy

As a result of the state's policy shifts, teachers have suffered a loss of autonomy in the classroom that has left many feeling alienated from their professional lives. One teacher in a school that had thus far maintained its bilingual program noted, "SAT nine and accountability have had a strong effect on us in the area of justifying everything that we do on paper. There is nothing about having kids fully bilingual. We're also losing a lot of teachers." All teachers interviewed expressed a disconnect between what they considered to be their students' greatest need—a creative and challenging curriculum—and what administrators at district and state levels considered to be of utmost importance. This growing tension has been exacerbated by mandates that do not take into consideration teachers' expertise. "There is a real lack of knowledge at the district and administrative level," one teacher pointed out. "It is very irrational. Teachers are trying to maintain integrity of their teaching program, but they're under close scrutiny." This scrutiny of teachers parallels the expectations placed on students to "produce" higher test scores. In fact, as several teachers suggested, the two are intimately related because students' performance on the SAT 9 is often taken as an indicator of their competence as teachers: "Teachers 'sweat it' every time SAT nine comes around; we dread it. We're being judged by it."

Thus, all of the teachers we interviewed, both those in schools where the bilingual programs had been dismantled and those where they had been maintained, expressed similar concerns about current trends in educational policies. Still, there were a few noteworthy differences between the two groups of teachers.

Specific Concerns of Teachers in Bilingual and Traditional Educational Settings

Teachers in schools that lost their bilingual programs in the wake of Proposition 227 emphasized the impact of the loss of primary-language instruction in combination with the increase in standardized assessment. In one teacher's words, "Doing away with bilingual education has hindered learning for children. Students are stressed out. We teach them how to take assessments." Thus, not only are students no longer able to rely on their primary language to help them make sense of material, but due to testing pressures, teachers are no longer able to offer them a rich curriculum, even in English. These teachers felt they were further impoverishing the educational experience of their language-minority students because they, too, had been denied the use of their linguistic talents and training to help their students make sense of material.

Teachers in schools where, thanks to waivers, bilingual programs were still in place expressed special concern that the emphasis on testing was eroding their programs and undermining their ability to maintain primary-language instruction. These teachers felt that the state's high-pressure, English-only accountability system was even more damaging to their primary-language programs than Proposition 227 had been. The state's accountability system privileges students' English language performance on the SAT 9 over other indicators of student achievement. Academic Performance Index scores threaten those bilingual education programs that remained intact after the passage of Proposition 227. "The only thing that really matters," one teacher explained, "are those

[English-language] test scores. And if we don't have that, we are not a good school." Students' learning in their primary language becomes irrelevant. This calls into question bilingual educational practices and encourages bilingual teachers to transition children to English earlier.

Principals

We found that principals' philosophical positions on bilingual education significantly influenced how they perceived the relationship between Proposition 227 and the state's English-only accountability system. Those who were strongly in favor of bilingual education shared their teachers' feelings of powerlessness in a system that appeared to them to involve interconnected policies. One principal in a school forced to dismantle its bilingual program felt that anti-immigrant sentiments were behind the state's policies regarding standards and assessment of language-minority children. In her words:

> I see it all wrapped up with [Propositions] two-o-nine, two-twenty-seven, and one-eighty-seven. I see there are a lot of people in the state who wish these children would just go away and are using them as scapegoats for the years of underfunding in the schools, and not addressing the real problems. They're our little victims. The teachers, also, are victimized—having to present material the kids aren't even ready for. They too are so caught up in the standards of the state of California, and they know very well the children aren't ready for it.

Thus, according to this principal, the introduction of APIs and the requirement that all children be tested in English were only the latest in a series of moves by state-level politicians and policy makers to reduce immigrant and native Latino student access to educational opportunities. This administrator also expressed frustration at her own loss of control over the way her school and its students would be ranked and judged by the state: "Having to test them in English is a travesty like everything else. I do what I'm supposed to because my job is to implement board policy. So we have to do it, but it's really terrible during testing time. I can see so many kids struggling." This feeling of powerlessness has, according to this principal, affected morale at her school among both teachers and pupils.

In contrast, principals who did not have a strong philosophical commitment to bilingual education appeared to see no conflict between the success of language-minority children in schools and the new assessment system. In their view, the English-only testing mandate and the strict standards were helping to hold schools accountable for addressing the needs of English-language learners. Proposition 227 and the English-only testing mandate helped these principals' schools become "more focused, [with] fewer things we're trying to do" (also, see Sloan, chapter 5). Although these principals saw connections among the various state policies, in their view the outcomes for language-minority pupils were positive.

One principal's school had adopted a "much more direct instruction" literacy program, similar to Open Court. He mentioned that it was Proposition 227 and English-only standardized testing that had encouraged this switch. He also said he was pleased with the results in terms of an increase in test scores. When asked whether he saw any connection between Proposition 227 and SAT 9 testing, this principal responded, "It's helping in our case, because we have about seventy percent LEP and our test scores went WAY up." Some of the credit belonged to their new literacy program, he explained, but "All these things are tied together. It's not just any one thing." This principal's conclusion that the English-only instruction mandated by Proposition 227, combined with a more direct instructional approach to literacy, has helped raise his LEP students' test scores seems to support teachers' assertion that at the administrative level, curricular decisions are being made on the basis of how programs affect standardized test scores rather than on how they affect children's educational experience.

Much of the difference of opinion among principals regarding the high-stakes, English-only testing of language-minority students appeared to originate in the subjects' personal viewpoints on the efficacy of bilingual education. Yet regardless of their attitudes toward the connections, all of these principals agreed with teachers that the various policies converged to affect language-minority students in interconnected ways. According to the professionals who manage the schools and classrooms of language-minority students, an English-only testing mandate and accountability system has had at least as much effect on the curriculum and school experience of language-minority students as Proposition 227.

Specific Concerns of Principals in Bilingual Schools

Like their teachers, principals in schools that had maintained their bilingual programs noted that some of the most devastating effects of English-only testing have been forced early transitions into English and an increase in test preparation and English curriculum in bilingual class-rooms. The principals also reported an increase in conflicts among staff members at their schools, and underlying all of these effects, the further erosion of primary-language instructional programs.

These principals (again, like their teachers) seemed especially con-cerned about English-only testing. The overarching theme among those we interviewed was that the English-only testing mandate is inappropriate. As all five of these principals explained, testing students in English who are not receiving English literacy instruction yields no important information about the students. Worse, it places students and teachers in the awkward position of being judged on material they have not studied. Results of the English-only tests are not valid, these principals maintain, yet the results of Spanish-language tests such as SABE are not taken into account in the statewide school ranking system. As one principal angrily asserted:

> Not only [is it] unfair, it's almost idiotic. Whoever thought it would be prudent to assess a student in a language they are not being in-structed in. . . . Whoever made those rules, it doesn't make sense. Two-twenty-seven allowed us to maintain bilingual education if par-ents approve, for us to instruct kids in their primary language in con-tent while they're learning English. Parent waivers are a provision of the law. And our parents have requested bilingual programs. And then they turn around and make those kids take a test in English. It's wrong. It's part of the conservative agenda to enforce English-only instruction, to put as many barriers in the way as possible to bilin-gual education.

It is difficult, in the face of the English-only testing requirement, to con-tinue in good conscience to instruct children in their primary language. According to the same principal, "We know we're doing the right things, using best practices, helping the kids learn English and the content areas in the best possible way . . . yet when you're judged in the newspaper by that [API] score, you can't help but feel badly about it."

CONCLUSION: IMPLICATIONS OF CALIFORNIA'S ENGLISH-ONLY POLICIES ON LATINO LANGUAGE-MINORITY STUDENTS

Since the passage of Proposition 227, additional policy shifts, including high-stakes testing, supplemental curriculum focused on English acquisi-tion, and increased accountability have converged to significantly impact the education of language-minority students. The effects of these multiple policies have not been uniformly positive, and the implications for the future are not promising.

Our findings reveal that teachers in schools that maintained, and schools that eliminated, bilingual education following the passage of Proposition 227 are experiencing these policies as top-down reforms. This has in effect reduced teacher autonomy with respect to classroom instruction. Current educational trends posit higher test scores and a school's API ranking as the primary educational goals of students and teachers. According to the teachers we surveyed, this misplaced focus has led to the impoverishment of student learning. Further, for bilingual educators, this focus has resulted in the erosion of their primary-language instruction and curriculum. The educators with whom we spoke saw the intersection of Proposition 227 with other reform attempts as encouraging teachers to teach to the test and to transition students into English at a faster rate than effective teaching practices for second-language learners would advise. Principals' philosophical position regarding bilingual education and Proposition 227 factored into how they perceived the effect of the various state policies on language-minority students, but they all resoundingly agreed with teachers that the policies were converging in California's classrooms and having a powerful impact on students.

California teachers' projections of the impact of high-stakes testing on their language-minority students find strong parallels in the work of McNeil and Valenzuela (2001). Drawing on emerging research on high-stakes testing and on their individual investigations (McNeil, 1988, 2000; Valenzuela, 1999, 2002), the authors identify alarming educational trends associated with the implementation of the Texas Assessment of Academic Skills (TAAS) testing in the state's public schools: TAAS-based teaching and test preparation are usurping a substantive curriculum; TAAS is divorced from children's experience and culture; and TAAS is widening the educational gap between rich and poor, between mainstream and language-minority students (McNeil & Valenzuela, 2001).

The educational trends in California and Texas are similar. Both states use one test to determine academic outcomes for students. Both have placed a tremendous emphasis on school ranking and are seeing a drastic increase in the implementation of mandated scripted reading programs at the expense of known, effective instructional practices for second-language learners. Like Texas, California is moving toward a more and more prescriptive educational system, discrediting the cultural and linguistic assets students bring to the classroom. According to McNeil and Valenzuela, the TAAS system is "playing out its inherent logic at the expense of our poorest minority children." Our data indicate the same is true for California's policies. The accountability system supports subtractive English-only programs for Latino students (García, 2001). Nor is California's approach aligned with empirical information related to optimal and effective schooling for language-minority students (August & Hakuta, 1997). Presently, three years after full implementation of Proposition 227 and two years after implementation of state accountability policies, SAT 9 scores for California's Latino students statewide continue to show underachievement. And significant achievement gaps persist between Latino, White, and Asian students. Our research findings indicate a very negative prognosis. In both the short and long terms, the multiple-policy push toward "English only" appears poised to exact a great price, especially on the educational outcomes of California's Latino·students.

NOTES

1. There are many examples of such efforts: the California State Department of Education funded programs to better train infant and toddler caregivers (California State Department of Education, 1998); the U.S. Department of Education launched reforms in federally funded education programs (García & Gonzalez, 1995; United States Department of Education, 1997); the National Academy of Education initiated discussion of standards-based reform (McLaughlin, Shepard, & O'Day, 1995); the Roundtable on Head Start Research (part of the National Research Council) undertook an issue analysis of research needed to produce a thriving future for Head Start among a highly diverse population of children and families (Phillips & Cabrera, 1996); the National Council of Teachers of English and the International Reading Association developed language arts standards (NCTE/IRA, 1996); and the National Association for the Education of Young Children issued a position statement regarding linguistic and cultural diversity (NAEYC, 1996).

2. Moreover, teachers, administrators, and school board members can be held personally liable for fees and damages should a student's parents or guardians sue for failure to enforce the provisions of the initiative.

3. In developing its position statement, the AERA relied on the 1999 Standards for Educational and Psychological Testing, which represent a professional consensus between AERA and the American Psychological Association and National Council on Measurement in Education.

4. In an initial assessment of Proposition 227 implementation in selected districts and schools, García and Curry (2000) note that a combination of factors influenced implementation strategies. In general, interviews with school district personnel and teachers reveal that districts with longstanding bilingual program policies tended to pursue parental waivers, which allowed them to maintain existing programs. As a result, district-wide efforts were made to ensure waivers at

each school. At the local level, principals played a key role in ensuring that parents were informed of parental waivers by holding school-wide meetings and sending letters home translated in the appropriate language.

REFERENCES

Alamillo, L., & Viramontes, C. (2000). Reflections from the classroom: Teacher perspectives on the implementation of Proposition 227. *Bilingual Research Journal, 24*(1–3), 155–67.

American Educational Research Association. (2000). *AERA position statement concerning high-stakes testing in preK–12 education.* Retrieved December 13, 2001, from http://www.aera.net/about/policy/stakes.htm

August, D., & Hakuta, K. (1997). *Improving schooling for language minority children: Research agenda.* Washington, D.C.: National Research Council.

California State Department of Education. (1998a). Education Code, Section 300–340.

California State Department of Education. (1998b). *Fostering development in a first and second language in early childhood.* Resource Guide. Sacramento, CA: Author.

California State Department of Education. (1999). *Public school accountability act.* Retrieved March 24, 2004. Available at: http://www.cde.ca.gov/psaa/

Foorman, B. R., Francis, D. J., Fletcher, J. M., Schatschneider, C., & Mehta, P. (1998). The role of instruction in learning to read: Preventing reading failure in at-risk children. *Journal of Educational Psychology, 90*(1), 35–55.

Gandara, P. (2000). In the aftermath of the storm: English learners in the post-227 era. *Bilingual Research Journal, 24*(1–3), 1–13.

García, E. (2001). *Hispanic education in the United States: Raíces y Alas.* Lanham, MD: Rowman and Littlefield Publishers.

García, E., & Curry-Rodriguez, J. (2000). The education of limited English proficient students in California schools: An assessment of the influence of Proposition 227 in selected districts and schools. *Bilingual Research Journal, 24*(1–3), 15–35.

García, E., & Gonzalez, R. (1995). Issues in systemic reform for culturally and linguistically diverse students. *College Record, 96*(3), 418–31.

García, E., & Palmer, D. (2000). Voices from the field: Bilingual educators speak candidly about Proposition 227. *Bilingual Research Journal, 24*(1–3), 169–178.

McLaughlin, M., Shepard, L., & O'Day, J. (1995). *Improving education through standards based reform.* National Academy of Education, Panel on Standards-Based Education Reform. Stanford, CA: Stanford University.

McNeil, L. M. (1988). *Contradictions of control: School structure and school knowledge.* New York: Routledge.

McNeil, L. M. (2000). *Contradictions of reform: The educational costs of standardization*. New York: Routledge.

McNeil, L. M., & Valenzuela, A. (2001). The harmful impact of the TAAS system of testing in Texas: Beneath the accountability rhetoric. In M. Kornhaber & G. Orfield (Eds.), *Raising standards or raising barriers? Inequity and high-stakes testing in public education* (pp. 127–150). New York: Century Foundation.

Moustafa, M., & Land, R. (2001). *The research base of Open Court and its translation into instructional policy in California*. Retrieved March 24, 2004. Available at: http://instructional1.calstatela.edu/mmousta/The_Research_Base_of_Open_Court_and_Its_Translation_into_Instructional_Policy_in_California.htm

National Association for the Education of Young Children. (1996). NAEYC Position Paper: Responding to linguistic and cultural diversity—Recommendations for effective early childhood education. *Young Children*, p. 12.

National Commission on Excellence in Education. (1983*). A nation at risk: A report to the nation and secretary of education, United States Department of Education*. Washington, D.C.: The Commission: Superintendent of Documents U.S. GPO distributor.

National Council of Teachers of English/International Reading Association. (1996). *Standards for the English language arts*. Urbana, IL & Newark, DE: Authors.

Phillips, D., & Cabrera, N. (Eds.) (1996). *Beyond the blueprint, directions for research on Head Start's families*, National Research Council. Washington, D.C.: National Academy Press.

Policy Analysis for California Education. (1998). *Californians speak on education reform options: Uneven faith in teachers, school boards and the state designers of change*. Berkeley, CA: Author.

Stiles, J., Cohen, J., Elkins, Z., & Gey, F. (1998). *California Latino demographic databook*. California Policy Seminar, Berkeley, CA.

Stritikus, T. (2000). *Proposition 227: A qualitative analysis at the classroom level*. Doctoral Dissertation. University of California, Berkeley.

U.S. Department of Education. (1997). *No more excuses: The final report of U.S. Hispanic Dropout Project*. Washington, D.C.: Author.

Valenzuela, A. (1999). *Subtractive schooling: U.S-Mexican youth and the politics of caring*. Albany: State University of New York Press.

Valenzuela, A. (2002). High-stakes testing and U.S.-Mexican youth in Texas: The case for multiple compensatory criteria in assessment. *Harvard Journal of Hispanic Policy, 14*, 97–116.

Wells, F. (2001). Zip codes shouldn't determine our students' future. *California Educator, 5*(8), 6–8.

White House Initiatives on Educational Excellence for Hispanic Americans. (2000). Report of the White House Initiative. Washington, D.C.: U.S. Department of Education.

8

The Centurion: Standards and High-Stakes Testing as Gatekeepers for Bilingual Teacher Candidates in the New Century

BELINDA BUSTOS FLORES AND ELLEN RIOJAS CLARK

Promoters of teaching standards and policy makers have an erroneous, misguided, and misplaced faith in competency testing. President George W. Bush (2001), for example, contends that testing helps ensure equality and that it is racist *not* to test. We disagree that standards tout accountability—in the form of high-stakes testing—as crucial to educational reform. As educators who work with minority, prospective, bilingual-education teachers in a large, urban public university, we see what the policy makers do not: the arbitrary outcomes and unnecessary conflict, pain, and struggles faced by these students as they pursue their goal of becoming certified teachers. We are repeatedly confronted with evidence of the inequities of schooling and high-stakes testing. Our experience reveals that far from being a model of educational reform, Texas is a perfect example of why the dictates of policy do not always translate into good practice.

In this chapter, we review some of the key efforts to reform teacher education, including the escalation of high-stakes competency testing, and trace their effects on the supply of minority bilingual education teachers in Texas. State and federal legislation that ties funding to test-based accreditation has prompted local colleges and universities to initiate additional layers of competency testing of their own. The result is a new set of barriers limiting the number of minority teacher candidates—and this at a time when great shortages of teachers who can meet the needs of the state's rapidly changing school population already exist. On the basis of our previous research and the results of a case study (reported here) we conducted recently, we contend that teacher testing in Texas serves as a gatekeeping mechanism for prospective bilingual education teachers (Clark & Flores, 2002; Flores & Clark, 1997; Flores, 2001). Existing tests have an inherent lack of predictive validity as a measure of teacher competence. We argue that there should be alternatives to competency testing and that competency should be assessed using multiple measures. Furthermore, as Hood and Parker have proposed (1989), state legislatures and university departments of education should be "pressured to allow minorities more of a determining role in the shaping of the tests" (p. 519).

TEACHER EDUCATION REFORM EFFORTS: THE PROLIFERATION OF COMPETENCY EXAMS

In Texas, teacher accountability became a political issue in 1986–87, the first year all teachers were required to pass the Texas Examination of Current Administrators and Teachers (TECAT) to be certified to teach (Clark & Flores, 2002; Flores & Clark, 1997; McNeil, 2000). The TECAT did not, however, sufficiently reduce the number of existing "incompetent" professionals, or at least not in policy makers' estimation. Two additional tests were implemented: the Pre-Professional Skills Test (PPST), an entry exam that was supposed to confirm the competency of teacher candidates; and the Examination for the Certification of Educators in Texas (ExCET), which was designed as an exit competency test for prospective teachers. Initially, only teacher candidates were required to take the PPST. Later, policy makers decided that all entering undergraduates should pass a minimum competency test. In 1987, the Texas Assessment of Skills Program (TASP) exam was designated as an entry, state-mandated test for first-time students at all state public colleges and universities (Boylan, 1996; Clark & Flores, 2002; Flores & Clark, 1997; Matthews, 1993). These entry and exit tests are described later in more detail.

Texas Assessment of Skills Program

All freshmen entering Texas public colleges and universities are required either to have been exempted from taking the TASP or to have taken and passed it (some limited alternatives are noted later). The exam tests students in reading, writing, and mathematics. TASP passing standards (set by the state and regulated by the Texas Higher Education Coordinating Board [THECB]) require a minimum scale score of 230 out of 300 in the reading and mathematics portions and a minimum scale score of 220 out of 300 in the writing portion. Exceptionally high scores on the Scholastic

Aptitude Test (SAT), American College Test (ACT), or the Texas Assessment of Academic Skills (TAAS) will exempt a student from taking the TASP (see Figure 8.1).

According to the THECB, in 1998–99, only 10.8% of Latino students, as compared to 76% of White students, were exempted from the TASP on the basis of their ACT, SAT, or TAAS scores. In 1999–2000, the number of Latino exemptions increased to 13.3%. More university-bound Latino students were exempted (23.1%) than community or technical college-bound students (9.4%) (THECB, 2000). Significantly, it is among the latter group that most nontraditional, ethnic minority teacher candidates are found.

For 1999–2000, on initial attempt, Latinos had a 33.8% overall passing rate and Whites had a 60.4% passing rate (these rates include exemptions as well as passes). On their first try, all students were more likely to pass the writing portion (69.3%) as compared to the reading (61.4%) and math (42.0%) sections. Failing the test on its first administration decreases the likelihood of passing on the second administration (THECB, 1995, 1999, 2000). In 1999–2000, 35.2% of the Latino test retakers passed on subsequent attempts, as compared to 49.7% of Whites who retook the exam. Again, across students in all ethnic groups, retesters were more likely to pass the reading portion (54.64%) of the test than the writing (51.1%) or math (49.7%) segments. Boylan (1996)

FIGURE 8.1
TASP Exemptions

Test	Minimum Scores Required	
ACT	Composite Scores of 23, with	
	Individual English Score	19
	Individual Mathematics Score	19
SAT-recentered	Composite Score of 1070, with	
	Verbal Score	500
	Mathematics Score	500
TAAS*	Reading	Index score of 89
	Writing	Scale score of 1770
	Mathematics	Index Score of 86

Note. *A minimum index score of 70 is considered passing on the reading and writing portions of the TAAS. A minimum of 1500 out of 2400 is considered passing on the TAAS writing.

concluded that students who fail the TASP more than twice are at an increased risk of dropping out of college. It is likely that students' performance suffers as their stress levels increase with each subsequent attempt at the test. Remediation does help some students pass the TASP in subsequent trials (Boylan, 1996; THECB, 1995; 1999), but others are "stopped out" (Tinto, 1987) from pursuing a college degree.

Over the last several years, the state has offered some alternatives for demonstrating mastery on the TASP (THECB, 2001). For example, the "B-or-better" rule allows students who complete remediation in the TASP subject area they did not pass to fulfill the TASP requirement by passing a required college core course in the subject area with a grade of "B" or better. The state now also gives the universities more flexibility in determining whether a student has fulfilled TASP requirements. Nevertheless, most universities continue to require all students to take the TASP prior to enrollment in college-level course work. Thus, the exam continues to be a gatekeeper, especially for minority students.

Examination for Certification in Texas (ExCET)

All teacher candidates must register for and pass the Examination for Certification in Texas (ExCET) in specific areas to be certified to teach in Texas. Each ExCET exam is a criterion-referenced, multiple-choice competency test (i.e., the type of certification sought determines the number and type of ExCET tests to be taken). According to the Texas Education Agency (TEA, 1994, p. 1), "The purpose of the ExCET is to ensure that each educator has the knowledge necessary to begin teaching in Texas public schools or to be granted a professional certificate. ExCET tests are related to the job which is required at the entry-level." Elementary generalist teachers must pass two tests for certification. Bilingual education teachers, however, must take three tests to be certified: Professional Development, Comprehensive/Bilingual Education, and Texas (Spanish) Oral Proficiency Test (TOPT). Bilingual early childhood teachers must take all of these tests plus the Early Childhood test, for a total of four exams (early childhood generalist teachers have to pass three tests). See Figure 8.2 for an overview of entry and exit exams required by the state of Texas.

The Professional Developmental test for elementary teachers "measure[s] pedagogical knowledge in areas such as instructional planning and methodology, curriculum development, classroom management, assessment and evaluation, and principles of education" (TEA, 1994, p. 6). The

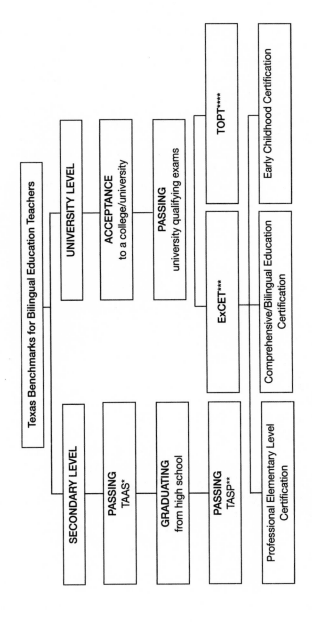

Texas Benchmarks for Bilingual Education Teachers

SECONDARY LEVEL
- PASSING TAAS*
- GRADUATING from high school
- PASSING TASP**
  - Professional Elementary Level Certification
  - Comprehensive/Bilingual Education Certification

UNIVERSITY LEVEL
- ACCEPTANCE to a college/university
- PASSING university qualifying exams
  - ExCET***
  - TOPT****
  - Early Childhood Certification

Mandated testing for Texas teacher candidates, 2002.

*TAAS = Texas Assessment of Academic Skills

**TASP = Texas Assessment Skills Program Exam; required of all entering college students. High scores on TAAS, SAT, (Scholastic Aptitude Test), or ACT (American College Testing) result in exemption.

***ExCET = Examination for the Certification of Educators in Texas. Test is criterion-referenced: type of certification sought determines number and type of ExCET exam required.

****TOPT = Spanish Oral Proficiency Exam. Required for bilingual edcators.

Comprehensive/Bilingual Education test measures foundations and principles of bilingual education, content knowledge, and ability to apply pedagogical knowledge to particular content. The Early Childhood test measures principles and developmentally appropriate practices for the Pre-K–K grade levels. The TOPT measures Spanish oral language proficiency; to pass, students must demonstrate an advanced level of proficiency.

The TEA permits school districts to hire prospective teachers after they have completed their degree and certification requirements, but before they have taken the appropriate ExCETs (first-year employed teachers have one year within which to pass the tests). Teachers who have not passed their specialty ExCET can, unfortunately, be hired only in a non-specialty setting (e.g., general elementary). The hiring district dismisses teachers who subsequently take and do not pass the ExCET needed for their specialization.

COMPETENCY EXAMS AS GATEKEEPERS

Ethnic minority students are not entering institutions of higher education or the teaching profession for various reasons, including lower rates of college eligibility and enrollment, and higher rates of attrition (Valencia, 1991). The high cost of tuition and the opportunity for other career options may be other contributing factors (Recruiting New Teachers [RNT], 2000). A declining interest in the teaching profession may also be due to the TAAS-driven curriculum (Flores, 2001). In addition to these factors, however, and an arguably more important influence, is the gauntlet of competency tests that must be endured to reach the goal of becoming a bilingual education teacher (Valencia & Aburto, 1991a).

The most recent ExCET data reveal that White, nonminority teacher candidates continue to have higher scores and a higher passing rate on their first attempt than their minority counterparts (State Board of Educator Certification [SBEC, 2001]). As Table 8.1 shows, White candidates' first time and cumulative passing rates are higher than those of Hispanic candidates, and Hispanic candidates' passing rates are higher than those of African American candidates (SBEC, 2001a, 2001b, 2001c). Minority students' passing rates rise on their subsequent trials, but they remain well below those of their White counterparts. Moreover, over a three-year period, from a pool of approximately 15,000 Hispanic teacher candidates, 11–12% did not pass the ExCET, even upon re-taking the exam. Thus, a single measure denied approximately 1,500 Latino teacher candidates the opportunity to teach.

TABLE 8.2
Texas Statewide Annual ExCET Passing Rates by Race/Ethnicity

	White		Hispanic		African American	
Year	First Attempt	Cum. Score	First Attempt	Cum. Score	First Attempt	Cum. Score
9/1/00–8/31/01	93%	96%	79%	89%	73%	84%
9/1/99–8/31/00	93%	95%	80%	88%	75%	81%
9/1/98–8/31/99	93%	96%	80%	88%	74%	80%

Adapted from SBEC reports, 2001.

Detailed analyses of competency test outcomes in Texas and other states confirm the role that these exams play as gatekeepers for ethnic/racial minority students. For example, after an examination of data from six states that use competency entry or exit exams and that have a high density of Latinos, Valencia and Aburto (1991a) noted some interesting findings. They concluded that ethnic minority students were challenged more by the basic and general knowledge tests than by those that focused on general professional knowledge and classroom observations. Valencia and Guardarrama's (1995) analysis of the 1991–1992 Texas PPST and ExCET data led to additional conclusions about the effects of high-stakes testing. Noting evidence of a high failure rate for minority students, the authors confirmed that entry competency tests served as gatekeepers for prospective minority or bilingual education teachers. They also found that the Professional Development component of the ExCET presented ethnic minority students with the most difficulty.

We conducted a similar study with bilingual early childhood teacher candidates (Flores & Clark, 1997) and identified both the Professional Development and the Early Childhood ExCET tests as key areas of difficulty. On the professional test, although an 88.5% passing rate was reported for all elementary examinees, Latino students had only a 66.5% passing rate. A lower overall passing rate was reported for universities with larger Latino enrollments. On the Early Childhood test, Latino students had a 47.85% passing rate compared to an overall passing rate of 75.1%. These data led us to conclude that the ExCET tests, especially the professional and early childhood exams, were primary gatekeepers for future Latino bilingual early childhood teachers. However, we also noted

other factors that may have contributed to higher failure rates: (a) a high
degree of key courses taken with adjunct faculty; (b) course work taken
over an extended period of time and on a part-time basis; (c) excessive
credit hours taken per semester; or (d) too many exit exams taken on the
same day (Flores & Clark, 1997).

THE INTERSECTION OF HIGH-STAKES TESTING AND
UNIVERSITY POLICY

Despite policy makers' and politicians' tendency to take the usefulness of
competency tests as given, there is little empirical research that confirms
a positive relationship between Texas' competency tests and actual
teacher performance. Studies that used the National Teacher Exam
(NTE) as a measure of teacher competency (e.g., Daniel, 1993; Moore,
Schurr, & Henriksen, 1991; Pultorak, 1991) found a lack of correlation
between the NTE Core Battery and performance. The Educational Testing Service (publisher of the NTE), explicitly cautions that the test does
not predict teacher performance (Pultorak, 1991; Valencia & Aburto,
1991b).
    Furthermore, issues of validity and reliability have not been ade-
quately addressed for teacher competency tests (Valencia & Aburto,
1991b; Haney, Fowler, Wheelock, Bebell, & Malec, 1999). Melnick and
Pullin (2000) warn that "Given the concerns about validity and reliability
with (teacher) tests . . . assurance[s] about teacher quality are ephemeral at
best" (p. 273). These limitations have not, unfortunately, prevented the
spread of competency exams. Not long after the implementation of the
ExCET exams, some Texas universities began adding exit requirements
of their own, designed to enhance students' scores on the state's mandated tests. State colleges and universities have a vested interest in their
students' scores: institutions with large numbers of low-scoring students
risk losing their accreditation—not only for certifying teachers, but for
granting any degree. Moreover, despite a recent warning from the National Council on Research that "lawmakers shouldn't rely on teacher-li-
censure tests as the sole basis for comparing teacher-education programs
or for withholding funds" (Basinger, 2001, p. 4), federal funding and licensing decisions are tied to competency test scores as well. Shaker
(2002) notes:

> With the inception of Title II of the Higher Education Act (Public
> Law 105-244, [1998]), the federal government has begun a process

of employing such [competency] tests not only for entry to the class-room by individuals, but for determining which institutions of higher education will have the right to prepare candidates for licensure. (p. 65)

Policies like these restrict access to educational opportunities for all students, but, as we show in the case study that follows, they are especially damaging to non-traditional, minority teacher candidates.

CASE STUDY: TITLE VII "HOME-GROWN" TEACHERS

Background

During fall 1995, the University of San Cuilmas[1] was awarded federal funding for a Title VII bilingual education teacher preparation project to prepare "home-grown" teachers.[2] Twenty students were selected to participate in the project. Of these, twelve successfully completed their degree and certification requirements within a two-year period. The remaining eight are the focus of this case study. Among the students selected to participate in the project, the majority (16 out of 20) were individuals who had been attending the local community college and who had worked for numerous years as bilingual paraprofessionals. The school districts employing these paraprofessionals had recommended them as candidates for the university's Title VII project during the fall 1995 and spring 1996 semesters. In addition to having their districts' recommendations, the candidates had to satisfy the following program entry requirements: (a) have a minimum GPA (grade point average) of 2.5; (b) have completed a minimum of 30 hours, but preferably 45 hours or more, in the core curriculum; and (c) have taken and passed the TASP. Some candidates were admitted to the project conditionally because they had not passed all three sections of the TASP.

These future teachers were placed in a cohort and were carefully followed throughout their program of study by university faculty and staff. They were also monitored for completion of the TASP requirements. For some, passing the TASP required extensive remediation, especially with the math section.[3] (Nontraditional students typically find the math portion of the state-mandated tests the most difficult, especially when their own high school experience occurred many years prior to enrolling in college). All of the paraprofessionals had gone to school over a number of years and had accumulated their college hours slowly while working full time. Their overall grade point average ranged from 2.8 to 3.2 (on a 4-point scale). Once in the project, they all completed their program of study within three years; some did not have to do student teaching because they had served as paraprofessionals for over five years.

During the fall 1999 semester, the university hired an ExCET director whose main responsibility was to monitor the passing rates of completing students and to implement a plan for increasing first-time passing rates. Although the university's overall passing rates were comparable to the state's average, some administrators remained concerned about the first-time pass rates and the overall number of retakes. Equally worrisome was the provision in the 1998 reauthorization of the Title II Higher Education Act (described earlier) that authorized rescinding a university's accreditation and ending its federal aid if students' test scores were too low. The university decided to direct the teacher certification office, for the first time, to require all completing teacher candidates to take a university-administered "qualifying exam." Significantly, all prospective elementary teachers were required to take the same comprehensive test, regardless of specialty area. Moreover, teacher candidates were not allowed to take their state-mandated test until they had taken and passed this qualifying exam and had completed all but the last methods course and student teaching. In the past, each teacher candidate had taken the state test as recommended by the advisor. Now, rather than taking the test when they felt ready, teacher candidates had to first pass the university's qualifying exam and then prepare for the state-mandated exit exam.

Sample

As a follow-up to the university's Title VII project, we examined the undergraduate records of 20 students who had been successfully teaching in area school districts. We were saddened to find that 8 of these 20 first-year bilingual education teachers were no longer in their original positions despite the following: They (a) generally had an above-average GPA, with an overall GPA of 3.0; (b) had received excellent field observation ratings, ranging from 4.3 to 5.0 (on a five-point scale), from their cooperating teacher; and (c) had earned outstanding letters of recommendations from their supervising teachers. As first-year teachers, these candidates on average had received ratings of "exceeding expectations" on their cumulative teacher evaluation. They were well liked by administration, faculty, parents, and children. When they completed their program of study, they had no difficulty securing employment in the school district that had recommended them for the program. The reason these eight "home-grown" teachers had not retained their teaching positions after the first year was because they had not been able to pass the university qualifying test (and thus could not take the state-mandated ExCET exams).

Analysis

When we examined the data more closely, patterns emerged. We noted that the eight "home-grown" teachers themselves had been educated in schools located in low-income districts. We posited that these teacher candidates' prior schooling might be a factor in their inability to pass the university-imposed test. Historically (and even at present), these resource-poor districts have been staffed by individuals not prepared as educators, some of whom are not teaching in their field of study, lack certification or appropriate credentials, or have been prepared through alternative certification routes (Valencia, 2000). Our position is that poor schooling coupled with exclusionary gatekeeping mechanisms resulted in a lack of equal opportunity. Although our position may appear contradictory—unlike some of their "teachers"—our candidates had completed a program of study leading to teaching credentials. In support of this position, we defer to Darling-Hammond's (2000; 2002) findings indicating that university-prepared teachers are more effective than teachers prepared through alternative routes. Thus, we surmised that the educational system had failed these "home-grown" teachers when they were public school students, continues to fail them, and suppresses their aspirations of becoming teachers today.

We observed that in four of the eight cases, individuals who had great difficulty with the university's qualifying generalist test had no difficulty passing the state-mandated bilingual education comprehensive exam (some scored as much as 20 points higher on the stated-mandated exam than on the qualifying test). When asked how they accounted for this difference in their scores on the two exams, the "home-grown" teacher candidates pointed out that there were real differences in content between the two tests and that some or none of the responses on the qualifying generalist test would be appropriate for bilingual classrooms. This discrepancy was most apparent in the language arts section of the test because there are distinct approaches to the teaching of literacy for bilingual learners as compared to monolingual English-dominant learners. The students considered the bilingual education comprehensive exam to be "more on target" with what they had learned and studied. We also asked other students about their reactions to the two tests and received similar responses. We conclude that there is a curriculum mismatch between what bilingual education teacher candidates have learned and what is being tested on the university's "qualifying" comprehensive exam, a test specifically designed for generalist candidates.[4]

Another paradox was that the "home-grown" teachers had to wait until their very last semester before they could take the university qualifying test. Then, if they passed that hurdle, they had to take an additional three to four (depending on their areas of certification) state-mandated exams (see Figure 8.2). The infrequent administrations of the state-mandated exams during the academic year resulted in students having only one chance to take each of the tests during the regular semester (usually the student-teaching semester), and one chance during the summer semester before beginning their first year as full-time classroom teachers. These looming requirements, coupled with the stress of being first-year teachers, placed a heavy burden on the students. As the school year ended, eight of the "home-grown" teachers were faced with the reality that they would not likely have a job the next year because they had not passed the university's qualifying test or had not taken their respective state-mandated ExCET exams. An ill-conceived university policy thus threatened these students' career dreams and potentially diminished the state's supply of bilingual education teachers.

On our last check with the eight "home-grown" teachers in the sample, four had finally passed the state-mandated exams and were teaching; four still had not passed. One non-passing candidate was teaching in a private school, another was a substitute teacher, and a third was working for child welfare services. We could not establish contact with the fourth candidate.

University Policy as Gatekeeping

By implementing its own "prequalifying" test, the university effectively controls who takes the state exams. A university-imposed "qualifying comprehensive exit test" designed for generalist teachers results in barriers for other beginning teachers. The university's blanket policy may protect its accreditation and funding, but only at the expense of its students' welfare. Other universities have dealt with this dilemma in different ways. Some waive the qualifying comprehensive test for bilingual education teachers; others adjust the cutoff scores needed to pass the qualifying exams, and/or use the outcome as a diagnostic benchmark. This university refused to compromise on its requirement, even when challenged, but it did eventually opt to develop a qualifying bilingual education comprehensive test. Unfortunately, recent statewide certification changes further delayed the actual implementation of this bilingual education qualifying test.

The qualifying test continued to present difficulty for completing bilingual elementary education teacher candidates. All nine bilingual candidates who took the test during its most recent administration (fall, 2002) failed. Fortunately, upon employment, these candidates can register for the state-mandated exam without fulfilling the university qualifying exam requirement. The state mandated that universities cannot keep a "completer" (i.e., a teacher candidate who has graduated and/or completed all certification requirements with the exception of the ExCET exams) or an employed teacher candidate from taking the state-mandated exam.[5] However, school districts prefer to employ teacher candidates who have already completed all ExCET requirements. So, again, these candidates face a catch-22 situation (as the uneven employment outcomes for our "home-grown" teachers suggest).

THE CENTURION: NEW TEXAS TEACHER CERTIFICATION STANDARDS
BAR ENTRY TO THE PROFESSION

In yet another attempt to reform teacher education, Texas recently mandated changes to teacher certification programs, revamped and aligned teacher standards, and designed new teacher exit exams. Deplorably, these reforms are being made in the context of a current demand for 40,000 teachers and a predicted statewide teacher shortage due to a steady increase in attrition (Fuller, 2002). Under the new guidelines, future bilingual education teachers will have to choose either certification in early childhood through fourth grades (EC-4) or fourth through eighth grades (4-8). Additional content courses in math and science are required for these new certificates.[6] Some Latino and ethnic minority students will likely have had inadequate preparation in these areas because they may have attended schools in which a large majority of the teachers are not certified. Math and science teachers in low-income districts are especially unlikely to possess either a teaching certificate or a degree in these content areas (SBEC, 2002c). Furthermore, low-income schools often do not offer math or science course work beyond the third year of high school (Ovando & Collier, 1998; Valencia, 2000).

These new certification requirements, phased in fall semester 2002, may deter Latino students from considering the teaching profession. Those who do seek teaching credentials will likely be forced to choose the EC–4 certification because of the advanced requirements for the 4th–8th grade teacher certification. Thus, the new standards will likely shrink the number of Latino teachers available for grades five through eight.

Along with these new certification requirements, new exit tests known as the Texas Examination of Educator Standards (TExES) are being administered. The content of these exams is aligned with the new standards for EC–4 and 4th–8th-grade certification (SBEC, 2002b). Again, this kind of comprehensive exam will likely present the greatest difficulty for those Latino students who have had inadequate K–16 schooling experiences.[7]

CURRENT AND FUTURE DEMAND FOR ETHNIC MINORITY BILINGUAL TEACHERS

Nearly three-quarters (73%) of urban districts nationwide face an immediate and pressing need for bilingual education teachers (*The Urban Teacher Challenge*, 2000). Only 14% of K–12 teachers are ethnic minorities (Recruiting New Teachers, 2000). Given the overwhelming increase in ethnic minority student enrollment, it is unconscionable that the teaching force does not reflect this diversity.

Even in states that are highly populated with ethnic minorities, disparities are present. In Texas classrooms, for example, 40% of the students are Latinos; Latino teachers, however, represent only 16.3% of the profession (TEA, 2001). Enrollment in bilingual/ESL (English as a second language) classrooms has shown a steady 7.1% annual increase (TEA, 2001). Using various demographic trends, over the past ten years, several researchers have estimated and warned us about the looming bilingual education teacher shortage due to high-stakes testing (Reyna, 1993; Valencia & Aburto, 1991a; Valencia & Guardarrama, 1995). The bilingual teacher shortage also contributes to the steady increase in the number of teachers teaching out of field in the area of bilingual education as compared to other areas (Clark & Flores, 2002; Flores & Clark, 1997). Current Texas SBEC figures released in 2000 confirmed these predictions. Another teacher-demand study reported that 48% of Texas elementary teachers who had been hired in language minority settings lacked appropriate credentials (Texas A&M Institute for School–University Partnerships, 2001). The most recent data indicate that now nearly 50% of early childhood and 17% of elementary teachers assigned to bilingual classrooms lack appropriate credentials (SBEC, 2002b; 2002c).

The teaching force statewide is and has been predominately (75%) White (TEA, 2001); Latino first-year teachers make up only slightly more than 27% of the pool of educators (SBEC 2002a). The likelihood of dramatic changes reversing these bleak trends in the immediate future is extremely low. Relatively fewer numbers (15.3%) of Latinos as compared to Whites (77.3%) have sought teacher certification (SBEC 2002c; 2000d). The educational pipeline is not promising either. At the college level, Latinos still represent less than 5% of the total enrollment, and the enrollment continues to decline (THECB, 2001). Only 20% of all entering freshmen are Latinos, and of those, only 65% return after their first year (THECB, 1999). The relatively low number of ethnic minority students entering Texas colleges and universities reduces the pool of potential teachers. As early as the 1990s, the decline of African American students in higher education was also attributed to test bias and to the effects of standardized testing (Hood & Parker, 1991). Trends across the country are similar: Although 25% of minorities are college age, a mere 17% are enrolled in institutions of higher education (RNT, 2000). Yet despite these predicted trends, policy makers continue to make decisions that further reinforce harmful gatekeeping mechanisms.

Beyond demographic considerations, there are also pedagogical reasons for the recruitment and retention of ethnic minority, bilingual teachers. Valencia and Aburto (1991a) note that shared identity provides an important link between student and teacher, that students profit significantly from the presence of minority role models (see also Flores & Clark, 1997; Valencia & Aburto, 1991b; Valencia & Guardarrama, 1995); and that schools need to provide culturally-based curricula. Galguera (1998) found that minority students have a preference for teachers who mirror their bilingualism, ethnicity, and gender. In a recent study, the findings clearly demonstrate that both White and ethnic minority students academically benefit when taught by minority teachers within school districts that reflect ethnic representation and distributional equity (Meier, Wrinkle, & Polinard, 1999). A non-equitable situation benefits White students and not the ethnic minority student. A final reason for recruiting and retaining bilingual ethnic minority teachers is that mainstream teachers report feeling inadequate, unprepared to meet the needs of language and ethnic minority students

(Lewis, Parsad, Carey, Bartfai, Farris, & Smerdon, 1999; Monsivais, 1990; TEA, 1995).

CONCLUSIONS AND RECOMMENDATIONS

Politicians and policy makers are strong advocates of placing competency tests at the heart of educational reform. Educational researchers, however, have long argued against this approach. When Texas was first implementing the ExCET and PPST, for example, Melnick and Pullin (1988) predicted that such tests would neither improve teacher education nor enhance the performance of future educators. Spellman (1988) and Zapata (1988) posited that these "reforms" would further reduce the potential pool of minority applicants. As this chapter has shown, the negative predictions of these researchers (and others) have been borne out. In the end, high-stakes testing has not led to substantive reform. Quality education for all students has not transpired; nor has opportunity for all prospective ethnic minority teachers expanded. If we are truly committed to the education of all students and to the creation of an ethnically diverse cadre of educators, why do politicians continue to reduce this opportunity—as Flippo and Canniff (2003) recently argued—by "utilizing a single high-stakes test that . . . screens out minorities and language-diverse candidates from . . . classrooms" (p. 44)?

Our own examination of the inequities of teacher competency testing and standard reforms as indicators of accountability leads us to join in the condemnation of competency tests as invalid predictors of bilingual education teacher candidates' success in the classroom. Our case study (and our previous investigations) offers empirical evidence that paper-and-pencil tests do not assure teacher competency (Clark & Flores, 2002; Flores & Clark, 1997). When we examined the files for the Title VII "home-grown" teachers, we found they had been successful across a variety of indicators. The university's "qualifying test," however, threatened the pursuit of their professional goals. For some, the test was a temporary obstacle that resulted in a loss of income and self-confidence. For others, it was the end of the road; these promising candidates left the teaching profession.

Not only has competency testing dramatically eroded the number of ethnic minorities continuing in the academic pipeline (TEA, 1994), arbitrary, unjust, and invalid testing policies create a false illusion of objectivity. Empirical research shows little or no corroboration between teacher competency testing and actual performance. A better predictor of teacher effectiveness and performance is college grade point average (Daniel, 1993; Moore et al., 1991). In a recent study, Kinnison and Nolan (2001) noted moderate to weak relationships among TASP, GPA, and ExCET scores. Specifically, their data showed only a weak correlation between education course GPA and TASP scores. Weak to moderate correlations were observed between TASP and ExCET. Last, a moderate relationship was detected between education course GPA and ExCET scores. Kinnison and Nolan's study was marred by two glaring weaknesses: the lack of statistical significance and the lack of a more powerful analysis, such as multiple regression.

Despite the questionable validity and reliability of standardized testing in predicting teacher quality, Texas' policy makers continue on the disastrous path of reforming education through testing (Haney, Fowler, Wheelock, Bebell, & Malec, 1999). We contend, as Valencia and Aburto (1991a) advise, that the state would be better served with a more robust, multi-measure evaluation of teacher performance. Useful suggestions and cautions for alternative assessment of minority teacher candidates have been identified in the literature (Valencia & Aburto, 1991b; Valencia & Guardarrama, 1995). Guiding assessment decisions is Valencia and Guardarrama's call for a test-equity paradigm that

> . . . includes a combination of assessment strategies and instrumentation that focus on a system that is well-planned, clearly stated, and part of a continual process and whose goals and policies reflect an affirmation and commitment to ensuring equity for all students. Most importantly, the proposed assessment paradigm must deal in a proactive, responsible manner to eliminate test abuses associated with testing minority students. (p. 597)

One promising alternative to high-stakes testing is portfolio assessment, which appears to be a valid measure of teacher effectiveness (Curry & Cruz, 2000). Bond (1998) and Ladson-Billings (1998) suggest that accountability should reflect culturally responsive approaches appropriate for meeting the needs of ethnic minority students. In other words, to be retained at an ethnic minority school, teachers would have to demonstrate their use of cultural references in daily teaching and planning. In that way, educators would assist ethnic minority students in using their prior knowledge and experiences to better understand new academic concepts. Successfully performing teachers would benefit from such nonthreatening alternative assessment practices as portfolio and demonstration projects. Further, these types of practices would likely reduce the dwindling of the minority teacher pool.

Clearly, to truly improve education and make much-needed systemic change will require different strategies than those that have been proposed by promoters of the testing movement. However, the threat of loss of accreditation introduced by the 1998 Title II of the reauthorized Higher Education Act is likely to induce administrators at the colleges and universities that prepare teachers to formulate policies specifically designed to protect the institutions' status and viability. Thus, it is likely that universities in other states will follow Texas' lead and introduce "prequalifying" exams for their teacher candidates. For example, some Massachusetts universities now require students to pass the Massachusetts Educator Certification Tests (MECT) prior to entering the teacher preparation program (Melnick & Pullin, 2000).[8] Only 23 of 53 teacher preparation institutions in Massachusetts achieved the predetermined 80% passing rate, thus jeopardizing the certification status of 30 institutions (Melnick & Pullin, 2000). By requiring students to take the MECT to achieve entry, teacher-training institutions can protect their certification status. The high-stakes testing burden thereby falls exclusively on the individual.

Recommendations

With these institutional realities in mind, we make the following recommendations for a more equitable approach to educational reform.

- Use multiple measures for determining competency, including portfolio assessment, course grades, observational evaluations, and professors' recommendations.
- Require that states use psychometrically and theoretically sound competency tests.
- Require that state boards of education allow independent researchers to evaluate competency tests.
- Provide all students with diagnostic measures that assess their progress through their program of study.
- Design a program of study that incorporates content knowledge in meaningful ways in the teacher preparation program.
- Provide hands-on learning experiences and field trips to increase retention of content knowledge.

- Align curriculum with standards but avoid a test-driven curriculum.
- Provide supplemental instruction for gatekeeping courses, such as math and science, which will help nontraditional students acquire the knowledge and skills necessary to teach this content.

In addition, educational opportunity for all requires well-conceptualized strategies and requires the building of learning communities in which high schools, community colleges, and universities work together to recruit and retain prospective bilingual education teachers (Calderón & Díaz, 1993). Essentially, high-stakes tests pose as centurions guarding the gates into the teaching profession. Thus, we believe that subjecting individuals to an invalid and bankrupt system of high-stakes testing amounts to a denial of equal opportunity. And when such a denial is based exclusively on test scores, it is nothing less than institutionalized racism and oppression.

NOTES

1. University of San Cuilmas is a pseudonym used to protect the identity of the case study participants.

2. Title VII, now Title III, provides tuition, books, and stipend assistance to prepare bilingual educators. The term "home-grown" refers to investing in human resources, that is, classroom teacher aides, for capacity building of the local school district.

3. The "B" or better rule (described earlier) also helped some of the "home-grown" teachers clear the TASP hurdle.

4. Massachusetts' teacher candidates had similar difficulty responding to the literacy portion of their comparable competency exam because the theoretical framework being tested was different from the framework they had learned (see Luna, Solsken, & Kutz, 2000).

5. Because this rule did not take effect until September 1, 2001, it did not benefit the eight Title VII "home-grown" teacher candidates we were following.

6. Each university determines the number of semester hours candidates take to fulfill math and science standard requirements. For example, at this university, candidates pursuing Early Childhood through fourth grade (EC-4) certification take college algebra, and two Math for EC–4th Grade Teachers courses to fulfill math requirements. They also take 6 hours of lower-division science courses such as biology, geology, or chemistry and 8 hours of upper division science courses including labs in physical and earth/life science. Prior to the current re-

form, elementary candidates (1st–6th grade) took only college algebra and one Math-for-Elementary-Teachers course and 6 hours in science. Candidates pursuing the current 4th–8th grade generalists certification standards are required to have a greater in-depth knowledge in all areas, especially math and science; thus, candidates complete the same requirements as EC–4 candidates, plus an additional 6 hours in math, including conceptual calculus and 2 hours of science lab requirements. Fewer than 10 candidates had expressed an interest in pursuing the fourth-through-eighth-grade track, none who were bilingual teacher candidates. Currently, out of 400 potential teachers, about 30 are pursuing this track; only two are seeking bilingual credentials.

      7. After the implementation of the TExES during the fall 2003 semester, with faculty advocacy, university officials finally capitulated after learning that the "practice exam" provided by the state had no predictive validity, and that the practice exam could not be used as a qualifying exam. Although candidates are still required to take practice exams, the results are being used for diagnostic purposes.

      8. The MECT was originally designed as an exit test. During its first administration, however, it resulted in an approximately 50% failure rate for all teacher candidates, including 100% of all African American teacher candidates.

REFERENCES

Basinger, J. (2001, March 28). Tests should not be the sole barometer for judging teacher-education programs. *Chronicle of Higher Education*. Retrieved September 21, 2002. Available at: http://www.chronicle.com/daily/2001/03/2001032804n.htm

Bond, L. (1998). Cultural responsive pedagogy and the assessment of accomplished teaching. *Journal of Negro Education, 67*(3), 242–254.

Boylan, H. R. (1996). *An evaluation of the Texas academic skills program (TASP)*. Austin, TX: Texas Higher Education Coordinating Board. Retrieved July 23, 2000. Available at: http://www.thecb.state.tx.us/cfbin/ArchFetch.cfm?DocID=282andFormat=Html

Bush, George W. (2001). Texas Public Radio newscast. April 12, 2001, 12 p.m.

Calderón, M., & Díaz, E. (1993). Retooling teacher preparation programs to embrace Latino realities in schools. In R. E. Castro & Y. R. Ingle (Eds.), *Reshaping teacher education in the Southwest (A forum: A response to the needs of Latino students and teachers)* (pp. 53–68). Claremont, CA: The Tomás Rivera Center: A National Institute for Policy Studies.

Clark, E. R., & Flores, B. B. (2002). Narrowing the pipeline for ethnic minority teachers: Standards and high-stakes testing, *Multicultural Perspective, 4*(2), 15–20.

Curry, S., & Cruz, J. (2000). Portfolio teacher based assessment. *Thrust for Educational Leadership, 29*(3), 34–37.

Daniel, L. C. (1993, January). Predicting teaching performance: A multivariate investigation. Paper presented at the Annual Meeting of the Southwest Educational Research Association, Austin, TX. (ERIC Document Reproduction Service No. ED 357–029).

Darling-Hammond, L. (2000). Teacher quality and student achievement. *Education Policy Analysis Archives, 8*(1). Retrieved September 21, 2002. Available at: http://epaa.asu.edu/epaa/v8n1.html

Darling-Hammond, L. (2002, September 6). Research and rhetoric on teacher certification: A response to "Teacher Certification Reconsidered." *Education Policy Analysis Archives, 10*(36). Retrieved September 21, 2002 from http://epaa.asu.edu/epaa/v10n36.html

Flippo, R. F., & Canniff, J. G. (2003). Who is *not* teaching our children? The paradox of the Massachusetts test for educator licensure. *Multicultural Perspetives, 5*(2), 40–45.

Flores, B. B. (2001). The miracle of TAAS: Urban reality or legend? Implications for teacher preparation. *Journal of the Texas Association for Bilingual Education, 6*(1), 11–22.

Flores, B. B., & Clark, E. R. (1997). High-stakes testing: Barriers for prospective bilingual teachers. *Bilingual Research Journal, 21*(4), 335–358.

Fuller, E. (2002). Elements of demand for Texas public school teachers. State Board of Educator Certification. Retrieved December 15, 2002. Available at: http://www.sbec.state.tx.us/resrchdata/issuebrief.pdf

Galguera, T. (1998). Students' attitudes toward teachers' ethnicity, bilinguality, and gender. *Hispanic Journal of Behavioral Sciences, 20*(4), 411–428.

Haney, W., Fowler, C., Wheelock, A., Bebell, D., & Malec, N. (1999). Less truth than error? An independent study of the Massachusetts teacher tests. *Education Policy Analysis Archives, 7*(4). Retrieved February 16, 1999. Available at: http://epaa.ed.asu.edu/epaa/v7n4/

Hood, S., & Parker L. J. (1989). Minority bias review panels and teacher testing for initial certification: A comparison of two states' efforts. *Journal of Negro Education, 58*(4), 511–519).

Hood, S., & Parker L. J. (1991). Minorities, teacher testing, and recent U.S. Supreme Court holdings: A regressive step. *Teachers College Record, 92*(4), 603–608.

Kinnison, L., & Nolan, J. (2001). An examination of GPA, TASP, and ExCET scores for undergraduate teacher education candidates. *National Forum of Teacher Education Journal, 11E*(3). Retrieved September 21, 2002. Available at: http://www.nationalforum.com/19KINN~1.htm

Ladson-Billings, G. (1998). Teaching in dangerous times: Cultural relevant approaches to teacher assessment. *Journal of Negro Education, 767*(3), 255–267.

Lewis, L., Parsad, B., Carey, N., Bartfai, N., Farris, E., & Smerdon, B. (1999). Teacher quality: A report on the preparation and qualifications of public school teachers. *Educational Statistics Quarterly.* Retrieved September 21, 2002. Available at: http://nces.edu.gov/pubs99/quarterlyapr/2-feature/2-esq11-a.html

Luna, C., Solsken, J., & Kutz, E. (2000) Lessons from high-stakes teachers testing. *Journal of Teacher Education, 51*(4), 276–288.

Matthews, J. (1993). The politics and policy development in the TASP program. In *Performance assessment in teacher certification testing* (pp. 55–61). Amherst, MA: National Evaluation Systems, Inc., & American Educational Research Association.

McNeil, L. M. (2000). Creating new inequalities: Contradictions of reform. *Phi Delta Kappan, 81*(10), 728–734.

Meier, K. J., Wrinkle, R. D., & Polinard, J. L. (1999). Repesentative bureaucracy and distributional equity: Addressing the hard question. *The Journal of Politics, 61*(4), 1025–39.

Melnick, S. L., & Pullin, D. (1988). Implications of the use of teacher competency tests. *Education Digest, 53*(5), 10–13.

Melnick, S. L., & Pullin, D. (2000). Can you take dictation? Prescribing teacher quality testing. *Journal of Teacher Education, 51*(4), 262–275.

Monsivais, G. I. (1990). Latino teachers: Well educated but not prepared (An executive summary). Tomás Rivera Center, Claremont, CA, pp. 3–6. (ERIC Document Reproduction Service No. ED 372-887)

Moore, D., Schurr, K. T., & Henriksen, L. W. (1991). Correlations of National Teacher Examination Core Battery scores and college grade point average with teaching effectiveness of first-year teachers. *Educational and Psychological Measurement, 51*(4), 1023–1028.

Ovando, C. J., & Collier, V.P. (Eds.). (1998). *Bilingual and ESL: Teaching in multicultural contexts* (2nd ed.). New York: McGraw-Hill.

Pultorak, E. G. (1991). The NTE tests are more related to course work than teaching performance. *Education, 111*(3), 362–369.

Recruiting New Teachers. (2000). *Teaching's next generation: A national study of precollegiate teacher recruitment.* Belmont, MA: Author. Retrieved September 21, 2002. Available at: http://www.rnt.com or http://www.rnt.org

Reyna, M. (1993). *Summary of focus seminar: The critical shortage of teachers and other school personnel prepared to work with language minority students.* Austin: Texas Education Agency.

Shaker, P. (2002). Teacher testing: A symptom. *Teaching Education, 12*(1), 65–80.

Spellman, S. O. (1988). Recruitment of minority teachers: Issues, problems, facts, possible solutions. *Journal of Teacher Education, 39*(4), 57–63.

State Board of Educator Certification. (2001a). *Accountability System for Educator Preparation (ASEP) Accreditation summary report.* Retrieved May 12, 2002. Available at: http://www.sbec.state.tx.us/edprep/2001accredsummreprt.pdf

State Board of Educator Certification. (2001b). *ExCET pass rates and number of test-takers by test, 1992–2001.* Retrieved September 21, 2002. Available at: http://www.sbec.state.tx.us/resrchdata/ExCETpassrates9201bytest. pdf

State Board of Educator Certification. (2001c). *Statewide annual pass rates based on ASEP rules.* Retrieved September 21, 2002. Available at: http://www. sbec.state.tx.us/edprep/2001annpassrate.pdf

State Board of Educator Certification. (2002a). *Employment and attrition rates by teacher race and ethnicity and by certification route employment.* Retrieved December 15, 2002. Available at: http://www.sbec.state.tx.us/resrchdata/ Employment%20and%20Attrition%20Rates%20by%20Teacher% 20Race%20and%20Ethnicity%20and%20by%20Certification%20Route %20(Class%20of%201997).pdf

State Board of Educator Certification. (2002b). *Texas Examination of Educator Standards (TExES) by grade level.* Retrieved December 15, 2002. Available at: http://www.sbec.state.tx.us/stand_framewrk/TExES/texes.htm

State Board of Educator Certification. (2002c). *Who is teaching in Texas public schools? An analysis of in-field and out-of-field teaching in the 2000–2001 academic year.* Retrieved December 15, 2002. Available at: http://www. sbec.state.tx.us/Texas/whoteaching/2002Report

State Board of Educator Certification. (2002d). *Who's teaching in our schools? Reports.* Retrieved December 15, 2002. Available at: /https://secure.sbec. state.tx.us/Reports/WhoisTeaching/frm_whois_main.asp

Texas A&M Institute for School–University Partnerships. (2001). *Teacher demand study.* Retrieved May 4, 2001. Available at: http://partnerships.tamu. edu/publications/00-01%20supply %20 and%20demand%20study.pdf

Texas Education Agency. (1994a). *Educator assessment in Texas: 1992–1993 Report.* Austin, TX: Author.

Texas Education Agency. (1994b, May). *Teacher supply, demand and quality (Policy research project: Texas teacher diversity and recruitment, Report #4).* Austin, TX: Author.

Texas Education Agency. (1995, March). *Texas teacher preparation study: Interim report,* 1995. Austin, TX: Author.

Texas Education Agency. (2001). *Texas public school statistics: Pocket edition, 2000–2001.* Austin, TX: Author. Retrieved November 15, 2002. Available at: http://www.tea.state.tx. us/perfreport/pocked/2001/index.html

Texas Higher Education Coordinating Board. (1995, August). *Annual report on the TASP and the effectiveness of remediation.* Austin, TX: Author.

Texas Higher Education Coordinating Board. (1999, August). *Summary TASP test results for academic year 1994–1999.* Austin, TX: Author.

Texas Higher Education Coordinating Board. (2000). *Texas Academic Skills Program (TASP) summary of TASP/Alternative test (TASP/A) results academic year 1999–2000.* Austin, TX: Author. Retrieved December 15, 2002. Available at: http://www.thecb.state.tx.us/reports/pdf/0451.pdf

Texas Higher Education Coordinating Board. (2001). *Texas Academic Skills Program policy manual.* Austin, TX: Author. Available at: http://www.thecb. state.tx.us/reports/pdf/0425.pdf

The urban teacher challenge: Teacher demand and supply in the great city schools, 2000. Retrieved September 21, 2002. Available at: http://www.rnt.org/ quick/utc.pdf; http://www.rnt.org/quick/utc.pdf; or http://www.cgsc.org

Tinto, V. (1987). *Leaving college: Rethinking the causes and cures of student attrition.* Chicago: University of Chicago Press.

Valencia, R. R. (1991). The plight of Chicano students: An overview of schooling conditions and outcomes. In R. R. Valencia (Ed.), *Chicano school failure and success: Research and policy agendas for the 1990s* (pp. 3–26). London: Falmer Press.

Valencia, R. R. (2000). Inequalities and the schooling of minority students in Texas: Historical and contemporary conditions. *Hispanic Journal of Behavioral Sciences, 22*(4), 445–459.

Valencia, R. R., & Aburto, S. (1991a). Competency testing and Latino student access to the teaching profession: An overview of issues. In G. D. Keller, J. R. Deneen, & R. J. Magallán (Eds.), *Assessment and access: Hispanics in higher education* (pp. 167–194). Albany: State University of New York Press.

Valencia, R. R., & Aburto, S. (1991b). Research directions and practical strategies in teacher testing and assessment: Implications for improving Latino access to teaching. In G. D. Keller, J. R. Deneen, & R. J. Magallán (Eds.), *Assessment and access: Hispanics in higher education* (pp. 195–232). Albany: State University of New York Press.

Valencia, R. R., & Guardarrama, I. (1995). High-stakes testing and its impact on racial/ethnic minority students. In L. A. Suzuki, P. J. Meller, & J. G. Ponterotto (Eds.)., *Handbook of multicultural assessment: Clinical, psychological, and educational applications* (pp. 561–610). San Francisco: Jossey-Bass.

Zapata, J. T. (1988). Early identification and recruitment of Hispanic teacher candidates. *Journal of Teacher Education, 39*(1), 19–23.

9

—

High-Stakes Testing and Educational Accountability as Social Constructions Across Cultures

RAYMOND V. PADILLA

The theme explored in this chapter is that notions such as "high-stakes testing" and "educational accountability," which are hallmarks of some educational reform efforts, are social constructions (Berger & Luckmann, 1966) that can lead to the organization of schooling within very specific and narrow sociocultural frameworks. Although such sociocultural frameworks can go largely unacknowledged, their effects are significant. For example, through the current positivist and culture-of-measurement emphasis on testing and accountability, the dominant cultural framework decontextualizes local schooling practices (McNeil & Valenzuela, 2000), resulting in a severely distorted educational experience for some students. This chapter develops three major topics: (1) testing in relation to the culture of measurement; (2) the reductionist view of accountability and the need to counteract it; and (3) alternative social constructions of educational reform that provide a higher degree of sociocultural contextualization for diverse groups of students and the schools that serve them.

THE CULTURE OF MEASUREMENT VERSUS THE CULTURE OF ENGAGEMENT

Although high-stakes testing, such as the Texas Assessment of Academic Skills (TAAS) and the Arizona Instrument to Measure Standards (AIMS) has been critiqued from various perspectives (Haney, 2000; Hilliard, 1990; Klein, Hamilton, McCaffrey, & Stecher, 2000; McNeil, 2000; McNeil & Valenzuela, 2000; Mitchell, Robinson, Plake, & Knowles, 2001; President's Advisory Commission on Educational Excellence for Hispanic

Americans, 2000; Spring, 1998), little has been said thus far about the *cultural presuppositions* that undergird these testing practices. A culturally-based critique reveals that state-sponsored testing instruments and practices are part of a specific social construction of schooling, one that can lead to different consequences for various groups of students in terms of their schooling experiences and outcomes. Drawing (and perhaps even overdrawing) distinctions between the *culture of measurement* (which occasionally turns into the "cult of measurement") and an alternative *culture of engagement* helps clarify the ways in which schooling practices are socially constructed across cultures. Each of these cultural frameworks has its own set of deeply rooted assumptions about fundamental aspects of existence such as the nature of knowing, being, valuing, and purpose. Each also has its own fundamental goals, worldview, and influence on schooling practices.

High-stakes testing and educational accountability, two anchor points of recent educational reform efforts, so far are strictly framed within the culture of measurement. The chief goals here are the identification of merit and the distribution of material and social rewards based on that merit. Students are defined in terms of parameters whose values can be precisely measured. Using instruments developed under the sway of psychologism, beginning with Binet's intelligence test, assessment efforts have continued unbroken for almost one hundred years. The current reliance on high-stakes tests—measurement instruments that often are developed, tested, and administered by corporate interests (Spring, 1998)— is part of this tradition. The epistemological perspective of the culture of measurement is objectivist knowing, or what is called *saber* in Spanish (Padilla, 2000). Such knowledge is presumed to be universally valid and free from "subjectivist" influences or local perturbations. Under these conditions, a "norm" can be objectively set to any scale and various comparisons then can be made against that norm.

With respect to schooling practices, the culture of measurement strongly influences at least two important areas: teaching and curriculum. Teaching becomes highly decontextualized from larger pedagogical concerns. This can be seen in schooling practices such as teaching to the test (McNeil & Valenzuela, 2000) and in the overemphasis on process, credentialism, and test-taking competence. The abstract student becomes a reality and the real student becomes an abstraction whose learning and development can be determined only with the aid of a paper-and-pencil test and a presumed universal norm as a reference point.

With respect to curriculum, the culture of measurement leads to the isolation of people and schools. This isolation is driven by the evaluation of individual teachers, students, and schools through test taking, ratings, rankings, grading, and so on. Such individualistic evaluation is premised on a narrow range of curricular offerings, often limited to low-level, monolingual reading and writing skills and the rudiments of arithmetic and science (McNeil & Valenzuela, 2000; Ruiz de Velasco & Fix, 2000).

An alternative to the culture of measurement is the *culture of engagement*. The chief goal of this social construction is inclusion and human development in pursuit of democratic participation and *justicia* (justice). This goal is embedded within a worldview that values and fosters a culture of caring and inclusion (Freire, 2001; Reyes, Scribner, & Paredes Scribner, 1999; Trueba, 1999; Valenzuela, 1999). The epistemological foundation of the culture of engagement is local "relational knowing," or what is called *conocer* in Spanish (Padilla, 2000). Relational knowing has no universalistic or objectivist pretensions. It relies instead on local knowledge that is interactively acquired and validated. The norm is always locally contextualized and socially negotiated.

The influence of the culture of engagement on teaching and curriculum is quite different from that of the culture of measurement. With respect to teaching, the culture of engagement accepts students as they are and values their sociocultural context (Trueba, Spindler, & Spindler, 1989). It promotes student development by providing relevant learning, enhancing social competence, and engendering a sense of rootedness (García, 2001). Regarding curriculum, the culture of engagement emphasizes teaching teams, which develop and deliver curriculum as a group (Romo & Falbo, 1996), and studying integrated themes in the context of the daily life of the student and the community in which the student lives (González, Huerta-Macías, & Tinajero, 1998).

In theory, schooling practices can come under the sway of either the culture of measurement or the culture of engagement. In practice, differential political power privileges the culture of measurement. The consequences of this social choice are evident today in the profound teacher and student alienation (Romo & Falbo, 1996) that has led to teacher burnout, student violence, deteriorating schools, and widespread discontent with public education (Datnow, 2000). These conditions underscore the need for alternative social constructions of schooling practices.

THE PRACTICE OF ASSIMILATION VERSUS THE PRACTICE OF DIVERSITY

At the ontological (being) level, the culture of measurement is premised on an absolutist view of being. Thus, much as Shakespeare put it, "to be" has only one ontological alternative, "not to be." This cultural view contrasts with Spanish, which makes a distinction between absolute being, *ser*, and temporary or conditional being, *estar*. The absolutist view of being leads logically to the practice (some would say the malpractice) of assimilation. The goal of assimilation is to absorb all languages, cultures, and peoples into a melting pot of Eurocentric peoples and culture, and to destroy, enslave, or erase those not susceptible to such assimilation (Menchaca, 1997). The worldview of assimilation, based on absolutist ontology, presumes the superiority of Anglo-European peoples and culture. This presumption, in turn, supports the righteous imposition of this culture on all foreign peoples and the simultaneous elimination of all foreign languages and cultures (De León, 1998). The absolutist ontology holds that to be (in the sense of *ser*) is to exist in an evolutionarily determined hierarchy of human groups and their associated languages and cultures. These rankings are understood to be immutable, and those at the upper end of the hierarchy are to be preferred to those at the bottom.

The practice of assimilation has consequences for both teaching and curriculum. Its influence on teaching can be seen in the school practice of subtracting from students all foreign languages and cultural elements and replacing them with "superior" Eurocentric and Anglo-American ones (García, 2001; Valenzuela, 1999). Often, this cultural displacement is championed as being for the good of the student. The practice of assimilation shapes curriculum by emphasizing Anglo-American history and culture and attempting to erase the histories, languages, and cultures of all other groups. The English-only movement is an example of a particularly virulent version of this linguistic and cultural erasure (Hakuta, 1986; Krashen, 1996; Schmidt, Sr. 2000).

In contrast to the practice of assimilation is the practice of diversity, which fits well within the culture of engagement. The goal of diversity is to recognize, embrace, and celebrate the world's variety of languages, cultures, and peoples. Diversity is accepting of those who are different. It promotes the idea of *convivencia*, or getting along (literally, "living together"). The worldview of diversity is that all languages and cultures have inherent value and all need resources to thrive. Ontologically, diversity is based on *estar*, conditional or time-sensitive being. To be, in the sense of *estar*, is to exist in a historical and changing set of relationships across groups and cultures. Hence, all social and cultural hierarchies are historically conditioned, transient, and mutable (Freire, 1995).

The practice of diversity influences both teaching and curriculum. Because different languages and cultures are appreciated and shared, teaching becomes an additive practice (Valenzuela, 1999): New language and cultural elements are added to what the student already possesses. The curriculum emphasizes multiple languages, cultures, and histories, encouraging students from diverse backgrounds to see themselves positively.

Despite the affirming and inclusive nature of the practice of diversity, it is not the dominant framework. Instead, differential political power has led to the privileging of assimilation practices. The negative effects of this social choice include the following:

- The perpetuation of "White privilege" as a foundation for social relationships (McIntosh, 1989; Padilla & Chávez Chávez, 1995);
- The alienation of students and communities as a result of subtractive schooling practices aimed at removing foreign languages and cultural elements (Valenzuela, 1999);
- The loss of educational equity brought about by high student dropout rates and chronically low academic achievement among those who stay in school (Romo & Falbo, 1996; Trueba, Spindler, & Spindler, 1989);
- The perpetuation of impoverished communities.

As this list shows, social constructions of schooling practices can exact extremely high costs. Alternatives to the current culture of measurement need to be seriously considered.

THINKING DEFICITS VERSUS ASSETS

The culture of measurement often includes cultural deficit thinking (Trueba, Spindler, & Spindler, 1989; Valencia, 1997). The worldview of cultural deficit thinking, like that of assimilation, assumes the superiority of Eurocentered, Anglo-American language and culture (De León, 1998). All other languages and cultures are seen as deficient by comparison and, therefore, all must give way. Such views can strongly influence teaching. Students are seen as needing to be cleansed of their foreign languages and cultures; more wholesome Anglo-American language and culture can then be substituted for their home counterparts (Valenzuela, 1999). At the curriculum level, cultural deficit thinking emphasizes English-only instruction, teaching Anglo-American history exclusively, and inculcating Anglo-American values.

By contrast, the culture of engagement includes the thinking and rethinking of cultural assets. The goal is to accept all languages and cultures as valuable. The underlying worldview perceives all languages and cultures as having both assets and liabilities and seeks to use cultural assets to enhance schooling outcomes (García, 2001; Trueba, Spindler, & Spindler, 1989). No language or culture is assumed to be inherently superior to any other language or culture. Teachers working within this perspective value students from diverse language and cultural backgrounds. They also use language and cultural differences to enhance their teaching and their students' learning. At the curriculum level, an additive model of schooling is followed (Valenzuela, 1999). Students are given the opportunity to learn in more than one language, diverse languages and cultures are studied, and different values are acknowledged and examined. Most important, culture is defined as problematic and is critically examined (Freire, 1995) so that students can develop a global perspective and a secure sense of personal and cultural identity.

Unfortunately, it is cultural deficit thinking that currently holds sway, and it will continue to do so as long as those who hold cultural deficit thinking views also wield the most political power. But the consequences of cultural deficit thinking are serious. These include the demise of diverse languages and cultures (Fisherman, 1966), the entrenchment of subtractive schooling (Valenzuela, 1999) and its attendant failure to provide all students with a comprehensive, relevant education (Romo & Falbo, 1996), and the continued impoverishment of diverse language and cultural communities. In a world that is becoming ever more interdependent and interconnected (Figueroa, Wilkie, & Arroyo Alejandre, 1996), the value of cultural deficit thinking seems increasingly questionable.

SELF INTEREST VERSUS THE PUBLIC INTEREST

The culture of measurement often supports an extreme focus on self interest. The goal of this self(ish) interest is the pursuit of individual gain or benefit by virtually any means, with little or no regard for the common good or the condition of the physical environment. The worldview emphasizes the individual over the group and private gain over public good. Self(ish) interest is supported by a teleological perspective that holds that the purpose of human life is to achieve personal gain in a competitive social environment. Winners achieve their position as the result of their superior individual effort (variously augmented by government action). Losers have only themselves to blame for their failure (and thus should not complain).

This teleological perspective shapes teaching by casting students as individual, competitive learners. Students are individually tested, graded, and sorted as a basis for distributing rewards such as who goes to college and who gets into which occupations and positions of power (Spring, 1998). At the curriculum level, a focus on self(ish) interest promotes competition among students and supports academic tracking (Oakes, 1985; Romo & Falbo, 1996; Solomon, 1992) whereby students are sorted into different curricular strands according to their tested "ability," resulting in different outcomes for further study and narrowed career opportunities.

The culture of engagement, in contrast, shows greater concern for the public interest. The goal is to moderate the pursuit of individual gain by taking into account the common good and the condition of the physical environment. The worldview is that individual gain is subordinate to the common good and the preservation of a healthy environment. The role of government is primarily to promote the common good rather than to help individuals achieve private gain. The teleological perspective of the culture of engagement is that the purpose of human life is to promote community and a healthy environment. These views influence teaching in that students are seen as capable of learning through cooperation and collaboration. Rewards are provided for group as well as for individual effort. At the curriculum level, students of varying ability are grouped together and individual performance within group effort is rewarded. Democratic participation and democratic values are promoted (Freire, 2001).

Currently, self(ish) interest is privileged over the common good, with notable consequences: Schools reproduce existing social hierarchies (Bourdieu & Passeron, 1990; McNeil, 2000), stifle the upward mobility of students, retard the economic development of certain communities, and contribute to the degradation of the physical environment.

Social constructions of schooling significantly influence the goals educational reformers seek to implement (Berliner & Biddle, 1995). They also shape the set of probable educational outcomes that students are likely to experience. Given the likelihood that within a set of educational outcomes not all will be equally desirable, social constructions of schooling can have a powerful impact on students' life chances. Educational outcomes are determined not only on the basis of ability differentials in students, but also by differences in background characteristics over which students have little or no control (such as culture, language, gender, and social class) and by the quality of the schools the students attend (Romo & Falbo, 1996). When narrowly framed, social constructions of schooling can serve to severely decontextualize the learning process for certain students, putting them at a disadvantage compared to students for whom the social construction of schooling offers a more congenial and coherent connection to home and community (Trueba, Spindler, & Spindler, 1989).

A CULTURALLY-BASED ACCOUNT OF ACCOUNTABILITY

The problem of severe decontextualization of schooling can be seen not only in high-stakes testing but also in the socially constructed idea of accountability with which testing is frequently paired. Within the culture of measurement, accountability, like testing, becomes a narrowly defined program that can have a differential impact on educational outcomes and students' educational experiences. Students who fare the best under current accountability programs are those whose home and community most closely adhere to the underlying assumptions of the prevailing social construction of accountability. Students who come from homes and communities where these assumptions are different tend to do less well in school (McNeil & Valenzuela, 2000).

The decontextualization of accountability promoted by the culture of measurement occurs on several levels, not the least of which is the reduction of the semantic space related to the word "accountability" (see Haney & Raczek, 1994). Adherents of the culture of measurement assume that accountability is mostly about numbers and measurements based on numbers. However, both the English word *accountability* and its Spanish equivalent, *contabilidad,* share the same Latin root, *putare,* which means "to think." In Spanish, the verb *contar* means both "to count" and "to recount" in the sense of "to tell." Thus, in Spanish, accountability can be reported either by counting or by recounting, by numbers or by narratives. In its broader linguistic context, the English word accountability also includes as part of its semantic space the idea of an account, such as a story or narrative. However, the adherents of the culture of measurement tend to downplay the narrative part and limit accountability mostly to "the bottom line," a number or statistic that presumably tells the whole story about a student's learning and schooling.

The bottom-line approach to educational accountability can lead to severe decontextualization of the learning process and learning outcomes. Under numbers-based accountability programs, high scores on state or nationally sponsored tests become the educational goal for schools. To achieve this goal, students are required to master both substantive content and the heuristics of test taking. Thus, teachers shift instructional time from substantive content to drills designed to help students learn how to take tests. At the same time, the focus of the curriculum is redirected to cover whatever appears on the test (Spring, 1998). State-sponsored high-stakes testing displaces assessments of student learning that are based on a well-balanced local curriculum.

To be accountable is to be responsible for something, and the discharge of that responsibility is typically recounted through a narrative that presents facts, opinions, actions taken, and results achieved. Numbers may be an important element in the narrative report, but they are never the whole story, and they certainly do not speak for themselves. In other words, numbers, like all other kinds of information, must be provided some interpretive context before they make any sense (Lincoln & Guba, 1985). But the adherents of the culture of measurement rely on numbers for the whole story. Where policies require individuals to pass a test before they can be promoted to the next grade, otherwise knowledgeable students who simply do not perform well on tests can be retained in grade.

The classroom teacher may be well aware that a low-scoring student works at grade level on a daily basis, but if this competency is not proven by an acceptable score on a high-stakes test, the student must be retained (see Valencia & Villarreal, chapter 4, this volume). Ironically, high-stakes testing often is promoted as a strategy for decreasing the incidence of social promotion. Yet, these tests themselves can produce social demotion, an outcome that goes unnoticed by the adherents of the culture of measurement.

The blind eye numbers-based accountability that turns toward the social demotion of students is both an example and a telltale sign of how numbers-based accountability reflects a specific social construction of schooling. How a student performs in school is based on many factors that interact in complex ways. For example, school finance, the quality of teachers and teaching materials, students' level of health and nutrition, their family background, their home language, and a host of other factors influence school performance. Yet, the most noticeable consequences of high-stakes testing are those the individual student bears: promotion in grade or lack thereof; graduation from high school, or failure to graduate; acceptance to college or denial of admittance; and similar lifelong effects (Ruiz de Velasco & Fix, 2000; Solomon, 1992; Spring, 1998). High-stakes testing coupled with accountability makes individual students responsible for their own test performance as if none of the many factors other than individual effort and native talent, such as poor schools (Romo & Falbo, 1996), contribute to and shape performance. In numbers-based accountability, the state decontextualizes test performance and certifies the test taker as either competent or incompetent, worthy or unworthy of gaining access to community resources in pursuit of further education and advancement.

Under such circumstances, accountability unfairly punishes students and gives the state unwarranted power to label students in permanent and harmful ways (for a historic case of state centralism in pursuit of cultural hegemony, see Getz, 1997). As nearly all teachers agree, a student whose language background differs from the language of the test and who lacks English fluency will be disadvantaged in taking such a test. Test scores for these students need to be carefully interpreted to avoid inappropriate retention of students in grade level (Ovando & Collier, 1998). Yet, thousands of students with limited English proficiency are routinely subjected to high-stakes testing without taking into account their unique linguistic situation, let alone the quality and appropriateness of the instruction that they are receiving (See Ruiz de Velasco, and Alamillo et. al., this volume). The result is the mislabeling and excessive grade retention of students with limited English proficiency under the guise of numbers-based accountability programs. The culture of measurement sidetracks the thinking part of accountability and brings the full force of the state apparatus to bear on individual students and their school performance. With schools acting as handmaidens of the state's numbers-driven certification machinery, accountability becomes a means for maintaining existing social hierarchies on a broad scale and for exerting tighter control across large populations to determine who has access to public resources.

An alternative social construction of accountability can be formulated based on the culture of engagement (for other alternatives, see Valenzuela, 2002). *Engaged accountability* emphasizes through narratives the local, contextualized aspects of student learning. It fosters effective local decision making about student evaluation and proper placement in differentiated learning environments. Most importantly, rather than holding students solely responsible for school performance, it sees schools and communities as equally responsible for the academic achievement of their students (Reyes, Scribner, & Paredes Scribner, 1999).

Under engaged accountability, the thinking part of accountability is brought to the forefront. Teachers are empowered to make important decisions about how to teach and evaluate students under the guidance of local boards of education, whose members, in turn, are responsive to the wishes of local constituencies. Centralized state machinery plays no role in certifying which students may be promoted to the next grade level and which may not. Given that context is crucial to teaching and learning, evaluation of student performance should include multiple indicators of learning and a rich understanding of the circumstances under which the student is attempting to learn and the teacher is attempting to teach (Ovando & Collier, 1998). Reliance on abstract numbers or on a single test score is viewed as misguided and not likely to enhance student learning.

The idea of localism is an important aspect of engaged accountability. Emphasizing the local permits and promotes great diversity. Fostering diversity does not mean abandoning standards or quality. Rather, it means rejecting the universalist pretensions of the positivist culture of measurement; the culture of engagement challenges the supposition that all evaluations of learning are reducible to a single, one-size-fits-all package. Instead of supporting tests and assessment instruments that turn students into abstractions and subject content into disconnected bits of information that do not make sense in any particular place, engaged accountability programs would foster student learning within the context of students' everyday lives—incorporating family and community, for example (Chavkin, 1993; Torres-Guzmán, Mercado, Quintero, & Viera, 1994)—and within the context of positive, useful learning that can lead to social and economic advancement (Romo & Falbo, 1996). Engaged accountability programs would provide a thoughtful basis for the assessment of student progress, the effectiveness of schools, and the identification of community goals and priorities.

SUMMARY

The twin concepts of high-stakes testing and accountability programs are social constructions that result in different educational and life opportunities for various students. Subjecting the cultural assumptions that underlie tests and accountability programs to a cross-culturally based critique shows that high-stakes testing decontextualizes schooling and, as a result, disadvantages many students. Driven by a culture of measurement, both tests and numbers-based accountability programs turn students into parametric abstractions that centralized state apparatuses can label as worthy or unworthy. These assigned labels determine the resources available to individual students, such as access to advanced education and a desirable career. The labels also strongly influence where a student is likely to end up in the social hierarchy.

The culture of engagement, which places a premium on local context and negotiated social realities that seek to promote a more democratic community and greater equity in accessing resources, offers an alternative to the culture of measurement. Numbers are seen as only one (and certainly not the best) way to represent individuals and social situations; just as important, if not more so, are thoughtful narratives that provide a more complete and relevant account of teaching, learning, and schools. The culture of engagement makes no pretensions toward seeking universalist and objectivist knowledge. It sees the world in terms of ongoing transitions and transformations that must be reflected in the way students learn and are taught. It understands the role of centralized state power as limited to facilitating locally meaningful learning in the context of a just and democratic distribution of resources. Such learning, which presumes a substantial opportunity to learn with adequate resources, can provide students with the skills and emotional stability that will allow them to explore wider, nonlocal learning contexts driven by their own need to learn about the world and their community's need to participate effectively in state, national, and international arenas.

REFERENCES

Berger, P. L., & Luckmann, T. (1966). *The social construction of reality: A treatise in the sociology of knowledge.* New York: Anchor Books.

Berliner, D. C., & Biddle, B. J. (1995). *The manufactured crisis: Myths, fraud, and the attack on America's public schools.* New York: Addison-Wesley.

Bourdieu, P., & Passeron, J. C. (1990). *Reproduction in education, society, and culture* (Richard Nice, Trans.). Newbury Park, CA: Sage Publications. (Original work published 1970).

Chavkin, N. D. (Ed.). (1993). *Families and schools in a pluralistic society.* Albany: State University of New York Press.

Datnow, A. (2000). Power politics in the adoption of school reform models. *Educational Evaluation and Policy Analysis, 22*(4), 357–374.

De León, A. (1998). Initial contacts: Niggers, redskins and greasers. In R. Delgado, & J. Stafancic (Eds.)., *The Latino condition: A critical reader* (pp. 158–164). New York: New York University Press.

Figueroa, C. P., Wilkie, J. W., & Arroyo Alejandre, J. (Eds.). (1996). *Mexico and the Americas.* VIII PROFMEX-ANUIES Conference proceedings. Mexico City: Asociación Nacional de Universidades y Instituciones de Educación Superior.

Fishman, J. A. (1966). *Language loyalty in the United States.* The Hague: Mouton.

Freire, P. (1995). *Pedagogy of the oppressed.* New revised 20th anniversary edition. New York: Continuum.

Freire, P. (2001). *Pedagogy of freedom: Ethics, democracy, and civic courage.* New York: Rowman & Littlefield.

García, E. (2001). *Hispanic education in the United States: Raíces y alas.* New York: Rowman & Littlefield.

Getz, L. M. (1997). *Schools of their own: The education of Hispanos in New Mexico, 1850–1940.* Albuquerque, NM: University of New Mexico Press.

González, M. L., Huerta-Macías, A., & Villamil Tinajero, J. (Eds.). (1998). *Educating Latino students: A guide to successful practice.* Lancaster, PA: Technomic Publishing.

Hakuta, K. (1986). *Mirror of language. The debate on bilingualism.* New York: Basic Books.

Haney, W. (2000). The myth of the Texas miracle in education. *Education Policy Analysis Archives, 8*(41). Retrieved March 1, 2001, from http://epaa.asu.edu/epaa/v8n41/part1.htm

Haney, W., & Raczek, A. (1994). *Surmounting outcomes accountability in education: Paper prepared for the U.S. Congress Office of Technology Assessment.* Boston: Boston College, Center for the Study of Testing, Evaluation and Educational Policy.

Hilliard III, A. G. (1990). Limitations of current academic achievement measures. In K. Lomotey (Ed.), *Going to school: The African-American experience* (pp. 135–142). Albany: State University of New York Press.

Klein, S. P., Hamilton, L. S., McCaffrey, D. F., & Stecher, B. M. (2000). What do test scores in Texas tell us? *Education Policy Analysis Archives, 8*(49).

Krashen, S. D. (1996). *Under attack: The case against bilingual education.* Culver City, CA: Language Education Associates.

Lincoln, Y., & Guba, E. (1985). *Naturalistic inquiry.* Beverly Hills, CA: Sage Publications.

McIntosh, P. (1989, July/August). White privilege: Unpacking the invisible knapsack. *Peace and Freedom* 10–12.

McNeil, L., & Valenzuela, A. (2000). *The harmful impact of the TAAS system of testing in Texas: Beneath the accountability rhetoric.* In M. Kornhaber & G. Orfield (Eds.), *Raising standares or raising barriers: Inequality and high-stakes testing in public education* (pp. 127–150).

McNeil, L. M. (2000). *Contradictions of school reform: Educational costs of standardized testing.* New York: Routledge.

Menchaca, M. (1997). Early racist discourses: The roots of deficit thinking. In R. Valencia (Ed.), *The evolution of deficit thinking: Educational thought and practice* (pp. 13–40). Washington, D.C.: Falmer Press.

Mitchell, K. J., Robinson, D. Z., Plake, B. S., & Knowles, K. T. (Eds.). (2001*). Testing teacher candidates: The role of licensure tests in improving teacher quality.* Washington, D.C.: Committee on Assessment and Teacher Quality, National Research Council. National Academy Press.

Oakes, J. (1985). *Keeping track: How schools structure inequality.* New Haven, CT: Yale University Press.

Ovando, C. J., & Collier, V. P. (1998). *Bilingual and ESL classrooms: Teaching in multicultural contexts* (2nd ed.). New York: McGraw-Hill.

Padilla, R. V. (2000). *Sabiduría in the Chican@ context: Some epistemological notes.* Paper presented at the XXVII Conference of the National Association for Chicana and Chicano Studies (NACCS), Portland, OR, March 22–25, 2000. Retrieved April 6, 2001. Available at: http://coehd.utsa.edu/users/rpadilla

Padilla, R. V. & Chávez Chávez, R. (Eds.). (1995). *The leaning ivory tower: Latino professors in American universities.* Albany: State Universty of New York Press.

President's Advisory Commission on Educational Excellence for Hispanic Americans. (2000). *Testing Hispanic students in the United States: Technical and policy issues.* [Prepared by Richard A. Figueroa & Sonia Hernández]. Washington, D.C.: Author.

Reyes, P., Scribner, J. D., & Paredes Scribner, A. (1999). *Lessons from high-performing Hispanic schools.* New York: Teachers College Press.

Romo, H. D., & Falbo, T. (1996). *Latino high school graduation: Defying the odds.* Austin: University of Texas Press.

Ruiz de Velasco, J., & Fix, M. (2000). *Overlooked & underserved: Immigrant students in U. S. secondary schools.* Washington, D.C.: Urban Institute.

Schmidt Sr., R. (2000). *Language policy and identity politics in the United States.* Philadelphia: Temple University Press.

Solomon, R. P. (1992). *Black resistance in high school: Forging a separatist culture.* Albany: State University of New York Press.

Spring, J. (1998). *Conflict of interests: The politics of American education* (3rd ed.). Boston: McGraw-Hill.

Torres-Guzmán, M. E., Mercado, C. I., Quintero, A. H., & Viera, D. R. (1994). Teaching and learning in Puerto Rican/Latino collaboratives: Implications for teacher education. In E. R. Hollins, J. E. King, & W. C. Hayman (Eds.), *Teaching diverse populations: Formulating a knowledge base* (pp. 105–127). Albany: State University of New York Press.

Trueba, H. T. (1999). *Latinos unidos: From cultural diversity to the politics of solidarity.* New York: Roman & Littlefield.

Trueba, H. T., Spindler, G., & Spindler, L. (Eds.). (1989). *What do anthropologists have to say about dropouts?* New York: Falmer Press.

Valencia, R. (Ed.). (1997). *The evolution of deficit thinking: Educational thought and practice.* Washington, D.C.: Falmer Press.

Valenzuela, A. (2002). High-stakes testing and U.S.-Mexican youth in Texas: The case for multiple compensatory criteria in assessment. *Harvard Journal of Hispanic Policy, 14,* 97–116.

Valenzuela, A. (1999). *Subtractive schooling: U.S.-Mexican youth and the politics of caring.* Albany: State University of New York Press.

10

—

Accountability and the Privatization Agenda

ANGELA VALENZUELA

Let consumer choice concepts rule. That's a form of regulation. It's called the market.
—*House Committee on Public Education*
Chairman Kent Grusendorf

In this final chapter, I demonstrate how the state's version of accountability, which is at its core a business model, played into the hands of an emerging conservative political and economic elite, helping advance a privatization agenda aimed at implementing their ultimate form of accountability—the market. As I outlined in the introductory chapter, my work in the Texas legislature during its 78th session (2003) centered around advising State Representative Dora Olivo on her multiple-compensatory-criteria legislation. In addition, however, as a member of a local council of the League of United Latin American Citizens (LULAC), the oldest Latina/o civil rights organization in the nation, I participated in the legislative struggle over vouchers.[1] And, during the spring 2003 term at my home institution, the University of Texas at Austin, I taught a graduate course on Latina/o education policy. All three commitments spurred me, with the help of my graduate students, to stay well apprised of pertinent education legislation.[2] My focused study, observation, and analysis of the legislature's educational agenda during the 78th session also drew me into various political and public policy circles.

This combination of factors has provided a new framework for my understanding of accountability issues in Texas. Specifically, I have learned that answering the question of *why* Texas-style accountability fails Latina/o youth requires first examining several core features of the state's political and economic landscape, including points of convergence and divergence with Texas' Latina/o community and its leadership, especially LULAC. Accordingly, in this last chapter, I identify and discuss key legislation, political actors, and decisions that reveal a powerful underlying agenda to privatize education in Texas through various means, including vouchers.[3] I meld my observations with those of Shaker and Heilman (2002) and Apple (2000, 2001), whose theories and analyses provide complementary frameworks that help address the emerging political landscape of the actors in the Texas privatization drama, making these players' tactics and goals clearer.

In arguing that the current accountability system serves as handmaiden to the privatization agenda in Texas, I do not mean to suggest that all or even most of the players involved recognize or support this link between accountability and privatization. Nor do I mean to suggest that accountability—in all its components and complexity—reflects a rational, narrowly defined and focused strategy. To the contrary, what we have come to know as accountability in Texas is a shape-shifter, growing and changing to accommodate the latest outcomes of ongoing battles and compromises. Texas-style accountability reflects diverse sets of interests that roughly correspond to the following constituencies: parent, community, teacher, administrator, and school board organizations; Latina/o and African American educational leadership; the business community; and elected and appointed officials, including legislators themselves. There is nothing new about the presence of multiple agendas. They always pervade the political process—frequently in opposing and contradictory ways. My thesis rests on a different premise.

Apple (2000, 2001), in examining the political dynamics undergirding centralized, top-down educational reform in the United States today, theorizes that a powerful neoliberal, economic, and political elite exists, and he argues that this diffuse group's goal is "conservative modernization" (also see Hursh, 2003; Lipman, 2002). I maintain that in Texas, such an elite is both patently present and is the reason Texas-style accountability fails Latina/o youth. With members positioned from the offices of the governor, lieutenant governor, and House speaker, to the chairs and members of the core educational committees in the Senate and House of Representatives, to local-level businesspeople and philanthropists, this elite helped develop and now works within the current framework on educational accountability, while simultaneously explicitly supporting privatization efforts, including the hotly debated voucher issue during the 2003 legislative session.

To make my case, I develop my thesis by layering upwardly, first describing the shifting legislative and political context from which a dominant, conservative political and economic elite in Texas has emerged. This is a necessary point of departure because it reveals how the privatization agenda, emanating from a loose coalition of the business and religious right, became normalized sufficiently to encourage the development of a "new common sense" that now sustains proposals that in another era or a different sociopolitical context would be deemed extreme. Next, while tracing the rise of the conservative right, and especially the emergence of James Leininger as a key behind-the-scenes player, I also provide an assessment of the impact of the forward movement of the privatization agenda on the Latina/o community in San Antonio and on the LULAC leadership in Texas. Then I turn to the legislation that most clearly reveals the privatization agenda, splitting the discussion into a section that addresses proposals that did not include vouchers and a section that focuses on the voucher proposals. I close by drawing on the work of Shaker and Heilman (2002) and Apple (2000, 2001) to explain why Texas-style accountability fails Latina/o youth.

THE LEGISLATIVE AND POLITICAL CONTEXT

Republican Takeover in the House

As a result of the 2002 elections, which involved a gubernatorial race as well as other key races, a major political shift occurred statewide. Republican victories resulted in the first Republican majority in the Texas House of Representatives (88 Republicans versus 62 Democrats) since Reconstruction (Republican Party of Texas, 2002).[4] According to State Representative Pete Gallego (D-Alpine), in a speech delivered in Austin at the National Council de La Raza's annual conference,

> They [Republicans] were so excited that they decided that they were going to do this on their own. Because they had 88 votes, they decided that they really didn't need us, and they, you know, offered to buy us golf lessons. . . . "When we need you, we'll call you. And otherwise, you know, stay home." (July 10, 2003)

Beginning with a decision to stack committee chair positions with Republicans (thus abandoning a long-standing tradition of bipartisanship honoring seniority for these slots [McNeely, 2003]), the leadership of the newly configured House quickly signaled its partisanship. It also exposed its own woeful lack of experience, negotiation skills, and interest in compromise. Ultimately, this combination led to a quorum-busting walkout by Democratic legislators, who fled to Ardmore, Oklahoma, to avoid a vote on a redistricting map that would have increased Republican representation in Texas' congressional delegation.[5] In addition to illuminating the conservative privatization agenda in education, the shift in the state's political landscape, as played out in the legislature, provides insight into the ways that the accountability system itself is related to that agenda.

Budget and School Finance Crises

Despite the backing of a compliant Republican majority, implementing the wide-ranging changes that would accompany privatization seemed sure to meet with resistance. A solid political barrier, in the form of the state's looming fiscal crisis, stood firmly in the way of such proposals, as letters to newspapers and editorial columns throughout Texas made clear. Legislators entered the 2003 session facing a $9.9 billion deficit in general revenue funds for 2004–2005. This decline is attributed to economic recession; increased on-line purchases of goods and services (this form of consumerism undercuts rather than increases sales tax revenues); over-budgeted caseloads funding children's health insurance (a problem that had already produced a fiscal shortfall for 2003); and a lack of the kind of political leadership required to find new revenue to close these gaps (DeLuna Castro, 2003).

These conditions prompted sobering budget cuts across all levels of education—elementary, secondary, and university.[6] In kindergarten through twelfth grade (K–12), cuts were made in textbook purchases, teacher health insurance, services provided by the state's 20 regional educational service centers, and staffing at the Texas Education Agency (TEA).[7] Moreover, this revamping of the budget represents only one aspect of the crisis. The state also faces a school finance nightmare: As of 2003, 400 of the state's 1,034 districts have reached or nearly reached the upper limits on the amount of funding they can be allotted from local property taxes (the cap is $1.50 for each $100 in assessed property taxes [Keller, 2003]).[8] This issue remained unresolved at the close of the 78th regular session (June 2003); the legislature is slated to embark on a special session in spring 2004 to address the problem.

Education Policy Research Context

Even with the very real impediments to privatization created by the state's fiscal crisis, education policy research continues to provide fertile ground for developing and refining such proposals. Shaker and Heilman (2002) have written incisively on the current political context of inquiry in education. They make a two-part argument. First, the small number of academics who are involved in the development and passage of education policy created a vacuum that has since been successfully occupied by "advocacy academicians" who work under the umbrella of ideologically based interest groups. In lieu of an authoritative voice on education policy derived from the scholarly expertise of junior and senior faculty, a partisan research world now exists outside and separate from the academy, at state and national levels.

Second, this "parallel world serves to legitimize information which is ultimately used to discredit public institutions, open education as a new market for profit, and consolidate a 'conservative' world view" (Shaker and Heilman, 2002, p. 3). Examples of such partisan think tanks, nonprofits, and research organizations are the Cato Institute, Fordham Foundation, Heritage Foundation, Hudson Institute, Manhattan Institute, and many others that receive funding from wealthy benefactors such as Joseph Coors, David Packard, John Walton, and Texas' own James P. Leininger. Leininger, a medical doctor, businessman, and philanthropist for conservative causes such as vouchers, has emerged as one of the single most influential behind-the-scenes players in Texas Republican Party politics (Olsson, 2002).

By controlling the context and limiting the range of options, these groups constrain open inquiry. To be sure, all empirical inquiry is subject to bias and distortion. However as Shaker and Heilman (2002) point out, it is reasonable to assume that scholars and educators who place the interests of others ahead of their own are more invested in presenting valid accounts. This is certainly what I have witnessed in dealings between university faculty and politicians in the legislative events I have helped organize.[9] Conversely, the evidence produced by researchers funded through policy think tanks with carefully wrought agendas is often suspect. Before addressing the emergence of Leininger's public policy think tank, the Texas Public Policy Foundation (TPPF), it is important to mention a separate activity of his that has had tremendous implications, both for public support of vouchers and for divisive politics among Latinos in Texas.

The Courting of San Antonio's Latina/o Community

In 1994, James Leininger founded the Children's Educational Opportunity (CEO) Foundation. Four years later, in 1998, the CEO sponsored the

Horizon program. This project targeted predominantly Latina/o, low-income families living in San Antonio's Edgewood Independent School District, offering $4,000 vouchers to all students in grades K–12. Few missed the symbolism of the CEO Foundation's choice of Edgewood—where the landmark legal battle for equalizing school funding in Texas began (Kozol, 1991)—as the site for what was then the largest privately funded voucher program in the country. In the program's first year, 700 children received "scholarships" (the Foundation's term for vouchers) for either private or parochial school tuition. According to TPPF researcher Chris Patterson (2003), the Horizon program made $50 million in vouchers available, enough for every student in Edgewood whose family wanted one. By 2001, 1,139 students had received vouchers.

The mantra of the TPPF, and of select LULAC leadership in San Antonio who maintained that vouchers provide valuable opportunities, was (and continues to be) that parents should have choice and that no child should have to attend a poor or failing school (Fikac, 1997; Schrag, 1999). Thus, the CEO's Horizon program could not fail to benefit the community. The National Education Association (NEA), however, viewed the CEO's efforts in a very different light. During the 77th legislative session (2001), the NEA, along with the Texas State Teachers Association and Latina/o educational leadership, helped organize public opposition to the proposed voucher legislation. According to the NEA, "the basic political goal of the CEO was to undermine public education and generate support, especially from low-income parents, for tax-supported vouchers" (NEA, 1999).

Historically, LULAC at all levels—local, state, and national—has opposed vouchers. The shift among select state LULAC board members occurred contemporaneously with the emergence of the CEO Foundation. At a board meeting held in Fort Worth on December 6, 1997, state leadership decided to approve a legislative proposal supporting vouchers. Board members included leadership from the San Antonio LULAC council, which had links to Leininger (Olsson, 2002). According to former State Representative Henry Cuellar, a Democrat from Laredo who presented the proposed legislation before the LULAC state board, vouchers would allow students rejected from public schools with capped enrollment the option of attending a private school. The proposed legislation resulted in a heated dispute between state and national LULAC leadership, both controlled by members from Texas (Ray, 1997). Less than a week later, on December 10, national LULAC leaders and scores of local councils, as well as top Latino elected officials, denounced the voucher proposal at an Austin press conference (Ray, 1997). At the national LULAC meeting held in Corpus Christi, Texas, in February 1998, an

Austin-area council member called for the impeachment of both the concerned state director and the immediate past state director, as well as a national investigation (Cisneros-Lunsford, 1999a). These leaders were never impeached, but a storm of protest from local councils ensued statewide, ultimately leading to a reversal in LULAC's putative position, announced at the state convention in early June, 1998.

This defeat did not deter LULAC board members from San Antonio from establishing close links to Putting Children First (PCF), a pro-voucher organization endowed by Leininger. These ties were forged primarily through the formation of a corollary organization called San Antonio Parents for School Choice (Bryce, 1999; Cisneros-Lunsford, 1999b). According to PCF Executive Director Greg Talley, quoted in an interview conducted by a *Texas Monthly* reporter (Olsson, 2002), "My charge was to go out and get a broader voice. We had a big chunk of LULAC [the Hispanic advocacy group] board members, we had [Black Houston Democrat] Ron Wilson, and then we had some more traditional business guys." The San Antonio-based LULAC members still maintain their association with PCF, but they now desist from making public statements on behalf of LULAC.

The chief concerns of opponents to the Edgewood voucher program pertained to its adverse effects on the public schools—siphoning away much-needed funds, "creaming" the better students, and, as a result, lowering test scores in Edgewood ISD schools. With funding formulas tied to the number of students enrolled in a district, the Edgewood ISD was deprived of $4 million in state funding during the voucher program's first year of operation (Walt, 1999). Despite the loss of this funding and of hundreds of students, the district still earned the coveted "recognized" rating in 1999–2000 (TEA, 2000). In all previous years since the inception of the rating system (in 1994), however, Edgewood had received an "academically acceptable" rating—just above the lowest, "academically unacceptable" rating in the state's four-part rating scheme.

According to a widely cited evaluation study by Peterson, Meyers, and Howell (1999), the voucher program showed little effect on math and reading scores—the differences between voucher students and their comparison group in the Edgewood public schools were not significant. Nevertheless, concerns among Edgewood community members over the district's under-performing schools carried over into the 2003 legislative session, especially at the momentous March 18, 2003, voucher hearing, at which Edgewood parents on both sides of the voucher debate were vocal participants.

Vouchers as a solution to under-performance was challenged by a wide array of organizations and coalitions, including the formidable Coalition for Public Schools (CPS) (www.coalition4publicschools.org/). The Coalition is composed of education, child advocacy, civil rights, and religious organizations representing more than 3,000,000 members in Texas. The Texas Freedom Network (TFN), a 12,000-member organization with members in every legislative district throughout the state, waged a similarly aggressive campaign. In collaboration with the San Antonio Independent School District, the Coalition for Excellence and Equity in Public Education, a San Antonio-based coalition of community organizations and individuals that opposes vouchers, held a press conference on April 14, 2003. This anti-voucher briefing was attended by CPS and TFN representatives and other Coalition members, including Edgewood parents and PTA members, the Mexican American Legal Defense and Educational Fund (MALDEF), and several Mexican American members of the legislature.

The fight against vouchers by Latina/os was far from a solitary one; it was part of a broader struggle representing parent, community, and school-based interests statewide. Although vouchers and other privatization efforts were defeated in the 2003 legislative session, it is too soon to claim victory. According to the policy director of LULAC,[10] voucher legislation is likely to reemerge during the forthcoming special session on school finance.

Politically, the most unfortunate consequence with respect to Leininger's agenda were the divisions created within LULAC, particularly in San Antonio (Drosjack, 2003a; Garcia, 2003a; Pyle, 2003). LULAC councils have always functioned democratically as semiautonomous organizations, so the San Antonio members' stance does not threaten an ideological rupture. Rather, the issue is that these council members have succumbed to a narrow framing of options for educational reform, acting as if other proposals (such as substantive equity) were unavailable; and they have allowed themselves to become the public relations arm of a conservative agenda that otherwise seeks to remand social services to the realm of the family and the private sector of the community. The greatest irony, as Apple (2000, 2001) and others (e.g., McNeil, 2000) suggest, is that market-based ideas erode the very potential for the kind of collective deliberation and response that epitomizes LULAC's long history of supporting public schools and a reasoned approach to educational reform (San Miguel, 1987).

*The Emergence of the Texas Public Policy Foundation
and the Rise of the Conservative Right in Texas*

By all accounts, Leininger's TPPF[11] rose to prominence with the Republican takeover in the House, influencing the 2003 legislative agenda (Olsson, 2002; Villafranca, 2003). The TPPF advocates such conservative principles as limited government, low taxes, and school vouchers. The organization follows the Heritage Foundation's model of funding research by advocacy academicians and courting the media and politicians to influence the content and direction of public policy (People for the American Way Foundation, 1999; for an in-depth analysis of the far-reaching influence of the Heritage Foundation on the media, see Haas, Molnar, & Serrano, 2001).[12]

In addition to supporting this high-profile agenda, Leininger also regularly contributes campaign funding to candidates who support taxpayer-funded vouchers, or who indicate that they could be encouraged to do so. For example, in 1993, an organization founded by Leininger, the A+ PAC for Parental School Choice, helped elect to the Texas State Board of Education (SBOE) three candidates backed by the religious right (Stutz, 1996; also see Nathan, 1999; People for the American Way, 1999). According to Nathan (1999), with these changes, the board's membership swelled to six (of 15 total members) right-wing Christian Republicans who want to ban sex education, institute classroom prayer, and otherwise impose pedagogical theocracy on the public schools (Ludwig, 2003; Nathan, 1999). Commenting on the conservative decision making by the SBOE, veteran Republican State Senator Bill Ratliff offers the following:

> What this group [the TPPF] is all about is the drive for vouchers. . . .
> That's why they say the public schools are not rigorous enough, that
> we are still not doing enough. And the proof of that, they say, is that
> we dumb down our tests (cited in Hart, 2002).

In 2002, Leininger exerted his influence by contributing large sums to the election campaigns of conservative Republicans seeking top leadership positions in the state. Noteworthy electoral victories included those of Governor Rick Perry and Lieutenant Governor David Dewhurst, both of whom are sympathetic to vouchers (see especially Olsson, 2002). According to Craig McDonald, who heads an organization that tracks political campaign contributions,

> The kingmakers of the conservative, free-market movement have captured the governor's office, the lieutenant governor's office, and the speaker's office. . . . At the same time, they've been funding a conservative agenda. It's clearly their agenda that will be the one the leadership is looking for. (cited in Copelin, 2002)

Continuing the momentum built in the wake of the fall election results, during the opening days of the 2003 legislative session in January, the TPPF sponsored one of the largest policy gatherings in Texas history (Copelin, 2002; Sullivan, 2003). At this event, the incoming chairman of the nine-member House Committee on Public Education, voucher advocate Representative Kent Grusendorf (R-Arlington), led the discussion on the subject of school choice.

On the Senate side, where the stars were already aligned in favor of a conservative Republican majority, additional help came as the new lieutenant governor exercised his right to assign committee chairmanships. To chair the Senate Education Committee, Dewhurst picked Senator Florence Shapiro, a veteran republican who represents Plano, an affluent Dallas suburb. In recognition of her work on conservative causes, in 1999 Shapiro received a perfect score on the Christian Coalition's Legislative Scorecard.[13] She replaced another voucher supporter, Senator Teel Bivins, who had been nominated to this position during the 77th (2001) legislative session by then Lieutenant Governor Rick Perry. Less than a month after the TPPF policy event, Perry, now governor, expressed explicit support for vouchers in his State of the State address:

> And let's allow parents of children stuck in substandard schools to choose the best school for their child—whether that school is public, private, or religious. I know in this chamber there are Republicans and Democrats willing to take this step. They know what I know: When you give parents a choice, you give children a chance. (Perry, 2003)

In short, with the arrival of an eager cohort of conservative, provoucher legislators, the influence of key legislators and conservative foundations and organizations on state legislation was unusually direct in the 78th session. By funding politicians who support voucher programs, and supporting think tanks that obligingly draft ideologically influenced blueprints for reform, the state's new conservative elite helped ensure that discourse on vouchers and other privatization proposals were normalized and legitimated. As Apple (2000, 2001) maintains, the power of the neoliberal economic and political elite is their capacity to affect and indeed reshape the public's "commonsense" views of educational reform. I turn now to address these proposals for change.

THE PRIVATIZATION AGENDA IN THE 2003 LEGISLATIVE SESSION: NON-VOUCHER LEGISLATION

During the 2003 legislative session, committee chairpersons Kent Grusendorf of the House and Florence Shapiro of the Senate authored various legislative proposals that provide the most direct evidence of a clear privatization agenda in education. None became law. Still, these proposed bills conveyed a strong message that Texas is or should be poised for major changes in the way public dollars are spent. It should be noted, though, that despite the backing that these proposals received from powerful core Republicans, record votes on bills that made it to the House floor, namely, House Bill (HB) 1554 and Senate Bill (SB) 933, show that not all Republicans favor privatization proposals. Those same House votes also show that certain Democrats, most notably Ron Wilson, an African American representative from Houston, support privatization—thus revealing a modicum of success for the political right in the public relations battle between advocates for choice and advocates for public schools.[14] Sentiments in both parties, however, were shaped by a perceived cruelty in taking money from schools in a context of economic recession. Because of African Americans' and Latina/os' concentration in the public school system, it should come as no surprise that diverse segments of these communities weighed in on the voucher proposal (discussion follows).[15]

The privatization agenda figured most prominently in the following bills:

- HB 1133, which called for textbooks to be supplied to privately schooled children at public expense (authored by Grusendorf);
- SB 412 and companion HB 214, which allowed home schoolers to a) enroll in public schools part-time at district expense; b) receive free textbooks; c) participate in public-school sponsored extracurricular activities; d) be included in average daily attendance data; and e) be exempt from state assessments required of public school students. These proposals also included provisions that would authorize a school district to establish off-campus laboratories or other facilities (authored by Senator Shapiro and State Representative McCall [Plano], respectively);

- HB 1554 and companion SB 933, which called for the creation of virtual schools chartered by a public college or university (authored by Grusendorf and Shapiro, respectively).

Free Textbooks and Privileges for Privately and
Home-Schooled Children

Neither HB 1133 nor SB 412 made it out of their respective House and Senate committees. The fiscal notes for both were an obvious impediment. For HB 1133, the fiscal note states that there are approximately 230,000 children attending private schools in Texas. Based on these figures, as well as on the assumption that most privately schooled children would eventually seek to obtain free textbooks, the director of the legislative board calculated a cumulative, five-year net impact of $27,959,730.00 by 2008 (www.capitol.state.tx.us/). Similarly, the provision requiring the state to count home-schooled children on the basis of their average daily attendance (ADA) posed fiscal problems. The ADA count would directly affect the costs associated with textbooks, participation in extracurricular activities, and building and/or maintaining off-campus facilities, resulting in a major expense for taxpayers.[16] Positing a base of $4,700 on average for a student with no special needs and using a corollary assumption that of the 150,000 home-schooled students statewide, participation rates would range incrementally from 5% the first year the law took effect to 25% by 2008, a five-year, cumulative fiscal impact was estimated at $537,059,250.00.[17]

Another provision of SB 412, that home-schooled students be exempt from the state's testing system, bucked two trends: an ongoing effort to justify allotments in exchange for accountability, operationalized in terms of testing (McNeil, 2000); and a commitment to consistency in state-level attempts to bring all students under the aegis of accountability (Black & Valenzuela, in press). As with the other two, larger pieces of legislation (discussed next), the home-schooling bill raised explicitly stated concerns over "a lack of accountability." The proposal did make provisions for options and "choice," as its proponents maintained, but it also codified a decided inequity with respect to how privately, home-schooled children would be treated vis-à-vis the state's system of testing. In response to a question regarding why home-schooled children should not be tested, an attorney working on behalf of parents of home schoolers testified that parents' chief concern is that the state or local school district not have authority over what they teach at home (available on-line at www.capitol.state.tx.us/tlo/house/broadcast.htm). Thus, the bill's proponents sought to secure access to select curricula through public dollars while simultaneously adhering to their private definitions of curriculum and education. As the following summary will show, some voucher proponents' views toward testing and hence accountability render transparent a fundamental purpose. As conveyed in President George W. Bush's oft-expressed view that accountability is for "identifying failures," accountability is more about the politics of control over education than it is about children's learning. This focus then justifies a shift to a private schooling sector that not only lacks accountability but may also embody sectarian views that are contradictory to democracy.

Virtual Charter Legislation

HB 1554 and the companion SB 933 proposed to create a new type of charter school that would add to the charter system colleges and universities that use technology, particularly the Internet, to deliver instruction beyond a central campus. Although unstated in the legislation, the fiscal note for HB 1554 identifies home schoolers and some privately schooled children as the prime beneficiaries of the new form of charter (see www.capitol.state.tx.us/). Another important beneficiary of the proposed bills would be a private-sector vendor named K12, Inc., whose top official is former U.S. Secretary of Education William Bennett. K12, Inc. markets a computer-based curriculum. Bennett, along with other K12 lobbyists, worked aggressively behind the scenes to promote passage of this legislation (see Texas Federation of Teachers [TFT] Legislative Hotline 2003b, www.tft.org/).

    HB 1554 and SB 933 require instruction to be provided by certified teachers, but they also call for a problematic ratio of 1 teacher to 60 students in average daily attendance. The teacher is required to meet with each parent of each student four times a year. The high student-to-teacher ratio, combined with students' minimal contact time with the teacher (i.e., beyond e-mail, Internet access), was a topic of great concern in public testimony (available on-line at www.capitol.state.tx.us/tlo/house/broadcast.htm). In contrast to the distance-learning opportunities that currently exist in some districts, this legislation proposed a statewide charter and provided a mechanism for channeling funds specifically for sustaining this form of education. For example, each student would get a computer, printer, hard copies of instructional materials, and reimbursements for Internet-related expenses. The strongest arguments in support of the legislation focused on being able to tailor instruction to each student's actual level of ability and learning style, and so allow for progress in a self-paced manner. Access to certified teachers and an allegedly content-rich curriculum were also named as pluses. In Grusendorf's words, the legislation would be a boon for "those who would like the quality of a private education, but can't afford it" (quoted in Garcia, 2003b). Finally, the use of technology itself was deemed a significant advantage.

Opponents, who dubbed the legislation a "stealth voucher" plan (Garcia, 2003b), cited the following as important drawbacks: The bills were predicated on the unacceptable principle of using public money to subsidize the private sector of home schoolers, not to mention to enrich profit-seeking cyber-school owners and management companies such as K12, Inc. Equally important, the legislation's scope left out a significant body of students: This kind of charter school would be inaccessible to English-language learners and other special needs populations. Moreover, costs related to the state's purchase of computers and printers for students, as well as for reimbursing them for their Internet access expenses, would be prohibitive. Indeed, the cumulative, five-year fiscal note for this legislation totals $4,935,000.00 by 2008. Opponents also raised pedagogical concerns with respect to exclusively computer-based instruction and the lack of contact time with teachers, particularly for younger children. They mentioned privacy rights and the risks involved in protecting the identities of students located in anonymous districts. And, finally, they pointed to the lack of accountability in terms of state curricular standards, testing, and oversight by the TEA. Abetted by the state's fiscal crisis, the advocacy of numerous organizations, including the Coalition for Public Schools (www.coalition4publicschools.org/), eventually brought about defeat of the legislation.

THE PRIVATIZATION AGENDA IN THE 2003 LEGISLATIVE SESSION: VOUCHER LEGISLATION

House Bill 2465 called for a voucher system in the state's 11 largest districts; it was authored by Grusendorf, with Representatives Ron Wilson, Mike Krusee, and Glenn Lewis as co-sponsors. Termed "freedom scholarships," by Chairman Grusendorf, the author of HB 2465, this legislation would have allowed public school students in the state's 11 largest districts to attend private school at public expense.[18] In the original language of the bill, student eligibility was based on income. Students from families with incomes of up to 200% above the base level for qualifying for the free or reduced-cost lunch program would be considered eligible. Although initially aimed at benefiting minorities and low-income children concentrated in large urban districts, beginning in 2006 and pending approval from a local school board, any school district would be able to opt into the program.

Vouchers would entitle students to attend the accredited private school of their choice, providing there is space. In instances in which there are many applicants for only a few spaces, a random selection process would occur (the bill explicitly states that a private school may not discriminate on the basis of race, color, or national origin). Students would be required to take either the Texas Assessment of Knowledge and Skills (TAKS) or a norm-referenced instrument, and schools would have to publish the scores. House Bill 2465 also called for an evaluation to be carried out by researchers at the Charles A. Dana Center at the University of Texas at Austin.[19] The evaluation would assess the extent of program participation, student performance on (unspecified) "annual assessment instruments," student and parental satisfaction with the program, overall impact on public school students, and program impact on private and public school capacity, quality, and availability.

As with the home-schooling legislation described previously, individual allotments would be based on students' ADA. According to the March 18 fiscal notes for HB 2465 (www.capitol.state.tx.us/), the district in which the child resides would receive 10% of the voucher; the remainder would go to the private school. The 10% presumably would cover district-supplied transportation for scholarship students. The fiscal note put the districts' losses in revenue as a result of students' departure at $75 million by 2005. Economies of scale dictate that operating costs and overhead, often coupled with the challenge of rising energy and maintenance costs, especially for older buildings, remain regardless of fluctuations in student enrollment.

The public presence at the March 18, 2003, hearing on the voucher legislation was so immense that the hearing had to be held in the capitol's largest hearing room, with hundreds filling the auditorium and many spilling over into another room, where the hearing was telecast.[20] To be sure, many were present to hear 89-year old Nobel Laureate Milton Friedman speak in defense of vouchers. But even without Friedman, the controversial nature of the issue destined a large turnout.

The hearing lasted 10 hours, from 2:00 p.m. until 12:10 a.m. Of the approximately 100 individuals who had signed up to testify, 69 ended up being able to do so—32 witnesses for, and 37 against, vouchers. In addition to the expected attendance of civil rights organizations and parent,

teacher, administrator, and school board associations, many ordinary citizens were on hand—working-class Latina/o and African American parents, children, and community members—as well as activists. Various
pro-voucher groups were in attendance. Busloads of mostly Latina/o,
working-class parents of Horizon scholarship recipients came from the
Edgewood ISD wearing distinctive blue t-shirts. Leadership and community members from Dallas and Houston parochial schools were also well
represented, as were various African American community and church
leaders from east Austin, groups with long-standing grievances against
the Austin Independent School District.

Friedman's presentation was punctuated by raucous applause from
the audience, encouraging a contentious, if not competitive, spirit between voucher proponents and opponents that carried through to the end
of the hearing. After demonizing public schools as "government schools,"
and education as a "socialist industry monopolized by teachers "unions"
(field notes, March 18, 2003), Friedman acknowledged that the proposed
legislation would create the most far-reaching voucher program in the
history of the United States (Drosjack, 2003b).[21] Nevertheless, he critiqued the bill for not going "far enough," stating that what was needed
was a "completely free educational system." He also referred to privileges
that "rich, middle-class" parents have within the current system, because
of their freedom to secure the school of their choice. Parents opting for
private school, however, "pay tuition twice." "In a free-choice situation,"
he continued, "they [parents] would be part of a free market." Friedman's presentation thus set the stage for what turned out to be a highly
emotional debate, inasmuch as the formal structure of offering public testimony in committee hearings can be said to allow "debate."

Voucher Proponents' Views

Voucher supporters fell into several camps. On the one hand, there were
those who testified on the virtues of both choice and competition within
a free market of educational options. Echoing Friedman, many witnesses
conveyed their view that if public schools were forced to compete with
private schools, they would either have to improve or close down. This
notion of competition was most cogently expressed by Chairman
Grusendorf, who declared, "Let consumer choice concepts rule. That's
a form of regulation. It's called the market." Grusendorf's depiction of
the market as the ultimate form of accountability resonated with numerous witnesses who, asserting parents' rights, called for greater parental

control over and options in educational decision making. Many testified that parents would hold schools accountable with their decisions to support a particular school by sending their children there, or would withhold support by not sending their children there. As one witness (representing private school academies) put it, "Ultimate accountability is parental choice."

Others who testified cited neither choice nor competition, but concentrated instead on the failings of the public school system. Most subscribed to a conventional definition of educational excellence involving academic standards, testing, and the generation of comparable school ratings. Witnesses differed on the extent to which such methods should be applied to voucher recipients. Some argued that because testing drives curriculum, this would constitute government intrusion. In this vein, one speaker remarked that teaching to the test was a feature of public schools that should not be part of a private school environment.

A much different view was offered by a scientist associated with the Milton and Rose D. Friedman Foundation, who testified that parents with privately schooled children would benefit most from considering the statistical results on standardized tests. What private schools did with the results was a separate matter. A few voucher proponents conveyed a middle position, maintaining that the proposed legislation's requirement that students take either a standardized or norm-referenced exam, coupled with the Dana Center's evaluation study, were sufficient bases for determining accountability. Implied in both of these positions is the view that accountability, as currently defined, is valid. Most of the pro-voucher crowd, however, held less trusting and less sanguine views regarding both accountability and public schooling.

Indeed, accountability itself was often singled out as "the problem." A plurality of parents and community members, for example, referred to low academic standards that leave children poorly equipped for the global economy. They complained as well about low expectations and the continuing problem of socially promoting children (including their own) despite their inability to read or write. A Dallas-area parent decried the teachers and administrators who, through their testimonies, suggested that "everything is okay [with the public schools]." "It is a broken system," she charged, "even when 'recognized' [when it achieves a recognized rating]. The claim that we are taking money from the public school is not justified if the money is going into a system where it is getting wasted." Her allegation echoed the remarks of other witnesses who had drawn attention to the rising costs and what they defined as the diminishing returns associated with public education. Overall, though, costs were less of a focus for voucher proponents, compared to opponents. In fact, several community members condemned what they perceived to be schools' greater focus on money than on children.

One Latina mother from San Antonio testified that teachers in her daughter's public school told her that her child eventually would "grow out of" writing her letters and numbers backwards. Years later, teachers in the private school her daughter was newly attending suggested a formal assessment. Testing revealed the child to be dyslexic. As a representative from the Children with Disabilities Council (CDC) later testified, this mother fit into a particular category of parents present at the hearing—those whose children had suffered the consequences of not being properly diagnosed. The issue, the CDC speaker suggested, is less a private–public one, and more an indication of the range of teachers' and school administrators' knowledge of, and sensitivity toward, children with disabilities. It also underscores the unevenness with which schools apply federal disability guidelines.

Witnesses referred to various forms of research evidence in their critiques of schools without making explicit references to accountability itself. They mentioned, for instance, high dropout rates, very low rates of college attendance, and high remediation rates once in college. As a crowd, this group was quite impatient, booing and hissing those antivoucher witnesses who blamed parents for low performance or who used accountability data such as test scores to buttress their claims that public schools either are improving or are in less need for reform than the present call for vouchers would suggest. Perhaps the strongest anti-school language came from one of the cosponsors of the bill, Ron Wilson:

> If we're concerned about kids, we ought to be willing to do almost anything. Public education in this country is like a sinking ship. We ought to be throwing lifelines to kids, not trying to fix the ship. (cited in Pyle, 2003)

Several witnesses, including TPPF Director of Education Chris Patterson, invoked Texas history. "The great myth," Patterson said, "is that vouchers are some kind of experiment. When Texas established the public schools in 1876, it did so using a voucher system." (But see Blanton, 2004, who characterizes the schools as completely unregulated during the 1870s, approximating educational anarchy rather than a voucher system.) This rhetoric mirrored that of another defender of vouchers, who extolled Texans' "fiercely independent" character as sufficient justification for embarking on this experiment.

Voucher Opponents' Views

In response to voucher supporters' theoretical notions of choice and competition, various voucher opponents, including one Houston Independent School District school board member, suggested that choice already exists in the public school system, in the form of magnet programs and charter schools. Other witnesses argued that choice was less in the hands of parents and more in the control of private schools, who were free to decide whom to accept or reject. Along these lines, a Latina parent from the Northside District in San Antonio maintained that it is not "customer choice" that should govern parents' relations to schools, but rather, "customer voice." By this she meant that instead of abandoning their neighborhood schools, parents should become involved in them.

Some witnesses challenged the premise that choice does or should exist within schooling. A TFT representative, for example, noted that

> Whether we like it or not, we have a constitutional mandate for the state government to provide a public free education to students in the state of Texas. That, by its definition, is not a free market. They are compelled to attend these schools. And in being compelled, we have a responsibility as citizens to exercise diligence over what they are being exposed to and what we hope they are being prepared for as graduates of those schools.

Still others rejected the presumption of choice on the basis of the absence of a level playing field. Real choice does not exist unless the options are equal. A Texas Parent–Teacher Association (PTA) representative stated it in this manner: "If competition is truly what we seek, then give us a level playing field. Public schools are so full of mandates that we can't breathe. Meanwhile, private schools have none." This same PTA representative further challenged choice theory from the view that it is illusory: "Schools do not have the choice *not* to parent."

Vouchers also were vociferously protested as a matter of principle. An American Civil Liberties Union representative was among several speakers who argued that vouchers violate the separation of church and state. Religious schools, she offered, "lack freedom of expression and [children who attend them] have more censorship applied to [them because of] their status as students." She further lamented that "people think that they have to give up their civil rights in order to get a good education." These views aligned with those of several voucher opponents from conservative organizations like the Texas Eagle Forum, who argued that state funding of private schools would lead to government intrusion. A representative of the like-minded group Citizens for Freedom in Education asserted, "If there's only a test, that's too much regulation. If the test is a precursor to further regulation, this is another government string."

A Texas Freedom Network representative came at the problem from a different angle:

> At a time when our budget crisis in our state has already prompted legislators to consider measures like withholding textbooks and making up to $2.8 billion in cuts to our public schools, it is reckless to think about taking money out of our schools to subsidize private schools.

A representative from the League of Women Voters of Texas made a direct appeal to legislators:

> Transferring public funds will not improve public schools. They weaken the public school system. Texas is in an unprecedented fiscal crisis. You don't know how to fund the public school system. Why do you wish to take funds from the public school system and fund the private school system? How can you live with yourselves?!

A concern raised by and discussed among the education committee members themselves pertained to the potential for discrimination, despite the legislation's nondiscrimination clause. I testified that a decision not to discriminate is not necessarily a decision to include or be inclusive of children, either in terms of their special needs or with respect to diversity in the curriculum. Adding to similar concerns expressed by numerous witnesses, I noted that the language of the legislation fails to mention whether English-language learners, disabled children, low socioeconomic-status children, females, or those belonging to a faith that is different from that embraced by the school would be protected from discrimination. Nor did the bill mention whether a private school may discriminate when there are many more applicants than spaces available. The same witness from the Citizens for Freedom in Education organization, mentioned previously, expressed her view that private schools *want* to discriminate on the basis of religion. Private schools do not want their philosophy diluted by having to admit students of a different faith or creed. Her testimony failed to address others' concerns, however, such as whether these private schools might also want to discriminate on the basis of other characteristics, either because of a lack of fit or an inability to offer needed services.

Huge portions of voucher opponents' testimonies were far less impassioned than these examples. They addressed stock concerns such as the notion that private schools are not accountable to the public for their actions or outcomes generally, and that the legislation did not go far enough in trying to guarantee accountability on the part of these schools. Many questioned the need for vouchers at all, given that the Texas educational system recently has demonstrated significant improvement, primarily in the form of higher test scores. Others referred to research evidence showing that voucher programs do not significantly improve the educational achievement of students. Another significant concern was losses in revenue to public schools due to student departure.

In contrast to the rounds of testimony from voucher proponents that children are still graduating from public schools with poor reading and writing skills, much of the discourse on achievement that opponents offered was laudatory. It departed from the unquestioning premise that the current accountability system is valid and fair. The Houston school board member, for example, referred to the Broad Prize for Public Education that the Houston Independent School District (HISD) won for closing the gap between minorities and nonminorities.[22] Her testimony also focused on the underappreciated benefits associated with being part of the public school system. Besides educational choices, she referred to the availability of athletics, special education, and English as a second language programs—many of which are not offered in the private sector. She concurred with an education committee member who suggested that the public schools may not be doing a good enough public relations job regarding the benefits of public schooling.

An interesting, if unfortunate, element of the testimonies of several anti-voucher witnesses was the tendency to place the primary burden of responsibility for poor performance on the students and parents themselves. Even a seemingly benign comment about parents "who aren't supportive of their kids" from a representative of the Texas Classroom Teachers Association drew protests from the crowd of Latina/o parents seated around me. A similar reaction occurred when the League of Women Voters representative declared,

> It's pathetic to hear people blaming the schools, teachers, and administrators when the issue that the biggest item that controls whether a student does well is parental concern. What this bill says is that we have given up on public education.

The audience was equally pained when a Latino Southwest Independent School District (SISD) board member from San Antonio stated emphatically that "parental involvement *is* the answer," after mentioning the strides the SISD had made and the amount of money that would be taken away from the district if the legislation were passed. Unknowingly, these witnesses hindered their own cause when they marshaled a technicist, pro-accountability discourse. The parents' boos, challenging body language, and discourteous comments about such witnesses spoke volumes. In this regard, those on the political right sounded more grounded and sympathetic to the notion of troubled schools than those on the left.

Perhaps the most obvious reason for the displeasure I observed among audience members was the overwhelming representation of parents that day—the auditorium was literally overflowing with parents who obviously cared about education. Another possible explanation lies in the emergence of a racially coded categorization of Latina/o parents as uncaring to simultaneously explain student under-performance and absolve schools of their responsibilities (Valenzuela, 1999). Indeed, numerous parents reacted against "the data" and also against the institutional discourse on costs associated with vouchers. It may be tempting to dismiss their views as either emotional or unrealistic, but the raw nerve that was tapped when parents were blamed for student under-performance suggests that they believed their sincere expressions of despair with the public school system were being ignored or dismissed as unrepresentative.

In short, pro-accountability rhetoric seemed to fall on deaf ears. This dynamic reveals the limits to accountability. Schools and districts may be able to raise test scores, but this does not in itself denote a responsible stewardship of the public's trust. Proclamations such as the availability of choice in public schooling, for example, defy a lived experience of limited options for poor people under any system. For this reason, in my own testimony, I appealed to that history of discrimination and exclusion, referring to the abuses of the current system, particularly the state's systematic distortion of the true dropout numbers (see McNeil, this volume).

Shortly after I testified, I spoke with several parents from Dallas. They told me that they had struggled deeply with their decision to support vouchers and that while they agreed with many of the points I made, they simply could not wait another generation to receive their due. I told them that as a parent myself, I understood their dilemma. As we parted ways, I contemplated how the "choice" that was offered to the community that day is one that would ultimately close off the very choices that we as a public need to hold onto—that is, the choice for shared, democratically governed, publicly funded schools.

Outcome

Although HB 2465 sailed out of committee with 5 voting for, 3 against, a lack of votes on the House floor kept it from moving forward. In a last-ditch attempt to secure its passage, Chairman Grusendorf tried to amend SB 1108, a noncontroversial dropout prevention bill, authored by both himself and Senator Shapiro. According to a TFN lobbyist with whom I spoke on the day of the vote on SB 1108 (May 25, 2003), the House Speaker did not allow him to do this because "he would have killed his own bill" (i.e., SB 1108).

WHY TEXAS-STYLE ACCOUNTABILITY FAILS LATINA/O YOUTH

My research on accountability has resulted in many invitations to give talks on the topic. Whenever I do so, I can count on being asked why there is such a great emphasis on test-based accountability. Another frequent question is whether I think the current fervor reflects the work of a conspiracy. Neither question can be answered simply. The Texas accountability story illustrates how communities need to be alert to the ways that national forces such as privatization, marketization, and de-democratization are taking hold. There is a national, even global, push on institutions to marketize those systems previously valued as public (see Lipman, 2002, and Hursh, 2003 for excellent analyses of the impact of neoliberal initiatives on Chicago and New York schools, respectively). Although the Texas case shows how this is not a monolithic system shift, the reader should not lose sight of the raw exercise of conservative power. It remains significant that a handful of individuals are able to both push their agenda through the sponsorship of candidates into state leadership positions and co-opt marginalized groups that the political right has starved with an unequal, often low-quality, system of education.

Work by Shaker and Heilman (2002) and by Apple (2000, 2001) renders this larger political landscape explicable. Shaker and Heilman (2002) describe a gaping hole in the world of policy making; fewer and fewer academics turn their attention toward policy, thus leaving the field wide open for the advocacy researchers and other powerful alliances that Apple identifies. Apple (2000, 2001) charts the growth of a dominant, neoliberal, economic and political elite with deep and defining commitments to freedom and choice, and with a primary goal of modernizing the economy by implementing "conservative modernization." At ground level, conservative modernization involves rightist transformations that bring disparate interests together, forming an odd combination that includes both market enthusiasts and backers of a regulatory state. In education, conservative modernization translates into supporting the notion that publicly funded schools belong in a competitive marketplace, while also promoting pedagogic uniformity and the implementation of "traditional" academic curricula, all under the guise of bringing "neutral" standards to bear.

A commitment to conservative modernization helps explain how leading politicians such as Chairman Grusendorf can be central to the evolution of numbers-based accountability and still "live with themselves" quite comfortably as they steer the state toward their goal of the ultimate form of accountability—the market. Grusendorf's seemingly hypocritical, or at least contradictory behavior of blocking Representative Dora Olivo's multiple criteria legislation can be reconciled. Although the Olivo bill would have improved accountability (see chapter 1, Valenzuela, this volume), Grusendorf's authoring and championing of legislation with no provisions for accountability as it is conventionally understood make sense if a "correct" notion of accountability as a market function is applied.

Shifting the focus this way, to take in the larger political panorama within which policy makers act, clarifies broad patterns of behavior as well as individual acts. Taking this perspective when considering the rise of Texas-style accountability is a case in point. Viewed in the context of conservative modernization, Texas-style accountability appears to be less a rational, carefully delineated model for improving education and more an eclectic collection of new and old ideas with varying levels of popular appeal and a hybrid set of champions—a political "grab bag" that has been deftly used by a powerful elite to move a larger agenda forward. I remind readers that although Representative Olivo had nearly all the support needed to pass her legislation, sleight-of-hand maneuvers by Grusendorf and others on the education committees in both houses kept it from becoming a reality (see chapter 1).

The well-funded, neoliberal agenda draws astutely on an array of contradictory power relationships as part of a larger strategy to make it difficult for subordinate groups to engage in meaningful political activity (Apple 2000, 2001). Included in this array are neoconservatives or social Darwinists such as President George W. Bush and core leadership in the Texas legislature, who fake equity by declaring their commitment to single-indicator accountability while simultaneously promoting vouchers that undercut educational equity, and failing to support adequate funding to provide all children with an excellent education. Insidiously, they deny the role that their own unearned privileges have played in their success while exploiting Americans' cultural appetite for testing students and rating schools (see Lemann, 1999, for an excellent cultural analysis of testing).

Another important source of power in the forward movement of the privatization agenda is contributed by "authoritarian populists," who construe education in moral, mostly Christian, terms and oppose the "secular humanism" of the public schools (Apple 2000, 2001). This group envisions an Edenic past when "traditional" values ruled the day. In its current makeup, Texas' State Board of Education subscribes to just such views (Ludwig, 2003; Nathan, 1999). By constructing the realm of the public as "bad" and the realm of the private as "good," the neoliberal elite exploits authoritarian populists' fears of the "other." This group is vulnerable to the view that changing demographics create "uncertainties" that need to be controlled with standardized curricula, instruction, and zero-tolerance measures. The belief in the importance of compulsory cultural homogeneity is especially evident in the enforcement of testing policies and practices that encourage a rapid transitioning of children out of bilingual education programs (Alamillo, Palmer, Viramontes, & García, this volume; Black & Valenzuela, in press).

Amid these groups is the new professional middle class, which seeks technical and managerial solutions to social problems (Apple 2000, 2001). As the voucher debate in the legislature reveals, neoliberals have used to their own advantage this middle-class group's "ivory-tower" naiveté that education can fix most social problems and that the state can legislate solutions to problems resistant to the powers of education. Most scholars, including all of the contributors to this volume, take a much different position regarding the role of education, emphasizing that educational outcomes reflect fundamental asymmetries of power that require political solutions.

Effective, equitable solutions, in turn, require good political representation in the legislature, on school boards, and among school administrators and teachers. Moreover, such leadership must also recognize how the seemingly innocuous language of "accountability" is part and parcel of a conservative political agenda that leaves ordinary parents and citizens struggling to find a new and effective vocabulary and voice that will enable them to participate equally and democratically in the broader institutional discourse on schools.

I would add that all three groups, the neoconservatives/social Darwinists, authoritarian populists, and the new professional middle class, are dangerously ready to equate efficiency with virtue. Concentration camps were efficient. So was slavery. Neither should we forget the oppressive American Indian boarding school system that deliberately aimed to "kill the Indian to save the man" (Spring, 1997). Similarly, the cynical reaction of many parents at the voucher hearing to witnesses' use of technicist, pro-accountability rhetoric underscores how effectively the accountability system, in its current incarnation, seems to perpetuate rather than ameliorate injustice.

The current model leaves too many poor and minority students behind, and their parents' patience is long since gone. They refuse to postpone until the next generation their children's access to the good life that a quality education promises. Even if vouchers ultimately will not serve their communities well, "choice" is seductive, stoking these parents' desire for a long-awaited release from rigid bureaucracies and sterile curricula. Most important, though, minority and low-income parents' backing of vouchers bears witness to the depths of their distrust of apologists for the current system.

The solutions to the state's unfinished work in education proposed during the 78th session of the legislature represent a significant challenge to the democratic notion that public schools are central players in the promotion of the common good. Albeit imperfectly, public schools are among the few remaining places for members of diverse communities to meet, communicate, and interact. In a general commentary with respect to neoliberal initiatives to increase citizens' isolation, McChesney states: "The net result is an atomized society of disengaged individuals who feel demoralized and socially powerless" (cited in Apple, 2001, p. 18).

The public school system is not and never will be perfect. Across- and within-district politics and inequities ensure a robust future for the harsh reality that equitable public schooling has never been common to all children in Texas. Yet public schools remain a precious space between the private realm of the family and the public realm of the market within which private interests can be pursued and where the market can be critiqued. The voucher hearing itself was an extraordinary, multi-voiced moment in democracy that, ironically—at least for many parents and community members, leaned heavily in support of an undemocratic, market solution to the lived educational story behind the numbers. It is easy to see how the legitimate grievances of poor, disenfranchised Latina/os and African Americans play directly into the hands of the promoters of the neoliberal agenda. Angry, impatient, too often deceived: This group is poised to barter its political soul.

Woefully absent in our statewide educational leadership is a strong, democratic voice calling for an invigorated public sphere in which accountability is not to the state but to a citizen public. To our detriment, the technicistic and economistic language of education has usurped both our commonsense ways of talking about schools and our collective ability to speak about public education as the bedrock of our democracy. Meanwhile, the battle over privatization in Texas shows no signs of abatement. As a frustrated colleague asked me in the aftermath of the voucher hearing, "Are we at the end of reform?" Only time will tell.

NOTES

1. I especially credit my association with LULAC at local and state levels for the analytical frame presented herein. Moreover, as of June 1, 2003, following the state convention in Fort Worth, I am now chair of the state LULAC Education Committee.

2. We developed a policy website that illustrates much of what we learned (http://www.edb.utexas.edu:16080/latino/).

3. Arguably, charter proposals—including several that were presented in the 78th legislative session—also reflect a move toward privatization (e.g., Bracey, 2001). I do not address these proposals because I limit my focus to those efforts that most explicitly reveal the interests of some parents of privately educated children and those of conservative organizations in pursuit of marketized schooling options.

4. In the previous legislative session, the House had 78 Democrats and 72 Republicans. In both sessions, the Senate was predominantly Republican (in 2003, there were 19 Republicans and 12 Democrats). Of the 12 Senate Democrats, 9 are minority, mostly Latino, legislators.

5. Senate Democrats also fled the state (to Albuquerque, New Mexico) for the same reasons that impelled the House Democrats to leave. Their grievances included the lieutenant governor's decision to override a Senate tradition that requires two-thirds of the members to agree to debate any proposal. Requiring only a simple majority—a numerical majority easily achieved by Republicans with no need to negotiate with or even listen to Democrats—is tantamount to losing substantial congressional representation for decades to come. Hence, the far-reaching implications of the Democratic walkout.

6. According to DeLuna Castro (2003), these budget cuts disproportionately affect Latinos who not only predominate among the poor and uninsured in Texas relative to both African Americans and Anglos (25% as compared to

18.8% and 7.3%, respectively), but who also comprise an increasing portion of the share of children in grades K–12 (42% as compared to 14% and 41%, respectively).

7. In addition to these direct cuts to public education, balancing the budget this past session also resulted in other legislation that adversely impacts poor and minority families, a loss of Medicaid coverage for more than 18,000 adults, and by 2005, 332,000 fewer children will have coverage. Income eligibility for the Children's Health Insurance Program (CHIP) was also changed, so that by 2005, 169,300 fewer children will be served (DeLuna Castro, 2003).

8. School finance in Texas is a very complex and dynamic issue. The state's contribution to public education constitutes 25% of the entire appropriations budget, but local property taxes still generate the lion's share of funding—$40.4 billion (58% of the state's $70 billion total budget in 2003). In the special legislative session, legislators plan to consider various proposals, including the possibility of replacing the current strategy of recapturing funds from 118 property-rich districts' tax revenues, a plan that has come to be known (pejoratively) as "Robin Hood." Other possible solutions include tax-base consolidation between districts, legislating new cost adjustments that take into account regional variations in teacher salaries, raising the statutory cap, subjecting the funding system to competition based on a certain definition of merit at the school and district level, and defining a level of adequacy for producing certain educational results, or a combination of these (Interim Committee Hearing on Public School Finance, Select, July 10, 2003; Joint Select Committee on Public School Finance, 2002). This array of options notwithstanding, adopting a plan deemed adequate for meeting the educational goals of the state is projected to be a driving principle for the 2003 special session. That is, because both state and federal education policy demand a diffusion of knowledge such that all children have a reasonable, if not excellent, opportunity to meet prescribed standards across grade levels, the constitutionality of the system and educational achievement are necessarily linked.

9. Except for attending an education policy event marking the ten-year anniversary of the Charles A. Dana Center (held December 3, 2002) that involved both faculty and advocacy researchers (www.utdanacenter.org/pressroom/anniversary.html), I have not been part of legislative gatherings that have included university faculty (apart from the events I organized).

10. Personal conversation, Ana Yañez Correa, February 14, 2003.

11. According to Nathan (1999), the TPPF received $1 million, or a fifth of its funding, from the philanthropist Leininger and his family.

12. Another noteworthy aspect of the conservative agenda are the legal firms like the Leininger-created Texas Justice Foundation (www.txjf.org), the Institute for Justice (www.ij.org) and the Legal Landmark Foundation (www.landmarklegal.org) that have successfully defended voucher programs in Florida, Cleveland, and Milwaukee (Pyle, 2003).

13. See Senator Shapiro's website (www.senate.state.tx.us/75r/senate/members/dist8/dist8.htm). The Christian Coalition was founded by Pat Robertson. It has a Texas chapter that supports school choice (www.texascc.org).

14. According to the Texas Federation of Teachers' legislative hotline (2003a), HB 1554 was voted down in the House by a margin of 79 to 63 (www.TFT.org).

15. To their credit, the Mexican American Legal Defense and Education Fund and the National Council de La Raza carried out consistent lobbying efforts against these proposals.

16. ADA serves as the basis for all state funding formulas. Through attendance policies, districts try to maximize their allotments because ADA drives their individual allotments that generate state aid in other areas, for example, bilingual education, special education, gifted and talented, and so on.

17. The fiscal impact of Shapiro's legislation was calculated on its identical companion legislation, HB 214. It should be noted that the only published fiscal note for this bill is based on a regular rather than a proportional ADA, according to the testimony of State Representative McCall (House Chamber archives, April 8, 2003; see www.capitol.state.tx.us/tlo/house/broadcast.htm). McCall testified that a proportional ADA would alter the fiscal note significantly.

18. It should be noted that African American State Representative Ron Wilson from Houston also had a voucher bill, HB 658, that was nearly identical to Chairman Grusendorf's proposal. Clearly, like LULAC, leadership within the African American community has been courted by conservative organizations. They have also formed their own organizations such as the Black Alliance for Educational Options (see Curry, 2002).

19. During the MALDEF trial (see chapter 1), testimony revealed that the Dana Center was heavily dependent on the TEA for many of its grants and contracts to both study and help implement the state's testing and accountability system (Treisman, 1999).

20. My description of the March 18th hearing is based on both my personal observations contained in field notes and a partial transcription of the audio-archived hearing, available on-line at www.house.state.tx.us/committees/broadcasts.php?cmte=400&session=78

21. An important caveat is that a subsequent amendment (C.S.H.B. 2465; see www.capitol.state.tx.us) to this legislation significantly reduced the number of children eligible to participate. The amendment introduced a new formula involving either 5% of eligible children in a district or an amount in scholarships equal to 3% of the district's maintenance and operating budget (based on revenue for the preceding year), whichever was the lesser. In the present discussion, I focus on the legislation in its original form.

22. The hearing occurred before it was discovered that many HISD high schools had manipulated their dropout data to achieve higher ratings (Schemo, 2003).

REFERENCES

Apple, M. W. (2000). *Official knowledge: Democratic education in a conservative age.* New York: Routledge.

Apple, M. W. (2001). *Educating the "right" way: Markets, standards, God, and inequality.* New York: RoutledgeFalmer.

Black, W. R., & Valenzuela, A. (2003). English language learners and assimilationist visions. In L. Skrla & J. Scheurich (Eds.), *Educational equity and accountability: Paradigms, policies and politics* (pp. 215–234). New York: Routledge.

Blanton, C. (2004). *The strange career of bilingual education in Texas, 1836–1981.* College Station: Texas A&M Press.

Bracey, G. W. (2001). *The war against America's public schools: Privatizing schools, commercializing education.* Boston: Allyn & Bacon.

Bryce, R. (1999). The pols he bought. *Austin Chronicle, 18*(22), 16–20.

Cisneros-Lunsford, A. (1999a, February 3). LULAC council forms voucher group. *San Antonio Express-News,* p. A1.

Cisneros-Lunsford, A. (1999b, February 9). Ouster of 2 LULAC officers sought. *San Antonio Express-News,* p. B1.

Copelin, L. (2002, December 10). Texas think tank's time has come: With the GOP controlling state government, group's vision could set legislative agenda. *Austin American-Statesman,* p. A1.

Curry, G. E. (2002, January 1). Do White conservatives fund Black voucher movement? *The Final Call.* Retrieved July 20, 2003, from http://www.finalcall.com/perspectives/voucher01-01-2002.htm

DeLuna Castro, E. (2003, July 12). Texas state budget for 2004–05 and implications for Latinos. Presentation at the National Council of La Raza annual conference, Austin, Texas. Also available at http://www.cppp.org/products/testimony/presentations/prs-nclr.pdf

Drosjack, M. (2003a, February 20). Parents protest pilot voucher program: San Antonio group says plan hurts poor district. *Houston Chronicle,* p. 21A.

Drosjack, M. (2003b, March 19). Pilot voucher program praised: Nobel-winning economist says it would help public education. *Houston Chronicle,* 30A.

Fikac, P. (1997, December 9). LULAC to join effort to shape voucher legislation. *Austin American-Statesman,* p. B2.

Garcia, G. X. (2003a, April 16). Pro-voucher S.A. group stirs up Austin firestorm. *San Antonio Express-News,* p. 1A.

Garcia, G. X. (2003b, April 24). House sinks bill for online charter schools. *San Antonio Express-News,* p. 1A.

Haas, E., Molnar, A., & Serrano, R. (2001). *Media impact of think tank education publications 2001.* Tempe, AZ: Education Policy Studies Laboratory, Arizona State University.

Hart, P. K. (2002, May 1). Right makes might. *Texas Monthly,* pp. 70–73.

Hursh, D. (2003). Discourse, power and resistance in New York: The rise of testing and accountability and the decline of teacher professionalism and local control. In J. Satterthwaite, E. Atkinson, & K. Gale (Eds.), *Discourse, Power and Resistance: Challenging the Rhetoric on Contemporary Education* (pp. 43–56). Stoke on Trent, UK: Trentham Books.

Joint Select Committee on Public School Finance. (2002, December). *Report to the 78th Legislature, December 2002.* Presented to the 78th Texas Legislature. Retrieved July 24, 2003, from http://www.house.state.tx.us/committees/reports/77interim/school_finance.pdf

Keller, H. (2003). Standards and accountability in 2003: Implementing the next phase of education reform. Policy brief. Austin, TX: Charles A. Dana Center.

Kozol, J. (1991). *Savage inequalities : Children in America's schools.* New York: Crown Publishers.

Lemann, N. (1999). *The big test: The secret history of the American meritocracy.* New York: Farrar, Straus, & Giroux.

Lipman, P. (2002). Making the global city, making inequality: The political economy and cultural politics of Chicago school policy. *American Educational Research Journal, 39*(2), 379–419.

Ludwig, M. (2003, July 9). New force in the fray on state's textbooks: "Intelligent design" adherents use science to question evolution. *Austin American-Statesman,* p. A1.

McNeely, D. (2003, July 17). Map would cost Texas in seniority. *Austin American-Statesman,* p. B1.

McNeil, L. M. (2000). Contradictions of school reform: Educational costs of standardized testing. New York: Routledge.

Nathan, D. (1999). Wallet and spirit. *Austin Chronicle, 18*(22), 22–26. Retrieved July 9, 2003, from http://www.austinchronicle.com/issues/vol18/issue22/pols.leininger.contr.html

National Education Association. (1999). At the local level: There's just no competition. *NEAToday Online.* Retreived July 9, 2003, from http://www.nea.org/neatoday/9905/atloclvl.html

Olsson, K. (2002, November 1). Mr. Right. *Texas Monthly,* p. 125.

Patterson, C. (2003, January 14). *Legislators guide to the issues 2003–2004: Education.* Monograph retrieved July 14, 2003, from the Texas Public Policy Foundation website: http://www.texaspolicy.com/research_reports.php?cat_level=1

People for the American Way Foundation. (1999, April 20). *Privatization of public education: A joint venture of charity and power.* Retrieved July 14, 2003 from http://www.pfaw.org/pfaw/general/default.aspx?oid=5091

Perry, R. (2003, February 11). Text of Governor Rick Perry's state of the state address. Retrieved July 20, 2003, from http://www.governor.state.tx.us/divisions/press/speeches/speech_2003-02-11

Peterson, P. E., Meyers, D., & Howell, W. G. (1999). *An evaluation of the Horizon Scholarship Program in the Edgewood Independent School District, San Antonio, Texas: The first year.* Policy brief from the Harvard Program on Education Policy and Governance. Retrieved July 14, 2003, from http://www.ksg.harvard.edu/pepg/pdf/edgex.pdf

Pyle, E. (2003, May 9). Class warfare: The Right is using poor minorities to push vouchers. But who benefits? *Texas Observer.* Retrieved July 14, 2003, from http://www.texasobserver.org/showArticle.asp?ArticleFileName=030509_f1.htm

Ray, S. (1997, December 11). Voucher program creates LULAC rift. San Angelo *Standard Times.* Retrieved July 20, 2003, from http://web.gosanangelo.com/archive/97/december/11/6.htm

Republican Party of Texas. (2000, November 20). Texas GOP makes solid gains in 2000 elections. Retrieved July 10, 2003, from http://www.texasgop.org/newsroom/newsDisplay.php?id=273

San Miguel, G. (1987). *"Let all of them take heed": Mexican Americans and the campaign for educational equality in Texas, 1910–1981.* Austin: University of Texas Press.

Schemo, D. J. (2003, July 11). Questions on data cloud luster of Houston schools. *New York Times.* Retrieved July 11, 2003, from http://www.nytimes.com

Schrag, P. (1999, November 23). The voucher seduction. *The American Prospect, 11*(1), p. 46.

Shaker, P., & Heilman, E. E. (2002, January). Advocacy versus authority: Silencing the education professoriate. *Policy Perspectives, 3*(1), 1–6.

Shapiro, F. (2001). The Senator's bio. Retrieved August 17, 2003, from http://www.florenceshapiro.org/bio.html

Spring, J. (1997). *Deculturalization and the struggle for equality: A brief history of the education of dominated cultures in the United States* (2nd ed.). New York: McGraw-Hill.

Stutz, T. (1996, October 16). $200,000 raised for religious conservatives: PAC seeks education board majority. *Dallas Morning News,* p. 17A.

Sullivan, M. Q. (2003, January 23). *Policy orientation bringing together top experts: Largest policy event in Texas history starts tomorrow!* Press release from the Texas Public Policy Foundation, retrieved July 11, 2003, from http://www.texaspolicy.com/press_releases_single.php?report_id=24

Texas Education Agency. (2000). *Academic Excellence Indicator System.* Retrieved July 14, 2003, from http://www.tea.state.tx.us/perfreport/aeis/2000/index.html

Texas Federation of Teachers. (2003a, February 19). *Vouchers, school finance, teacher contracts.* Texas Federation of Teachers Legislative Hotline. Retrieved July 8, 2003, from http://www.tft.org/legis/archive2.cfm?hotid=225

Texas Federation of Teachers. (2003b). *TFT Legislative Hotline Archive.* Retrieved July 8, 2003, http://www.tft.org/religiousright.htm

About the Contributors

Laura Alamillo is currently completing her doctoral studies at the University of California at Berkeley in the Education in Language, Literacy and Culture program. She has worked on the Proposition 227 Implementation Project at University of California at Berkeley, Harvard Immigration Project, and is currently completing a dissertation study on children's perspectives on Chicano children's literature.

Ellen Riojas Clark is an associate professor at The University of Texas at San Antonio in the Division of Bicultural Bilingual Studies. Her research interests include bilingual-education teacher preparation, ethnic identity, assessment, and gifted language minority students.

Belinda Bustos Flores is an assistant professor at The University of Texas at San Antonio. Her research interests include teacher self-concept and ethnic identity, teacher self-efficacy and beliefs, teacher preparation, effective teaching practices, and implications of high-stakes testing on bilingual teacher candidates.

Eugene E. García is Vice President for University–School Partnerships and Dean of the College of Education at Arizona State University. He has published extensively in the area of language teaching and bilingual development. His most recent books include *Hispanic Education in the United States: Raíces y Alas* and *Student Cultural Diversity: Understanding and Meeting the Challenge*—both published in 2001.

Elaine Hampton is an assistant professor in teacher education at The University of Texas in El Paso. Her research interests focus on educational reforms resulting from the global movement to a market economy. In her years as a teacher and now working with teachers, her firsthand knowledge of the impact of the standardized curriculum and accompanying tests motivates her research. She also researches the impact that U.S. factories locating in Mexico have on Mexican educational programs.

Linda McSpadden McNeil is the codirector of the Center for Education at Rice University and a member of the Rice education faculty. Her most recent book, *Contradictions of Reform: The Educational Costs of Standardization,* released in 2000, is having a strong impact on public understanding of the negative consequences of standardized reforms. Dr. McSpadden McNeil is a national leader in the area of school reform and writes extensively on educational quality, equity, and policy.

Raymond V. Padilla is a professor in the Department of Educational Leadership and Policy Studies at The University of Texas at San Antonio. He earned a Ph.D. in higher education from the University of California at Berkeley and a bachelor's degree in Spanish language and literature from the University of Michigan. He is the developer of HyperQual software for computer-assisted qualitative data analysis and the author, coauthor, and editor of various books and journal articles, including *Debatable Diversity: Critical Dialogues on Change in American Universities.*

Deborah Palmer is an advanced graduate student the University of California at Berkeley who began as a bilingual elementary educator in California. Her research interests include bilingual education policy and politics, and dual-immersion education.

Jorge Ruiz de Velasco is an education program officer at the William and Flora Hewlett Foundation in Menlo Park, California. Prior to joining the foundation, he was a senior research associate in the Education Policy Center at the Urban Institute in Washington, D.C., and a lawyer in the U.S. Department of Education's Office for Civil Rights. In addition to the J.D. (University of California, Berkeley), he holds a Ph.D. in political science and an M.A. in education policy and administration from Stanford University and an A.B. *cum laude* from Harvard College.

Kris Sloan is an assistant professor in early childhood at Texas A&M University. His research focuses on the ways high-stakes systems of accountability interact with and influence the work of teachers, as well as how such systems impact both educational quality and equity.

Richard Valencia is a professor in the Department of Educational Psychology and a faculty associate at the Center for Mexican American Studies at The University of Texas at Austin. Dr. Valencia has published extensively in the area of racial/ethnic minority education, with a particular focus on Mexican Americans (educational history; testing/assessment issues; social thought; demographic trends; educational litigation; factors related to intellectual/academic test performance; educational policy). His most recent book is *Chicano School Failure and Success: Past, Present, and Future* (2nd ed., RoutledgeFalmer, 2002).

Angela Valenzuela is an associate professor in the Department of Curriculum and Instruction and the Center for Mexican American Studies at The University of Texas at Austin. She is also the author of *Subtractive Schooling: U.S.-Mexican Youth and the Politics of Caring*, winner of both the 2000 American Educational Research Association Outstanding Book Award and the 2001 Critics' Choice Award from the American Educational Studies Association. Her research and teaching expertise are in the areas of sociology of education, urban education, and Latina/o education policy. She is also coeditor of the *International Journal of Qualitative Studies in Education*.

Bruno J. Villarreal is a doctoral candidate in the Department of Educational Psychology at The University of Texas at Austin. Mr. Villarreal's research interests focus on assessment issues with English-language learners, particularly on the gifted/talented. He is also currently working as a research assistant on a language test development project for bilingual Latino children.

Celia Viramontes was born and raised in East Los Angeles, California, the daughter of Mexican immigrant parents. She is a first-generation college graduate of Occidental College where she earned a Bachelor's degree in English in 1998. Currently a Ph.D. candidate in the Department of Ethnic Studies at the University of California, Berkeley and the recipient of a Ford Foundation Fellowship, her interdisciplinary scholarship focuses broadly on Chicano/Latino border studies, and Latino immigrant communities in California to examine how socially and politically conscious writers, political activists and community-based groups contest exclusionary political practices as embodied in Propositions 187 and 227.

Index